OBITUARY THEOLOGY

Reformed Doctrine
Of
Dying and Death;
Re.
Obituaries

Vernon G. Elgin

LUCAS PARK BOOKS
ST. LOUIS, MISSOURI

ISBN: 978-1-60350-006-7

Published by Lucas Park Books
www.lucasparkbooks.com

Contents

Dedication

I EXPRESS GRATITUDE

To One who is herself Seminary Trained:

a Practical Theologian, and *my Wife* of fifty-six years.

She gave me space and time and encouragement to fulfill a dream to write a book;

(And she moved in when Reader Mary died out.)

I EXPRESS GRATITUDE

For Family, Neighbors and Friends:

who at times spoke their "Noah" skepticism about my task;

and at other times, admitted closeted curiosity, like, "You are writing about obituaries?"

Ans. "No! About dying and death, as commented on in obituaries."

I wrote, in part, to delay an onset of depression, amnesia and Alzheimer's.

At first skeptics were only minimally encouraged about my success.

I accept at least fifty-one percent of the blame for their short sightedness;

in part, because of both the arcane subject itself,

and also because of my failure to promote myself defensively.

At times, I was not sure about the narrow way I was traveling.

But the longer I wrote and read,

the more confident I became about my ability to complete, and publish, the Project.

I EXPRESS GRATITUDE:

To all fellow travelers with me, from the beginning, or from somewhere along in the progress, and with me presently in spirit,

I EXPRESS GRATITUDE:

To a remnant increasingly excited about the Project.
They have persistently quizzed me about my
publication date.
I finally, somewhat facetiously, declared my deadline:
"The day before I die!
But I keep pushing back the date."
In exchange for revealing secrets about the writing
progress and themes, I extracted a promise: "Buy a copy,
hot off the Press!" I may have to open a Lending Library,
and charge "late" fees.

I EXPRES GRATITUDE:

For God and those, especially Jesus Christ, who have taught me how to die.
I am grateful also to all who have critiqued the text's
thoughts and words—
especially a professional reader, found frozen in her yard
on December 15, 2008;
and for those who have prayed, and made other spiritual
oblations of sacrifice,
and are now finally rejoicing in my publishing.

The Reverend Vernon G. Elgin, Ph.D.

Acknowledgments And Permissions

Scripture Quotations

Scripture Quotations come from the New Revised Standard Version of the Bible, copyright 1989, by the Division of Christian Education of the National Council of the Churches of Christ in the U.S.A. "Used by permission. All rights reserved." All Biblical Text comes from THE NEW INTERPRETER'S BIBLE, NEW REVISED STANDARD VERSION WITH THE APOCRYPHA, Copyright @2003 by Abingdon Press, 201 Eighth Avenue South, Nashville, TN 37202. (Certain quotes are from memory.)

Study Notes, Guides for Interpretation

Material is quoted from the "Study Notes" and "Guides for Interpretation" in THE NEW INTERPRETER'S BIBLE, NEW REVISED STANDARD VERSION WITH THE APOCRYPHA, granted by the Abingdon Press. (See Publishing data and address above.)

End Notes (Foot Notes) designate certain sources, and affidavits of permission.

Books, (Note: Publishing Information included with Footnotes); Creeds, Confessions, Commentaries

Books: Freeman, Morton S, *The Wordwatcher's Guide to Good Writing & Grammar,* Writers' Digest Books; Calvin, John, *Institutes of the Christian Religion, Books I-IV,* Presbyterian Board of Education; *The Constitution of the Presbyterian Church, (U.S.A),* Office of the PC(U.S.A.) General Assembly; Merton, Thomas, *No Man Is an Island,* Barnes and Noble, Inc.; Davis, John D. *et.al. Editors, The Westminster Dictionary of the Bible.* Westminster John Knox Press; Deitz, Bob, *Life After Loss, a Personal Guide Dealing with Death,* Fisher Books; Harrelson, Walter J. General Editor, Et. al. Editors, *The New*

Interpreter's Bible, New Revised Standard Version with the Apocrypha, Abingdon Press; Ross, Elisabeth Kubler-Ross, *On Death and Dying, Macmillan Publishing Company, NYC, NY.* Numerous Bibles, some out of print, but all Biblical Text References from *The New Interpreter's Bible, New Revised Standard Version with the Apocrypha.*

The Office of the General Assembly of the Presbyterian Church (U.S.A.), Louisville, KY: *THE CONSTITUTION OF THE PRESBYTERIAN CHURCH (U.S.A.);* PART I. *The Book of Confessions;* PART II. *The Book of Order.* Copyright by the Office of the General Assembly. (Confessions 1991, Order 2007.)

"Peace, Unity and Purity Task Force Report" from the Office of the Presbyterian Church (U.S.A.) General Assembly, 2006. Permission was channeled through the Permissions Desk of the Presbyterian Publishing Corporation, by Robin Howell and Dilu Nicholas. Ms. Howell, "Rights Manager," authorized permission to quote.

THE WESTMINSTER DICTIONARY OF THE BIBLE; edited by the Reverends John B. Davis and Henry Snyder Gehman, both Professors at Princeton Theological Seminary at the time of Publication of the Dictionary; Copyright 1944, by The Westminster Press, Philadelphia; based on *A DICTIONARY OF THE BIBLE,* Copyright 1898, 1903, 1911, and 1924 by "The Trustees of the Presbyterian Board of Publication and Sabbath School Work." Authorization for use of Copyright Material, from the desk of Robin Howell, Rights Manager, Westminster John Knox Press.

Material from Newspaper News Stories and articles (predominantly the *Seattle Times*), with permission from either the Newspaper Editor, or personally from the particular author of the text, permission most frequently granted by email or phone conversations; offered on occasion by another member of the News Staff. Permission from the Associated Press; Simon and Schuster (formerly Macmillan Publishers); National Geographic Society; Newspaper Reporter articles where compiled in cooperation with the Associated Press, if Reporter or News Editor indicated the necessity; where known and personal acquaintance with, direct quotes, and in certain instances, references, by personal contact, phone conversation or email correspondence.

Prayers, Hymns, Liturgical Resources

Material has been quoted according to standards of the Presbyterian Publishing Corporation, David Maxwell, President/Publisher, and from the following: Liturgical Resources from the Presbyterian *Book of Common Worship;* Hymn Lyrics from the *Presbyterian Hymnal(1989 edition);* and from the Presbyterian *Book of Common Worship Pastoral Edition*. The Books have been published by *"The Theology and Worship Ministry Unit,"* of the PC (U.S.A.); for the Presbyterian Church (U.S.A.), and the Cumberland Presbyterian Church; Published by *Westminster/John Knox Press, Louisville, KY*. Correspondence with the appropriate Units resulted in information that Permission to Quote was not necessary as all the quoted publications are in the Public Domain. (From the Desk of Robin Howell, Permissions Grantor for publications by the National PC{U.S.A.} offices.) Certain hymns or stanzas are quoted from memory. Where necessary, source has been recognized.

Note about Obituaries

At the beginning of the writing of the Book two years ago, contact regarding copyright was made with the News or Obituary Editors of two major Pacific Northwest Newspapers; and with two Funeral Directors at separate Funeral Homes in the Seattle area. The initial information was that "Obituaries are not newspaper copyright material." Writing the book proceeded.

In late summer, 2008, a conversation with another News Editor of one of the two area Newspapers contacted earlier, resulted in this clarification: "The copyright of an obituary belongs to the person who paid for its publication." Another editor stated, "No newspaper can give copyright permission for obituaries."

Contact was made with the Washington State Library Association and the King County Bar Association, and at their recommendation, a conversation took place with a Seattle copyright attorney. Information was given as follows: legally, copyright belongs to the person who paid for the publication in the paper—IF THE PERSON HAD NEGOTIATED THROUGH THE LIBRARY OF CONGRESS IN ESTABLISHING RIGHTS. With that information, and with encouragement from the Copyright Attorney, I proceeded to rewrite the Book. In my first writing, previous to obtaining all the information above, I identified very few of the obituary excerpts with the deceased's identity. In subsequent revisions, I have totally eliminated personal identity data except the information necessary to establish the integrity of the obituary, summarizing the situation and the information in the document.

As much as possible, I have obtained quoting permission from the Associated Press, Periodical Permission Desks, from writers themselves, or from survivors whom I know or have been able to contact personally.

Newspapers, Periodicals, and Others

Except where otherwise acknowledged, all obituary excerpts are based on documents printed in *The Seattle Times*, (then the combined *Times-Post Intelligencer* weekend editions, but currently the *PI* has shut down operations.) The same protocol applies to so many of the excerpts, that no other acknowledgment is made except this one—with deep appreciation to the Editor and Staff of the *Times*. The *PI* ended its publishing in early 2009. Other excerpts come from obituaries or obituary news reports in the following Newspapers or Periodicals: Tacoma, WA, *News Tribune;* Birmingham, AL, *Birmingham News; The New York Times;* Pittsburgh, PA, *The Pittsburgh Post Gazette;* The Cadiz, Ohio, *Republican; The Florence AL Daily Newspaper;* Eskridge, KS, *Mission Valley Herald;* Christ Church, New Zealand, *Daily Newspaper;* (We lived there 2002-4); *USA Today*, death news articles; Washington, IA, *Journal* ; Kent WA, *"Kent Reporter"*; Indiana PA, *Evening Gazette;* Kittanning PA, *Daily Leader Times;* Las Vegas NV, *Review Journal;* Boulder City NV, *Weekly News;* St. Joseph, MO *St. Joseph News-Press;* Maks

Goldenshteyn, *"Remembering the Forgotten," Seattle Times,* March 26, 2009; Norma Love and Associated Press, *New Idea in Mortuary Science: Dissolving Bodies,* St. Joseph, Mo, *St. Joseph (MO) News Press, 05/09/08;* World Report, *Seattle Times, After 700 Years Teen Gets Funeral,* Complied from Associated Press, *The Washington Post,03/25/09.* Excerpts lacking an identification source are from the *Seattle Times.*

Several quotations and references have come from the *"Christian Century,"* published bi-weekly at 104 Michigan Ave., Suite 700, Chicago, IL. Permission to quote articles from several editions has been granted from the permissions office of Ms. Christine Foust. Gratitude is expressed for alluding to their Mission Phrase printed on the Cover, "Thinking Critically, Living Faithfully."

Permission has been given by the *National Geographic Society* for quoting material from the February 2009 edition of *National Geographic,* Washington, D.C., article, "Where the Dead Don't Sleep," by A.A. Gill, Photographs by Vincent J. Musi.

Punctuation and Editing

Advantage has been taken in certain instances, of punctuation and other editing privileges, but within approved academic guidelines and University Education, one of the author's "majors" being English. Since *Obituary Theology* combines formal and informal style, both modes have been adapted for use. The two most referenced writing texts are: Morton S. Freeman (Forward by Edwin Newman), *The Wordwatcher's Guide to Good Writing and Grammar: Quick answers to pesky grammar and usage problems,* Writer's Digest Books; and Porter G. Perrin, *Writer's Guide and Index to English,* Scott, Foresman and Company. Several punctuation corrections were recommended from the Critical Readers.

Punctuation in general follows the author's education experience, from his Pennsylvania one-room or two-room elementary school years, "primary school" in some areas; and from his High School education in Elderton, Pennsylvania, Graduation, 1944; Virginia Polytechnic University (Virginia Tech), one year of University, courses predominantly in

Science and Math, Military Science and Cadet Training, (English also), through the Army Specialized Training Education Program; a professionally monitored self-study Psychology Course, while serving in the United States Army Air Corps, 1945-6; Indiana University of Pennsylvania, Baccalaureate in Secondary Education, graduating Magna Cum Laude, 1949; Seminary and Graduate Studies, Pittsburgh Presbyterian Theological Seminary, Master of Divinity and Master of Theology Degrees, 1952 and 1954 respectively; and The New College of the University of Edinburgh, Scotland, the Degree of Doctor of Philosophy in Theological Studies, 1960; sabbatical semester, The Union Theological Seminary, New York City, 1980; and numerous continuing education seminars in other Universities, and through Church and other Academically credited entities, both in the USA and Canada.

Forward

Obituaries serve both public and private interests; both the larger, extended society and the smaller personal one; the neighborhood and the household. At least one out of every six obituaries in the *Seattle Times*—more in Missouri, Alabama and South Carolina—contains a religious nuance or reference. For the purposes of this Book, the material classifies as "theology." Theology applies to information about the obituary Subject's church affiliation, circumstances surrounding the death including memorial commemoration or services, personal statements by or about the person, corpse disposition, greetings and personal messages for the soul to deliver when safe "under the shelter of the Most High," and most orthodox and unmistakably religious of all, Scripture sentences or allusions.

Theological material and nuance have caught my attention for many years. I have consciously or unconsciously critiqued the statements through my own theological bias, which is post-sixteenth century Reformation Presbyterian. I was born into Presbyterianism: first in the United Presbyterian Church of North America, which in 1958 became the United Presbyterian Church (U.S.A.); and in 1983 through a reunion of the UPC (U.S.A.) and the Presbyterian Church of the U.S. took on the name Presbyterian Church (U.S.A.). Not only was I born Presbyterian, I was baptized, converted, church-commissioned, professionally educated, ordained to its ministry of Word and Sacrament, and I was married, had offspring, and baptized and commissioned them into the PC (U.S.A.). I did the same for six grandchildren. It is the Church from which I now receive a pension, and in and with which I presume I will die. I have been a PC (U.S.A.) clergy fifty-seven years, and I currently travel globally, primarily in volunteer ministry. My wife, Marjorie's religious track has been parallel to mine, including graduation from the Pittsburgh (Xenia till 1958) Theological Seminary. We met at Seminary. *Obituary Theology*, the Book, concentrates more on dying and death, than on obituaries. Its main "portion" organizes into three sections: first, coming to theological terms with dying, and with the theology and the authority behind the dogma; second, last breath or the result of dying, commemorative services (if held, and if not, why not?), and disposing of the corpse; third, the personal and professional context of the deceased's life, and pragmatic counsel for survivors. Relative material from obituaries is excerpted. The Book will hopefully prove interesting and helpful to a variety of readers, both professional and amateur, both "sacred" and "secular." A Study Guide is attached for groups.

Extensive educational and professional experience have prepared me for writing the Book: a post-high school year as a seventeen-year old United States Army Air Force Cadet at Virginia Polytechnic Institute (Virginia Tech); Baccalaureate Magna Cum Laude Graduate, Indiana University of Pennsylvania (1949); Pittsburgh (Xenia) Presbyterian Theological Seminary, obtaining Masters' Degrees in Divinity and Theology (1952 and 1954); Ph. D. Degree in Theology, the New College, the University of Edinburgh, Scotland, (1960); and Sabbatical Study at Union Theological Seminary in New York City (1980). Continuing Education in Christian Faith, Ministry, and the Church and Social Justice issues was pursued at various institutions: the University of Iowa and Iowa Wesleyan; Yale Divinity School; Whitworth University, Spokane, WA; Princeton Theological Seminary; Chicago McCormick Theological Seminary; Vancouver (BC) School of Theology; four Interim Ministry Training Events at Montreat, N.C. and St. Catherine's in St. Paul, MN; Visiting Professor, Pacific Lutheran University in Parkland, WA and St. Martins College, Lacey, WA. After retirement I—and when able, my wife (herself a Pittsburgh Seminary graduate)—began itinerating the world, volunteering in mission, in New Zealand; Bali, Indonesia; Bogota`, Colombia; San Juan, Puerto Rico; and the University of Livingstonia, Malawi, Africa.

When I shared with a friend that I was writing a book on obituary theology; that my "List of Ten Goals" began with "To glorify God," and ended with, "To make $1 million," she quickly came back with, "Vernon, you would be better off purchasing a Washington State Lottery Ticket." I thanked her, and the next day I went to the Safeway Store and bought one. So far I am not better off financially. But I am more than better off for having the discipline and endurance to have written *Obituary Theology*.

Pre-Text
(Preface)

Two obituary excerpts introduce the "Pre-Text" of *Obituary Theology: Reformed Doctrine of Dying and Death; Re: Obituaries:*

HOLOCAUST SURVIVOR, PSYCHIATRIST, SEX THERAPIST, FLUENT IN SEVEN LANGUAGES: He was born in Europe, escaped Hitler, lived in several European nations, and Brazil, then came to the U.S.A., studied medicine, and became a prominent Psychiatrist. He was one of the first of his profession trained in "Masters & Johnson" therapy. He learned the language of most of the European nations, and "American" English. After two years in the U. S. Air Force he married Gayle in N.D., and they became the parents of three sons. He and Gayle became active in the Seabeck Christian Conference Center, which along with Eastshore Unitarian Church, is named as a designee of memorial funds.

SEATTLE BORN AND DIED, FAMOUS ARTHITECT BROTHER, NO SERVICES: She came to Seattle ninety-one years ago, by birth. Her Brother built "Northern Life Tower," now known as the "Seattle Tower." One daughter and one granddaughter survive. No commemoration service was held.

....

What do you call it: the introductory pages of a book? Traditionally, it goes by "Preface," or "Prologue," or simply "Introduction." What do you call it if you want to be creative? How about "Pre-Text," since the material serves as the pre-text of the book's main text?

Obituary Theology, the text, represents several years, not only of collecting and sorting obituaries, but also of theologically critiquing them. The more obituaries I read—principally daily in the *Seattle Times*—the more I kept asking myself about the religious material, "Where do these ideas come from?" They obviously have some theological background.

The more I pondered the matter, the less critical I became. Obituary theology, I concluded, emerges from grieving sources and difficult emotions, or at least different interpretations of the sources. Not all of them are formed by theological knowledge. Nor are many of the writers theological seminary graduates. Most obituaries reveal some knowledge of the Bible. Many of them are sincere expressions of "pop-theology." (The statement is not intended to be either derogatory or pejorative.) The documents emerge from deep suffering over loss, and penetrating grief. Someone close to the "Subject" has died. The survivors want others to know details about the life and death of their loved ones, and to inform those interested about closing commemoration or memorializing.

Both professional and personal experience—both my younger brother and sister's dying a few months past—sharpened my interest and curiosity in dying and death: the effects on survivors, and how the loss is reported. I added current obituaries to my collection, with the intent of writing a book about them someday. I finally settled on a subject and title. Then I started organizing the material. I struggled for a few weeks. I finally came to a "Sequential" decision; that is, organizing the material according to the order of events connected with dying and death.

First, you have to come to terms with your perception or factual knowledge that you or a close family member or friend is dying. Then you begin to realize that dying belongs to a universal process, and someday it will happen to you. Meantime, you have to deal with your feelings about losing someone who has endeared and influenced you. Along comes the "last breath," the death itself. That incident requires special "coming to terms with." Respect and custom, in most deaths, convince you to commemorate the deceased's life. You need to deal emotionally and administratively with a funeral or memorial service, or "no service." Perhaps the deceased had already decided. Disposition of the body must be made, both for legal and psychological reasons. Hopefully you had already obtained information about the program the person had desired, or worked out. Then there is an obituary to prepare. Depending on the extent of your involvement in writing it—again, hopefully the Subject had read *Obituary Theology* and had followed the advice of the author, and prepared an "autobituary"—you want to honor the deceased with theological, genealogical, professional and other details about their life. The whole middle section of the Book deals with these matters. The last section covers the more personal subjects mentioned in the last sentence, and moves into pragmatic concerns: the obituary, legal and other matters to take care of, and suggestions for many of the issues and problems that are endemic to the crisis.

Obituary Theology should prove to be helpful and interesting reading, in spite of the fact that the subject is neither popular, nor not necessarily nice or simple. The coverage of the material is unashamedly and admittedly theologically biased; the point-of-view about dying and death, and obituaries, settles on the theological ethos that grew out of the sixteenth century Reformation. The Author's lifelong commitment to the Body of Christ belongs to that tradition. He is a retired Presbyterian Church (U.S.A.) clergy. He has struggled, however, to write from an ecumenical perspective. He has aimed at being charitable with literature written for the most part by non-theologians.

In the midst of the journey a new book came to his attention, James Gustave Speth's, *The Bridge at the Edge of the World: Capitalism, the Environment and Crossing from Crisis to Sustainability*. (See "Acknowledgements" and "End Notes.") Speth reasons that a society that lives in Christ dies with gain, regardless of its religious diversity or commitment, irrespective of whether you spend your whole life in Galilee or go on mission to Mississippi, and is built, not on self interest, but on social solidarity. The author deals creatively with the commitment required of the Church to solve some of the issues in the current critical environmental crisis. The commitment requires, Speth insists, the following adjustments: "Moving from getting to giving, from individualism to community, from economy to ecology, from having to being, from satisfying wants to satisfying needs, and from being richer to being better."[1]

Do those moves sound to you like something you have heard before, a call to "deny yourself, take up your cross daily, and follow me?" If you think in those terms, you are a theologian.

Good luck on the maturity and theological insights that may confront or come to you as you read *Obituary Theology*. I am confident enough of myself and of my work, done hopefully with the spirit of God, to believe that reading the book will blow like a wind on your back and be strong enough to lift up many of the valleys and lower some of the mountains before you, and make straight the path for your feet, through the comfort of the risen Christ and the triumph of his Kingdom. Vernon G. Elgin

Section I. "Terms"

I.

Coming To Terms With Dying And Death

> *"I believe in.... Jesus Christ, his (God's) only son our Lord; who was crucified...."*
>
> The Apostles' Creed.

Obituary Excerpts

GIVEN OK TO GO TO JESUS: She grew up active in the Church, and stayed a member all her life. She sang in the choir, and accepted congregation leadership responsibilities. Her Family participated with her in church activities. Several family members were also with her while she was drawing her last breaths. They assured her that she had their OK to leave them and go to Jesus. She died shortly after. The family believes that she has joined their other deceased loved ones.

WITH THE LORD: The faith of the Seattle family is that their husband, father, and grandfather, has left them to be with the Lord. A service of commemoration for him was held at the Church of which he had been a member a number of years.

DEAD, AND GRATEFUL (An Autobituary): "I died today. (Date inserted).... I have had a great life, and I thank you all....in lieu of flowers, donations could be made to my Church, and to the local Hospice services....

....

Writing *OBITUARY THEOLOGY* started with composing a "List of Ten Reasons Why." Exultation headed the List; exaltation finished it. Glorification of God, of course, ranked first; boosting an ego and making a million dollars last. As organizing and writing and revising and evaluating the script accelerated, the List shrank; eventually it disappeared. Energy and joy and peace in being creative lasted, and a few of the list of ten was scratched. The joy of renewed acquaintance with Scripture, the satisfaction from a review and exploration of theology, and the contact with the memories of the dead through their obituaries—most of whom were strangers—reinforced a long-held desire to write some day about documents of the dead. The critical point-of-view is theological, particularly Reformed Theology, my theological ethos, pre-natal, I am convinced. As a Presbyterian, perhaps the word should be "predestined." It is anticipated that, since no writing about obituaries from a Reformation-obituary perspective has been produced, the Book will sell. If that prediction turns out to be the case, God be glorified—the exultation; the author appreciated, the exaltation. If the Book does not sell, the author's time has not been wasted. He has realized fulfillment of personal, intellectual and spiritual goals.

The somewhat arcane nature of the subject causes the author no anxiety about its successful marketing; in fact, he is looking forward to benign notoriety. That response will place him in good company, even Biblical society. Flood-man Noah's neighborhood grew curious about his boat construction, but not curious enough: "They were eating and drinking, and marrying and being given in marriage," going about their business as usual (Luke 17:26), "until the day Noah entered the ark." Soon the rain started.

Curiosity has emerged from the spreading rumor about a retired Presbyterian Church (U.S.A.) Clergy writing about the dead. Again, as it was in the days of Noah, some scoffed, some questioned, some expressed interest, and some became bored hearing about it. Nevertheless, the dream persisted, the computer kept recording, collecting of obituaries continued, and the writing picked up feverishly. The time has come for publication. The wisdom of Solomon has prevailed. He sang, or his female star did, "I adjure you, O daughters of Jerusalem, by the gazelles or the wild does; do not stir up or awaken love until it is ready." (Song of Songs. 2:7.) The connection? "Do not look for a publisher or send it off until the Book is ready. The Book is ready, the author's family is ready, curious friends are ready, and hopefully the Church and the world will be ready.

A theologian, or a critical reader need not read too many obituaries before one observation becomes obvious, a critical one: the religious or theological material the documents contain does not rise to the standard of Scripture, or of systematic or classical theology. It soon becomes obvious that neither Apostles, Reformers, Popes nor Seminary Professors composed the death biography. *Obituary Theology,* the Book, therefore does not take the reader on a classical philosophical, intellectual or imaginative adventure. In fact, obituary interest bows before dying and death treatment. The book examines church doctrine on dying and death, and obituaries, from two perspectives: a Reformed theological viewpoint, and a civil religion outlook, of which obituary information offers remarkable examples. The examination does not aim at condemnation or literary or theological criticism; it concentrates on appreciation, and fascination. To a less sophisticated degree, the goal corresponds to the mission of the periodical, *Christian Century,* as stated on the front cover page of its bi-weekly publications: "Thinking Critically, Living Faithfully." Readers of *Obituary Theology* will hopefully become more religiously discriminate, more spiritually literate, and more habitually loving from their literary exercise. Few sources publish religion and spirituality from a more eclectic and ecumenical viewpoint like obituaries. One reason may stem from the fact that obituary theology arises from suffering.

The ubiquity of suffering and dying inspires the Author's hope for book sales and readership. Dying persons journey through a process that terminates in death. The mysterious, somewhat dangerous, and always ubiquitous path from process to product—at times, seemingly impassable—leads through a wilderness that most mortals would rather not take. When their thinking settles on realism, however, and they accept the reality that the path is unavoidable and that traversing it can be successful, they are well along on the process toward survival. This state comes about by the process the Book entitles, "Coming to terms." The entire first third of the Book deals with that exercise. The goal focuses more on dying than on death, on victory rather than defeat, on leaving life on one dimension and entering it more fully on another. Regardless how far one progresses in life on earth, an even fuller experience of it awaits folk who think as the Gospel of Jesus Christ teaches. Coming to terms with, and actual realization of, eternal life puts a person on the path of everlasting life. Arrival at that goal immerses a person in a quality of life that is indescribable and irreversible. Life at that goal, so the author of life claims, finally deserves recognition as the winner.

For the moment stick to process, to the dynamics of dying. Vacillation may be a feature of dying: sometimes you want to, sometimes you hate to, sometimes you accept the fact that you have no choice, sometimes you take the matter into your own hands. The Apostle Paul came to this insight as he reflected in his letter to the Corinthians. After Christ changed Paul one hundred eighty degrees from the lifestyle that the Church persecutor seemed to have been progressing with, Paul realized something about life he had never experienced before. Of course, resurrection was one of his most dramatic discoveries. Meantime, he discovered some truth about life and death: life in Christ conquers the world, but in the meantime, death stays busy at work in the world. He himself knew that truth better than most people around him, even the Christians. He asked, "And why are we putting ourselves in danger every hour? I die every day! …I fought with wild animals at Ephesus. What would I have gained by it? If the dead are not raised, 'Let us eat and drink, for tomorrow we die.'" (1 Corinthians 15:30-34, selected.) The Apostle had come to terms with living while dying, and dying while living.

Coming to terms with dying, as Paul's testimony evidences, does not lead to despair or defeat, that is, if you come to terms theologically. Do not despair at this suggestion; you do not need a Seminary Education to think this way. Theology need not be a scary activity. To keep it from being dismissed as too difficult, arcane or scary; and to establish its credibility as a way to assist with both living and dying, the Book has adopted a brief and simple definition of theology: "Theology is human word about Divine word." For the time being accept that simplistic description, and trust that by the end of the Book you will be "more religiously literate, more spiritually discriminate and more habitually pious." If you achieve that goal—which you can—you will qualify for a theological diploma.

Now that some of the philosophy of the theology has been set forth, the path leads into areas of light, for some; of confusion, or darkness possibly for others. In order to stay more in light than in shadows, set yourself a goal: to come to terms with dying. Remember that the subject of "death" will come up in a later Chapter; dying demands our attention now. We have three professionals with whom to hold hands: Gloria, Lovelle and "Seattle Man." All three are dead, but they qualify for a front-runner position in coming to terms with dying by the facts that they were rather ordinary human beings, they suffered extraordinarily, and they had come to terms with living. Their nametags read: "Gloria," "Lovelle," and, rather than revealing the third person's name, please be content with calling him "Seattle Man."

By the day Seattle Man had died, twelve year-old Gloria and middle-aged Lovelle—a Seattle adolescent and a Portland-area "senior" woman—had already expired. The *Seattle Times* published obituaries of all three. Columnist Jerry Brewer, in a series of twelve articles, had chronicled adolescent Gloria Strauss' last days.[1] The girl had suffered four years with a rare blood disease, and she took her last breath in a local hospital. Columnist Don Colburn of the *Portland Oregonian* had followed the saga of the Portland resident, Lovelle Svart.[2] She had ended her time on earth via "death with dignity." (Oregon offers legal provisions for the dignity route out, and as of the two thousand eight elections, the State of Washington does also.) Lovelle swallowed a toxic drink while lying in her bed at home. The Seattle Man died, it appears, following natural complications.

All three of the deceased—Gloria Strauss, the adolescent; Lovelle Svart, the "death with dignity" woman; and the engineer from Seattle—had come to a point where they felt that they had suffered "long enough." Gloria's disease has already been identified; Lovelle had lung cancer; the Seattle gentleman, as noted, also had cancer. All three had shared at least one common blessing: they had died with loving family or friends either with them, or nearby. All three also shared a remarkable achievement: they had come to terms with their dying, each in his/her own special way; not necessarily in a "Reformed" tradition, but in a way marked by integrity of one sort or another; by courage, and above all, by suffering and struggle. Each had charted different routes, but each seems to have been convinced he/she would arrive where Divinely intended.

Adolescent Gloria had relinquished her seemingly irreversible fatal illness, and her uncertain future here on earth, into the hands of God. Gloria had settled on difficult terms to deal with, both here, and for the hereafter: when she died she would participate in the party that God had prepared for her. She was looking forward to it. Lovelle took matters into her own hands. She had struggled with her disease for several years. She had finally arrived at the decision to take advantage of the legal provision in Oregon regarding dying: she would end her life with a legally available drug. With the support of her aging Mother, personal friends, and the required counselor for the process, she organized her last days. Her death-life climaxed with a party. On that last afternoon she socialized with a group of friends, including the required representative, a Mr. Eighmey. Earlier in the day she had paid a last visit to her favorite "quiet place" in a nearby park. At the celebration, just before she started drinking her last drink, she and Eighmey quickly danced a polka. When the decided-upon time had arrived, she and her Mother went to Lovelle's room, and prepared the "cocktail." She started swallowing it. She later described the liquid as "the most god-awful stuff" that she had ever tasted. As she was about to take her first sip, her attendant asked her if this way of "going" were what she really wanted. Lovelle replied, "Actually, I would rather go on partying.... but yes." Mr. Eighmey ended his questioning of the dying woman with that enqury. She finished the liquid, and in a few minutes, embraced on her own bed by her Mother, supported by other family members, and with friends in a nearby room—and with compliance with the law regarding witnesses—Lovelle died approximately five hours after she had begun swallowing the lethal drink. A local television station filmed the scene; the tape aired later.

Lovelle's determination, her friends had become convinced, had contributed to her surviving as long as she had with lung cancer. Her five hours after initializing her last breath had not proved easy for her mother or her friends—or herself. Her death, available for viewing on web pages, gave the appearance of a dying woman having her own way, "The in-charge patient until the end," as she was described. About 10:30 P.M.,"Compassion & Control" volunteer, Jane O'Dell, announced that Lovelle's pulse had stopped. Her skin had turned pallid and her fingernails pale blue. Each last breath demanded more than a minute. The Newspaper reported, "Eighmey (the "Compassion and Control" official delegate) leaned over at 10:42 P.M., his ear to her chest to listen for a heartbeat. He stepped back, shaking his head, and he spoke in a quiet voice, 'She's gone.'" Lovelle Svart had breathed the last of many labored breaths. As Mr.Eighmey said, "She's gone." Where? The safest minimally factual answer could read something like, "From us." Her dying was over, ending on whatever terms she in her deepest heart and mind had come to. Those closest to her had become convinced that Lovelle Svart had come to what she perceived for her to be the best way "to go," both as a process and a product.

Gloria Straus' last days contrasted dramatically with Lovelle's. Several visitors had buoyed her spirit, creating a party atmosphere in her hospital room. No encouragement, however, had supported her like her own faith. She had grown up in it. Her devout religious family all believed that God had assisted their beloved child—and themselves. Her parents, in particular, had encouraged her in her steadfast trust in God. She had also had encouragement from her School, St. Philomena Catholic, in Seattle. Principal Sandy Smith complimented the dying girl: "The abundance of her love would flow to whoever was in the room with her." At her public Memorial Commemoration in the School Gymnasium, the Rosary was recited. "It was Gloria's favorite prayer," Parish Priest, Father Vanderberg commented. She had told him that she never felt pain when praying it.

Gloria's terms for dying were less autocratic, more suppliant, than Lovelle's. She believed, with her parents, that God would heal her, one way, at one time, or another. Nevertheless, she wanted a farewell party, and she believed until her last breath that one would be waiting for her. After she had died, her family conceded that, instead of a final earthly celebration as her reward, the girl had received many more lasting greetings. Reporter Brewer wrote, "Gloria was granted a party ticket to heaven." The many attendants at her funeral concurred. A few moments of solemn partying even intruded into her funeral. An announcement was made that her youngest brother was observing his first birthday that day. Father Vanderberg turned the news celebrative; he asked the congregation, "How can we keep from singing?" The Congregation couldn't; they broke into "Happy Birthday." In his closing story about the girl, Columnist Jerry Brewer wrote: "Gloria's party was about more than her.... it was about how her loved ones say she had touched people through her unselfishness" Her father commented, "Her legacy will reign." (From Mr. Brewer's October 5 *Seattle Times* Article, with his permission.)

Gloria, Lovelle and Seattle Man had come to terms about their readiness to die, and Gloria and the Man testified to how religion had assisted them to that point. Both of them also had firm convictions about the life beyond their years on earth. Both were amateur theologians.

A reference in John may be a tribute to their faith and their confidence about their life beyond death: "Those who love me will keep my word, and my Father will love them, and we will come to them and make our home with them." (John 14:23.) The post-death extension of the "home" situation is, "And when you die, we will bring you to your final home to live with us." This hope was also shared by Paul: "Whether we are awake (living) or whether we are asleep (dead), we may live with him (the Lord Jesus Christ) who died for us." (1 Thessalonians 5:9-10.) Paul's theology added a Christian postscript: Jesus not only died for us, he also was raised for us.

The terms persons come to when dying depend on a number of variables: Did you grow up in a Christian home? Are you a believer? Do you track off to Church regularly to worship God? Does dying bother you? Do frightening dreams about the process occasionally rob you of sleep?

"When I was a child"—to introduce a sentence from Paul's letter about love, 1 Corinthians 13—I thought about dying, like a child. The Charles Lindbergh Son's kidnapping happened when I was five years old. A photo in our daily paper triggered my anxiety. The front-page image showed a ladder leaning against the house and resting on the sill of the child's bedroom. The Lindbergh house resembled the Elgin's. For several nights in a row my Dad took me outside before I went to bed to prove to me that no ladder was there. In a few months I was ready to go to bed without a parent going through anxiety-relief rituals with me. It helped that my brother and I slept together, and our sisters' bed was also in the same room. As in Paul's letter, after a few weeks, "I put an end to childish ways." (Vs. 11.) I presume I had come to a five year-old child's terms about dying. I had trouble with my bedtime prayer, "Now I lay me down to sleep.... if I should die before I wake." "Mum" assured me that I would show up "tomorrow morning" at the breakfast table for my Wheaties, porridge, homemade bread, and sweet, whole-cream, coffee.

An Australian family of our acquaintance recently faced coming to terms with dying when their little boy, probably six years old, died. I was pastor at the Second Union Church in San Juan, Puerto Rico when we first met the family; Elizabeth was pregnant at the time. Her sister was one of our members. They had had a Texas background. Elizabeth was having a troubled pregnancy. They had a boy, David, and he not only had birth problems, he also had blood problems. He had received aggressive medical treatment, including chemotherapy, almost since birth. He has had a high priority on our personal prayer list since he was born. He died in the spring of 2009, in Brisbane. Like Gloria, the girl introduced earlier, David was loved and prayed for by medical staff, neighbors, friends and churches all over the world. His rare disease would not submit to treatment. The family modeled endurance, holding fast to their Christian faith and hope.

Upon David's death, we sent Elizabeth and Ben our sympathies. I reminded the family of an incident from King David's experience with grief, when his first little baby died. The infant had been conceived as a consequence of the King's lust for Bathsheba. Upon learning of her pregnancy, the King arranged for her husband's almost certain death in the front line of a battle with a formidable foe. The son would have been heir to the throne. During the child's pre-death illness, David mourned publicly and self-denying. As soon as the child died, David washed, put on clean clothes, and started eating normally. The palace staff was shocked, and whispered about it. They could not understand why he was not mourning the child's death. The King responded, "While the child was still alive, I fasted and wept; for I said, 'Who knows? The Lord may be gracious to me, and the child may live.' But now he is dead; why should I fast? Can I bring him back again? I shall go to him, but he will not return to me." (2 Sam. 12:22-3.)

Elizabeth responded to our sympathy letter as a woman who had come to terms with dying and death. She wrote:

"We really appreciate your prayers throughout our journey with David, and now, with us, as we begin a new journey. We miss David a whole, whole lot, but praise the Lord that His grace has been right here with us enabling us to set our eyes on the hope we have in Christ. We see this as an answer to the many prayers that are going out on our behalf, and as a testimony to His Amazing Grace. God is good."

Elizabeth added a word about how far the testimony of David's dying and commemoration service had reached. Many of those attending his funeral were non-Christians: ...hospital staff, colleagues from Ben's (David's Father) company, and friends. "It was wonderful that they all came out (from the service) uplifted by the tone of hope and joy," Elizabeth wrote. "We pray that the lives that were touched by David's testimony would be seeds planted in fertile soil, and that they will bear eternal fruit. ...We feel very blessed and loved. The Lord bless you." Ben and Elizabeth. (Quoted by permission.) Surely many of those who had cared for David while he was dying had come to terms with his—and possibly their own—death.

From a Reformed theological perspective, grace is prevailing. It attaches to Jesus' words, "I am the resurrection and the life." (John 11:25.) The Apostle Paul's confidence is a rock of strength for believers! "...suffering produces endurance, and endurance produces character, and character produces hope, and hope does not disappoint us...." (1 Corinthians 5:3-5.); and, "Just as sin exercised dominion in death, so grace might also exercise dominion through justification leading to eternal life through Jesus Christ our Lord." (Romans 5:21.) Elizabeth and Ben are enduring through the terms in those Scriptures.

Not every grief-stricken family or person arrives at terms that satisfy or comfort them. Arrival depends significantly on which of three attitudes you take toward dying and death: ignore it (aggressively or passively); defy it (intellectually or blatantly); or greet it (graciously, even thankfully).

Ignoring dying probably proves the most popular of the three positions. It places you in the woods with Rip Van Winkle, or in a decaying plantation like "Gone with the

Wind," and Scarlet O'Hara at Tara; and in a pit of pessimism with Qoheleth, the "Teacher-Preacher-Philosopher" in the Biblical Book, Ecclesiastes. Qoheleth had a favorite mantra, "Vanity of vanities! All is vanity!" (Ecclesiastes 1:2 and elsewhere.) "Vanity" in Hebrew can also be translated "breath." Ignoring "last breath" thwarts the purpose in living toward it.

To ignore death is foolish and dangerous, for the reason mentioned earlier: death's inescapability in most non-arbitrational terms. When Jesus prayed in Gethsemane, out of his agony on the Thursday night before Passover-Preparation Friday, "Let this cup pass from me," he was allowing suffering to trump reason and mission. The two energies returned before he rose from his knees, and he added, "Thy will be done." Ignoring death raises suspicion about amnesia, procrastination, cowardice, and, above all, ignorance of the truth.

Defy. Defying death may turn out more pitifully than ignoring it. (Notice, the word is "defy," not "deny.") Defy describes the solution that the ignorant and belligerent settle on. Deny acquiesces to passive acceptance. Think of the difference between an agnostic and an atheist. Defy and atheist are in one camp; deny and agnostic are across the firing line from them. The difference lies in passivity, or at least non-activity. The mind does not settle on coming to terms; it lets terms settle on it.

Taking a defiant attitude toward death moves you farther away from Qoheleth's tent, and closer to Job's flap. Job found a psychological-theological platform to question divine justice; he doubted and argued with God, and continued the argument with counselors who had supposedly come to him on a mission of consolation. (Their theological terms were reviewed a few sentences back.) Job found unacceptable the suggestion that if he would confess his sin, he would experience restoration. The friends' problem was their wrong premise. Job did not recant his defiant mood until God took the initiative and engaged him in a personal encounter. He then came to his senses: his problem had not been sin; it had been sight! Upon gaining new theological insight and making a firm commitment to it, his health and prosperity returned. He capitulated to the Lord: "I know that you can do all things, and that no purpose of yours can be thwarted." (Job 42:2.) In fact, he was rewarded with double portions of his previous accumulations, except for the number of children: no change, ten before and ten after. If he had the same wife, or only one before and after, she would have borne twenty children. How many women would hang around a troubled man to achieve that record?

Saul of Tarsus lived in defiance of the Gospel until Jesus came to him in a mysterious epiphany, blinded him, rebuked him for persecuting the Church—tantamount to persecuting Jesus—and called him to a death-defying mission. When he experienced blindness as part of his Damascus Road conversion package, he was instructed to hasten to Damascus for help. He was directed to Ananias, a firm disciple there; he was to be baptized, and then he came to terms with the call to the mission that Jesus had planned for him. Jesus gave this tribute to one whose defiance initially was intolerable; but Jesus saw the potential: "For he is an instrument whom I have chosen to bring my name before Gentiles and kings and before the people of Israel; I myself will show him how much he must suffer for the sake of my name." (See Acts 9.) A similar contradiction would have happened if early in April 1945 Adolf Hitler had converted to Judaism, and on "V.E. Day" had been sent to New York City to promote Zionism.

Greet. Greeting death softens its threat, shatters its scare and neuters its nerve. Dying persons—living, healthy persons as well—may choose how to greet death while alive; but more important, how to face it with surer armor when it attacks. Appropriate greeting can create a quiet and peaceful demeanor. Anxiety may not totally disappear, but it may act like an injection of the serum that could inoculate many people against the swine flu in the year 2009. When it comes, whether tortuously painful or benevolently peaceful, death's onslaught had better have been anticipated. "You know neither the day, nor the hour," Jesus said about his return.

The same ignorance applies to death, unless a sick person commits suicide. Or unless an Oregonian or Washingtonian goes the "death with dignity" route. Paul prescribed one greeting tactic: "Do not worry about anything, but in everything by prayer and supplication with thanksgiving let your requests be made known to God. And the peace of God, which passes all understanding, will guard your hearts and your minds in Christ Jesus." (Philippians 4:6-7.)

That supplication and its fulfillment may achieve the epiphany Jesus had after overcoming Satan's temptations at the beginning of his ministry. Jesus refused to accept Satan's terms, with this result: "The devil left him, and suddenly angels came and waited on him." (Matthew 4:11.) Greeting death is far different from lying down in the middle of a busy freeway, or on a bullet train railroad track. Jesus described and illustrated it in many ways. This distillation may help, from Jesus' own words: "If any want to become my followers, let them deny themselves, and take up their cross, (Luke inserts 'daily') and follow me." (Matthew 16:24.) Live literately, think discriminately, and love habitually.

Coming to terms with dying makes the same demands as coming to terms with living, in spite of the fact that you had no choice in your conception or birth. Aside from Jesus Christ and certain of the prophets and early Church missionaries, few viewpoints compare with St. Francis of Assisi's petitions in his renowned "peace" litany: Where evil is being sown, the Saint intoned, let me sow good: where there is hatred, love; injury, pardon; doubt, faith; despair, hope; darkness, light; sadness, joy. He then concluded: "O Divine Master, grant that I may not seek so much to be consoled as to console; to be understood as to understand; to be loved as to love. For it is in giving that we receive, it is in pardoning that we are pardoned, and it is in dying that we are born to eternal life." (St. Francis' prayer may be found in most volumes of devotional literature. My memory has etched it, and if I forget or need prompting, I can find it in the Presbyterian *Book of Common Worship.)* The Hebrews Epistle offers a sample of the terms Jesus came to: "For the sake of the joy that was set before him, (he) endured the cross, despising the shame, and has taken his seat at the right hand of the throne of God." (Hebrews 12:2.)

I, myself, have stood, and knelt, at deathbeds when the evidence of coming to terms with dying proved undeniable. The saints who in my experience have arrived at that apogee have relied heavily on divine assistance. Their saintliness has given me epiphanies of hope and joy. A woman named Leta—either nearing or into her ninetieth year when I became her pastor fifty-seven years ago—brought me fearfully and dangerously close to heaven. Her personal epiphany transported my literate, discriminate and habitual imagination heavenward, and then it returned me to her bedside. I was making a pastoral call on the bedridden parishioner. I dared, after checking it out with her, to sit on the edge of her bed. We held hands. She announced that she wanted to share the most spiritual experience she had ever had. Some months earlier, she said, "Jesus came into my room. He stood at that same bedpost against which you now lean your back. The room lit up. Jesus looked as he might have appeared in his transfiguration: radiantly illuminated. He had few words. He began, 'Leta, your mansion waits. It's beautiful. All the bathrooms have gold fixtures, and there is not a medicine cabinet in the whole place! No crutches, no wheel chairs, no dressings for wounds. It has everything you need without anything pain-killing or prosthetic.'" Leta interjected, "I had to ask the meaning of that word. He told me. And then he kissed me and left. I have never experienced a peace like it before. I wanted to go home with him that day. But he said, 'Not yet.'" Both Leta and I cried. Leta had come to terms with dying.

Then there was Gladys in Puerto Rico. Early in my first days of ministry with the Second Union Church of San Juan, a member of the congregation took me to visit her. She was recovering from complications connected with lung cancer. The Season was Advent. After prayer, she requested a chorus from one of her favorite hymns, "Angels We Have Heard on High." We joyfully and loudly burst into "Gloria…in excelsis Deo…!" We sang it, and her smile stretched, in its effect, across the room. From then until the day she died, on every visit with her, and at her funeral, we sang, "Gloria....Deo!" (On one occasion I brought an even broader smile when I suggested we alter the words a bit, instead of "Gloria," we sing "Gladia...." Her faithful husband, Carlos, son of a deceased Baptist Pastor, drowned out both of us. It was beautiful. I have also prayed at bedsides where the dying had no beauty at all, and "Gloria..." seemed inappropriate. Breathing turned strained and noisy. The last breath ended with forced gasps and a ghostly-eyed grimace. The gestures, nevertheless, communicated that the dying person had come to terms with the mind and spirit of the risen Christ.

In her iconic book ON DEATH AND DYING Swiss Psychiatrist and Author, Dr. Kubler-Ross (published 1969), offered suggestions on why coming to terms with death may be more difficult for some than others. The psychiatrist maintained that death is so "distasteful" that it presents itself as a subject almost impossible to think about.[3] The Psychiatrist claimed that at a deep unconscious level, the human mind refuses to, or cannot, deal with death's trauma. Human beings cannot imagine, or think of being gone, having discarded mortality, and having put on immortality.

Distaste of death does not necessarily distract believers from greeting it. While he was on the cross, thirst, and probably hunger as well, not to mention his pain from the nails, did not direct Jesus into delirious defiance and a change of mind. He did not cry out, or if he did, he was not heard yelling, "Get me down off this damned tree." Distaste is response of those defying such an end, rebelling against the suffering that may last for years before it comes. Distaste may also prompt ignoring your end, regardless of whether you are currently miserably dying or vibrant with good health. Greeting trumps defying or ignoring death.

As he did in so many human experiences, the Apostle Paul left a record of swallowing what he anticipated was coming. His "spoonful of sugar that makes the medicine go down" had been first handed him in his Damascus Road conversion. His conversion introduced him to a feast of preaching the cross and establishing churches before, to use his own metaphor, he would get stung. His years of service had their periods of external strife and internal struggle: rejection, imprisonment, torture, balancing the good he would do, with the bad he wouldn't do, and then when wanting to do good, he would find bad so close at hand and heart. He wrote to the Philippian Church about the paradox at the center of his dilemma: "For to me, living is Christ, dying is gain." (Philippians 1:21.) The Apostle admitted that he preferred dying, but that goal would prove selfish and disadvantageous to the Congregation. He lived with the conviction that God wanted him alive for some time yet. He had no intention of searching for a "god-awful tasting" drink, or a gun, or a knife, or a rope, or a bottle of pills! (Even if they had been available.) He stated his confidence again in a Philippian Church context, "I can do all things through him who strengthens me." (Ibid. 4:13.) So can any person, with perhaps a little help from a Pastor or a Counselor or one's family.

Occasionally a person has come to terms with the attitude: "I am going to get dying over with!" At this desperate moment a dying person may receive a parole; or some encouragement like a proverb or a poem stanza, maybe even one like in the "Song of Solomon," (8:6): "Love is strong as death, passion fierce as the grave." (The one problem of using this verse is that the love Solomon had in mind in composing the line was physical, "eros" love, not "agape" or "philio." But if you are dying, what difference does etymology make?) One dying person began her autobituary classically:

> "What greater gift is there than love?
> What richer asset shared than that of time with
> loved ones?
> What grander voyage taken than that in spirit?
> Of these, we say, there are none."
>
> *(Source not named; the composition may be original.)*

The Obituary Column in a recent weekday edition of the *Seattle Times* substantiates the claim made earlier about religious indifference in the Pacific Northwest. Of the approximately forty documents, three contained "religious" vocabulary or references. One asserted that the deceased had gone to a better place, and is dancing. Come to terms? Another concluded that the deceased Wife, Mother, Grandmother's dying had welcomed her into a homecoming, and the family is now joyfully celebrating life with Jesus. Come to terms? A third document stated, as many obituaries do in cases of long-married couples, that the man's earthly departure had resulted in a heavenly reunion with his wife. Come to terms with dying? In my judgment, all three of the above had enough "Spirit" in them to qualify for a "Yes" answer—at least as far as I can judge or affirm, based on my Reformed theological position.

One or two caveats about terms and dying, particularly on contemplation of the mystery of "what happens afterwards." The first concerns purgatory. Purgatorial repentance, restoration and re-housing assignments following death have no place in Reformed Doctrine—except denial. Passages of Scripture that suggest otherwise must be carefully "exegeted." A more orthodox position on judgment is found in Jesus' parable, "The Rich Man and Lazarus"—not the Lazarus Jesus raised from the dead, the brother of Mary and Martha. The Lazarus of the Parable was a poor man, the selfish elitist a rich man, probably a member of one of the powerful and prestigious religious establishments. He refused to allow starving Lazarus even into his garbage can. Death reversed their social and economic status. Lazarus went to Abraham, that is, heaven, or Paradise; the rich man to Hades. He had a vision of Lazarus enjoying all the luxury he had never had access to before. When he became writhingly parched he requested Abraham to send Lazarus "down" with an ice cube, or its equivalent. Abraham said he would not, nor could not, meet the request; the great Chasm between heaven and hell was like the new Israel wall in Jerusalem, making it almost impossible—or at least time-consuming—for Palestinians to move into Israel territory. The rich man began—too late—to feel compassion for his five living brothers. He requested

Abraham to send someone to them with the message of the Gospel, or in the rich man's own words, "Warn them, so that they will change their ways." Abraham responded that such an imposition on God's decrees was not necessary: "They have Moses and the prophets; they should listen to them." The rich man had a response: "No, father Abraham; but if someone goes to them from the dead, they will repent." Abraham closed the conversation, "If they do not listen to Moses and the prophets, neither will they be convinced, even if someone rises from the dead." Message: you decide your hereafter here! (Monastic Saint and author of profound spiritual literature, Thomas Merton will remind us of this truth in the last Chapter of the Book. Don't peek!) Purgatory is powerless, useless, and superfluous for believers who work to be theologically literate, discriminately studious, and habitually and lovingly pious.

The other caveat deals with communications sent along with the "going" for the "already gone." The gesture is presumptive; the assumption is that the going person will arrive at the place where the previously deceased has already arrived. That fortune may or may not be the case. You may respond, "Well, to err is human...." Wrong. Alexander Pope had either never read Genesis or did not believe it. If I had been Pope's editor, I would have drawn a line through "human," and written either: "To sin is human...." Or, "To err is to sin...." Eve and Adam were made in the image of God, and until the serpent trumped perfection, a "Utopian" ambiance lasted. But it changed. The consequences have already been considered.

Whether you die of cancer, or from mocking God by not taking care of your body, or by some other shameful abuse, as in HIV-Aids; or whether you die of "old age" and "natural causes;" or in an Airline tragedy, or by suicide or murder—however and whenever you die, coming to terms with your own or a loved one's dying, or the imminent prospect of it, benefits you with broad coverage. However, do not aim at being an expert in the process. What you train for may be as illegitimate and irrelevant and redundant in heaven as a Presbyterian Pastor. A dying person does not need to qualify as a "super-death-delegate" to be eligible. Teenagers die in car wrecks, young soldiers die in Iraq, young women die of invasive cancer, middle-aged bachelors succumb to heart attacks, some old and feeble or diseased should die, but live to be a hundred years old, the last decade spent in a Nursing Home. Regardless of its "godawful" distaste, its nasty sting or a pleasurable reception, the best terms in which to die, according to the Christian Faith, are the following:

- baptism, if you or your superiors have taken advantage of its availability, or you are mature enough and disposed toward its acceptability; baptism, however, does not guarantee that the baptized person will "fall asleep;" that is, die in Christ;
- greeting death unafraid, in spite of its penalty; in trust that Christ rose from the dead, and his resurrection guarantees ours;
- a record of having loved God, and your neighbor as yourself; and compassionate enough, if necessary, to allow the poor your garbage if that is all you have to share;
- a record of worship and service in the Church, promoting Christ's kingdom on earth as it is in heaven, including sustenance from "eating his body" and "drinking his blood; " again, not a requirement. Jesus said, "I have other sheep that do not belong to this fold. I must bring them also, and they will listen to my voice. So there will be one flock, one shepherd." (John 10:16.) Another reminder: when it happens, you will be saved by grace, not by "Church," not by doing good, not by the righteousness of your spouse, not by memorizing Scripture, not even by saying, "Lord, Lord…," but only by doing the faith of Jesus Christ, in whom you have believed. (Matthew 7:21-3.)

The wisdom of God says that whether we live or whether we die, we are the Lord's. Many obituaries give testimony that that relationship is the one in which their subject had died. Surely those persons had no more anxiety about dying than about stubbing a toe. If you die with a minimum struggle with breathing, and in relative peace and quietness, you will verify that you had come to terms with the cross of Jesus Christ. No one can come higher than Paul, in the terms already quoted. "For to me, living is Christ, and dying is gain," the Apostle wrote. And Jesus said to Martha at her brother's grave, just before Jesus brought him out—alive: "Everyone who lives and believes in me will never die." (John 11:26.)

What words do you hope to quote—from memory, if you are conscious—as you are dying? My choice would be the thoughts I usually rehearse at night before I go to sleep, Jesus' dying words, "Father, into your hands I commend my spirit." (Luke 23:46.) What words would you like to hear him say when you first meet him fact-to-face? My choice would be, "Truly, I tell you, today you will be with me in Paradise." (Luke 23:43.) Can you "top" those? If you can, you have come to superlatively supernatural terms with dying. Coming to terms is safe enough.

II.

Coming To Terms With Theology

"I believe in God...." The Apostle's Creed.

ENGINEER, AMATEUR THEOLOGIAN, APPROXIMATING RENAISSANCE: His final destiny, according to his obituary, had been accomplished in his death: the Lord had gathered him into his arms. Devoted to family, friends and community, and a Veteran, his philosophy held that life's glass never stays half-empty or half-full; it always overflows. His optimism, energy and mentoring skills had touched many lives. Following a struggle with fibrosis, he had "passed away" peacefully at home. All who had the privilege of knowing him will sorely miss him, the almost Renaissance imitator. He was buried at Tahoma National Cemetery. A Commemoration of his life was scheduled for later in the spring.

....

The Las Vegas *Review Journal* would have considered it a privilege to print the complete text of the above obituary; the *Journal* obituary pages have particular spiritual integrity. They begin Biblically: "The Rock....a faithful God, without deceit, just and upright." (Deuteronomy 32:4.) "Your steadfast love is as high as the heavens; your faithfulness extends to the clouds." (Psalm 57:10.) Classical poetry follows the Scripture references: Gratitude is the fairest blossom, which springs from the soul. (Henry Ward Beecher.)....Death is the Golden Key that opens the Palace, Eternity. (John Milton)." (Punctuation as in the original.)

Obituaries in most major daily newspapers, like the excerpt above, contain spiritual data: tributes to the faith of the individuals; suggestions about the deceased's post-death spiritual destiny; occasional references to their ease of, or courage in, dying; comments about their Church affiliation and involvements; announcements of a funeral, frequently at their Church; and an occasional inclusion of verses of Scripture. Regardless of whether the information classifies as theology, especially as Reformed dogma or that of most mainline religions or upstart denominations, the intent justifies the sentences: they honor the deceased's faith journey. They may inspire readers to do likewise.

The theology in obituaries tends toward subjectivity and sentimentality. Regardless of its taste, vocabulary, polish or orthodoxy, it qualifies for consideration in *Obituary Theology.* Any information that has a connection with religion qualifies for comment. If you want to critique it you may use your own theological outlook as a standard, or the theology in this Book. *Obituary Theology* was not written to be judge, only a comparison. To repeat, this Book aims primarily at being a thesis on the Reformation dogma of dying and death, written from the viewpoint of a retired Presbyterian Church (USA) Pastor. Reformed theology claims its base in Scripture. Though they may have Scriptural allusions, obituaries are not published as comment on Scripture. If they reflect Biblical understanding about dying, the intent is probably more coincidental than intentional, and probably fits the belief and lifestyle of the Subject (being) who has just died.

A cultural religious icon—referred to in the previous chapter—that has influenced the positions taken in *OT* (which henceforth will serve as an abbreviation for *Obituary Theology,* not *Old Testament)* is the biweekly periodical, *Christian Century.* Words that define the magazine's mission, "Thinking Critically, Living Rationally," appear on the cover. The challenge in reading the magazine is first, to think, and to read the material with reason and discrimination; and second, to reflect objectively on what is read, and live with more enlightenment. The assumption of the editors appears to be that discriminatory thinkers make good believers, and good believers make perceptive thinkers.

No matter how smart a person is, however, a reader can penetrate Jesus' thinking only according to the measure of faith (grace) bestowed on you. How many of us rise to that level? The playing field is leveled: geniuses bear the same standards of accountability as dunces. The *Century* obviously wants Christians to be thinking readers, as well as hearing-doing-saving disciples.

Jesus had men among his Twelve—and women among his students—who, if they were living in the present century, would have benefited from a subscription to the magazine. Thomas, John, Philip, James, and then the lately-become Apostle, Paul, would have received their money's worth, if they had had access to the magazine. They combined hearing and doing in such consistency that they surely would have became beneficiaries of Jesus' promise about those who treat the Gospel with the reverence and obedience it deservers: "We (Father and I) will come and make our home with them." (John 14:23.)

Coming to terms with theology, and especially the theology of dying and matters related to it, requires a clear understanding of what you are coming to terms with; otherwise how will you know if you have arrived? The definition that *Obituary Theology* has settled on, as already alluded to, combines the two Greek words that form the root of the discipline: *Theos* (God) and *Logos (word.)* Combine the two for a definition of theology, and you come up with—as already stated: "Theology is human word about Divine Word." The definition could also apply to Scripture knowledge, with a slight alteration: "Scripture knowledge is inspired human interpretation of the inspirited Divine Word." If you have ever thought deeper about dying and death than how sad it can be, and how it may hurt physically and psychologically, and how dislocating the experience will prove, and whether I will go to heaven or hell, you have thought critically, therefore, theologically. You are ready to think deeper.

The reader does not need to think within the bounds of Reformed Theology—even if you know what the bounds are—to think critically and weigh rationally, either the obituaries excerpted in the Book, or the author's comments on them. The Book approaches the subject and the resources of *OT* from a moderate Protestant viewpoint. Reformers of the Sixteenth Century stressed the Bible as the authoritative truth about God, the Church as preserver of the truth, and the believer as a member of the priesthood of all believers. The *Apostles' Creed* summarizes orthodoxy, and the Holy Spirit guides the Body of Christ as heirs and builders of the Kingdom of God. Students in Reformed Seminaries, atn least more than half a century past, and possibly today yet, memorized principles of Reformed theology by an acrostic: TULIP: Total depravity, Unconditional election, Limited atonement, Irresistible grace, and the Perseverance of the saints.

Reformed Theology also formed the basics of the theological system of the Church of my—and my wife's—spiritual background, The United Presbyterian Church of North America (1858-1958). The foundation theological UPNA document contained "The Great Ends of the Church." In 1958 the UPC (NA) and the Presbyterian Church (USA) merged into the United Presbyterian Church of the United States of America, and retained "The Great Ends" as a basic Reformed theological statement. The same base was kept in 1983, with the reunion of the UPC (USA) and the Presbyterian Church (US), to become the Presbyterian Church (USA). The opening pages of the new Church's *Constitution,* Part II, "The Book of Order, Form of Government," Chapter I. Preliminary Principles, No. 2, enumerate "The Great Ends of the Church:" "The proclamation of the Gospel for the salvation of humankind; the shelter, nurture, and spiritual fellowship of the children of God; the maintenance of divine worship; the preservation of the truth; the promotion of social righteousness; and the exhibition of the Kingdom of God in the world." The System of Reformed Theology embraced by "The Great Ends" shapes a Reformed agenda for the Church, and for its living the Word in the world.

Four features of Reformed Theology have been singled out as the theological base for *Obituary Theology:* **Essence, Source, Deliverance, and Acceptance. Praxis,** a fifth feature, deals with application or practice of the faith. Since it is the pragmatic characteristic of the discipline, it will be applied more to the matters dealt with in the last Chapter of *OT,* "Knowhow."

Coming to terms with theology, then, as it relates to the goals of *OT,* begin at the beginning, and the beginning is **essence.** Scholars, and even the less scholarly, may object. Their protest may advocate that <u>Essence</u> is embarrassing and intimidating—too reductionist, too ethereal, too foreign to incarnation and too abstract. A response may ask, Who or What is more abstract than Spirit (John 4:24), or unsearchable judgment and inscrutable ways (Romans 11:33)? Or the name God gave for Moses to claim his authority from. "I am that I am," or "I will be who I will be." Think of essence of God as God in God's own self; "God unpeeled," or unrevealed, remembering that God declared that no one can look on God and live. When Moses came down from the mountain, even though he had kept his face veiled while receiving the Ten Commandments, his countenance nevertheless glowed; as did Jesus' at the Transfiguration. Meditate also on Genesis 1:1: "In the beginning God. (Was God awake?)"

In his first chapter to the Romans the Apostle Paul railed against those who by their ungodliness and wickedness "suppress the truth" that God is. Of course, Paul argues, God is, and God is known primarily because of what God does or has done. God can be known because God has made self-knowledge plain: "Ever since the creation of the world his eternal power and divine nature, invisible though they are, have been understood and seen through the things he has made." (Romans 1:2.) Paul's statement alludes to feature numbers two and three in the introductory list to the features of theology, but the statement about God as essence is clear. God is the essence of theology, and the essence of God is "eternal power and divine nature."

One of the most helpful statements about essence in the Bible is alluded to above, the one God delivered when Moses was in the midst of receiving his Mt. Horeb call through the Burning Bush that eventually resulted in his leading the Exodus of God's chosen people away from Egypt. (The statement was repeated when the Ten Commandments were delivered.) At Sinai a theophany (appearance of God) brought Deity and the Prophet together. A storm played a dynamic prelude to the encounter. Thunder and lightning were clapping and flashing, bursting the clouds; trumpet sounds were blasting, and smoke moving like a little child in competition with the clouds. The sky was turning black. A riveting sentence introduces their meeting: "Moses drew near to the thick darkness, where God was." (Ed. The God of light in thick darkness? What a funeral text! See Exodus 20:21.) When Moses demanded a confirmation of the Divine presence he was encountering, he received the answer "YHWH," translated, "I am what I am, (or 'I will be what I will be....')" As observed, four Hebrew consonants form the word-name "YHWH," later popularized in Biblical translations as "Jehovah."(Gospel writer John would make etymological use of the concept behind God's name in seven Gospel "I am" statements. John's purpose was, of course, to underscore his emphasis on Jesus as "very God of very God."

The Jacob's Well conversation about God between Jesus and a Samaritan woman—touched on in other contexts in *OT* —turned into an "essence" talk. The conversation began when Jesus asked a Samaritan woman for a drink. She expressed her surprise at a male Jew being willing to talk to a Samaritan female. She was further surprised when Jesus addressed her morality. In her hopes of diverting him, she boldly—or ignorantly—settled on theology. She asked Jesus to settle an issue that segregated the unorthodox, mixed-blood Jew-Samaritans from real "Jews." Samaritans worshiped on Mt. Gerizim, within sight of the two of them; the "real" Jews worshiped on Mt. Zion in Jerusalem. Jesus said that Mountain choice makes no difference. He then stretched the Samaritan's theology with the statement: "God is spirit, and those who worship him must worship in spirit and truth." She went home and shared her new insight into the essence of God. Men of the village headed for the well, and a mini-Pentecost took place. The new Christians returned to Samaria and said to the woman, "It is no longer because of what you said that we believe, for we have heard for ourselves, and we know that this is truly the Savior of the world." (John 4, particularly vs. 42.) The primary insight about essence that emerged from Jesus' being thirsty was, "God is spirit."

The *Westminster Dictionary of the Bible* article on "God," (p. 206) deals in essence with great generosity.[1] Fifteen attributes of God are listed. Many of them, however, connect with deeds. God in essence wants to be known. Thanks be to God for allowing humanity to know about and of God's essence, and to commune with God in essence. But do not make an image of that essence, or worship the image, in spite of the difficulty of relating to one who cannot be seen or heard graphically, or concretely, or materially.

John Calvin's brilliant contributions to theology five hundred years ago—2009 celebrates his 500th birth—as one would expect, included insight on essence. Calvin insisted that discovering who God is comes from meditation on what God does; again, essence is a product of revelation. The nature of God always occupied a central place in Calvin's thinking. He asserted that God clothed the Creation with essence wrappings. Calvin also attributed human experience—*Cognitio experimentalis Dei*—with an essential role in the discovery of essence: "No man can take a survey of himself but he must immediately turn to the contemplation of God, in whom he 'lives and moves.'…. And no man can come to the true knowledge of himself, without having first contemplated the divine character, and then condescended to his own…. His (God's) essence indeed is incomprehensible, so that his Majesty is not to be perceived by the human senses; but on all his works he hath inscribed his glory in characters so clear, unequivocal, and striking, that the most illiterate and stupid cannot exculpate." (*Institutes*, Book I. Chapters 1, 2, and 5.)[2]

Chapter Two of The *Westminster Confession of Faith* outdoes the Westminster Dictionary of the Bible in identifying "essence." On precursory examination, the *Confession* seems to contradict Calvin. One difference between the *Confession* and the *Dictionary* is the number of "essences of the Essence" of God, and how they are perceived. The *Dictionary* lists twenty-two "is's" of God, about half of them stating how God's essence is known by what God does. One of the purest "essence" statements is found in Chapter 2, #2: "God hath all life, glory, goodness, blessedness, in and of himself; and is alone, in and unto himself, all-sufficient, not standing in need of any creatures which he hath made, nor deriving any glory from them, but only manifesting his own glory, by, unto, and upon them; he alone is the fountain of all being, of whom, through whom, and to whom, are all things; and hast most sovereign dominion over them.... He is most holy...."[3]

An obituary in a 2007 edition of the *Seattle Times* introduces a man who came into contact with God's essence. The document differs from many obituaries in at least two ways. First, and most importantly, it insists that Christian experience of God is by grace, "God's unmerited favor." Second, it relies on Scripture for authentic theology. (It is also a longer than the average document.) It features three photos: the first, a "Senior Age" picture, with the following passage of Scripture: "For I am already being poured out as a drink offering, and the time of my departure is at hand. I have fought the good fight, I have finished the race, and I have kept the faith." (2 Timothy 4:6ff.) The other two photos hint at the devout life of a man of the Church.

God is the essence of theology, and being is the essence of God. Jesus came to earth as a divine being. However, according to Paul, he did not bring the total package with him; before he left heaven for Bethlehem he had "emptied himself," not totally, but of the totality of divine essence, as the Philippian Epistle (2:7) asserts. The next sentence, verse 8, says, "He humbled himself." His humility form was "slave," and out of that slavery came the water of life, the bread of life, and the blood of eternal life.

Paul reminded the Churches that he organized his theology around one aspect of God's essence that is capable of, worthy of, and compulsory for, imitation: "Let the same mind be in you that was in Christ Jesus, who though he was in the form of God...emptied himself, taking the form of a slave...." (Philippians 2:1-11.) Jesus was and is eternally, except for the few years when he was "incarnated" and on earth, the essence of God, therefore, of being. God is one essence, and three in being, and all three beings are God in essence. And they are eternally so, except for the Incarnation.

Source introduces the second feature that one experiences, or is searching to experience, about God. Again, as with Calvin, knowledge and experience and conviction of the source of "all things"—God—comes to a human being, in large part, by thinking critically and living faithfully, or *Cognitio experimentalis Dei*. A living person, no less seriously than a dying one, comes into a deeper relationship with God, hence Jesus Christ, by coming to terms with God as source of human life on earth. God is the source of all sources. The Logos, or Word, claims the same attribute: "All things came into being through him (the Word, or Logos, or Jesus), and without him not one thing came into being." (John 1:3.) The discharges from the Source, John insisted, are light and life. (Ibid. v. 4.) Paul's understanding heads for infinity: "For from him, of him and to him are all things." Another translation reads, "Source, guide and goal of all that is." (Romans 11:36.)

In her new book, *Sovereignty,* theologian Jean Betake Elshtain offers a helpful comment about how essential source is in coming to terms with God, particularly as Sovereign. (The concept has crucial meaning for dying and death and resurrection.) "To understand God truly, we must see God not only as the **center** of a great order of reality, but as its **absolute source.** The world exists because God chose to create it. God could choose a different world, or no world at all, at any moment. God's will replaces God's reason as the measure of sovereignty."[4] To know and understand God truthfully, "thinking critically" requires seeking God's will, which reveals God's essence. The revelation motivates living rationally, because faith is rational. God as source never goes dry, or takes sight off the sparrow, the seedling, or the fruit. God is, in essence, the divine being who promotes peace and justice in and for the whole creation. At the end of the Sixth Day, "God saw everything that he had made, and indeed, it was very good." (Genesis 1:31a.) And God wants it kept as pure and undefiled as when it came from the Source as possible. But in a "fallen world" God's want cannot possibly be realized.

Deliverance features prominently with theology. It brings theology nearer to the acceptance feature. Deliverance closer connects the God of essence and source with the God of human "know ability" and an expectation of contact and obedience. Sovereignty and Source impact the good that God delighted in the Sixth Day.

In deliverance Source-Essence takes on many guises; incarnation is the most crucial. God leaves heaven to make theology a tool of creation and communication, as Paul wrote to the Romans (1:18-20.) Creation is transformed into a phenomenon that makes discernment of God's eternal power and deity unavoidable. God was so gorged by the goodness of essence, that God had to expel it, share it. God, the essence of good plans and good results, and useful for the creation, sorts out what the earth and its human citizens need. The Creator Source-Essence entrusts to the human creation dominion over the Garden and everything created. It is something worth talking about, even bragging about, and God will begin the talk. The communication system had been part of the original plan. Eve and Adam will be the first to do God-talk. If only they had been born better equipped to do Satan talk, or to shut their mouths at the right time—that is, before taking a forbidden bite.

Deliverance keeps God eternally active. God in wisdom determined to create mission and ministry for human activity. The Church will be formed and privileged to assist in the deliverance: a big act of trust on God's part! If the

Church ever needs deliverance, Plan B will have to be set in place. No created, normal human being has the blood for it.

Deliverance in the meantime has attracted great minds, created a variety of instruments, and called a band of committed travelers. The primary deliverers in the Old Testament came from the ranks of the Law and the Prophets, and the devoted priests of the sacrificial system, and the servants who spent long hours in the Temple and the Synagogue—without computers, iPods or projectors. They included those who accepted responsibility for training children in the way they should go, attracted youth to the scripture handed down through the ages orally and written, and equipped adults in the theologies of the Old and New Covenants. Parents gave their sons and daughters to foreign tongues and poorly governed lands, and missionaries gave their lives willingly and unconditionally to those who in Jesus' sower-seed-soil paradigm fit the bad-soil behavior of rock throwers, courage chokers and pleasure perverts. (Remember Stephen, Acts 7:54-60.)

The fourth feature of theology, as it relates to obituary theology, **acceptance**, calls the Church to attention. Once God as God exerts inexhaustible Divine Essence in creating the world and everything in it, and endows humanity with the ability of discernment, human beings have no excuse for not knowing and responding to God. One of the first imperatives is for humans to acknowledge the special endowment of our species, *imago dei.* Your acceptance of yourself as an advantaged creature, meaning you are capable of receiving and discovering the knowledge of God and figuring out some of the mystery of the plan of God's will, vindicates God's going to the bother. Paul recalled the courage of God in doing these favors: "We have this treasure (Sic. the Gospel) in clay jars, so that it may be made clear that this extraordinary power belongs to God and does not come from us." (2 Corinthians 4:7.)

One of the first attempts at deliverance resulted in reverse-acceptance. The delivery scene was the Garden of Eden, and the rejection of the word came from Eve and Adam. The history of acceptance would be marked by episodes of contrariness, argument, rebellion, repentance and resolve. Noah, Abraham (and Sarah), Moses, Isaiah, the four Gospel authors, Peter on the day of Pentecost, Paul, and John author of "The Revelation" would play the leading roles in the Biblical chronicle of acceptance.

However, no event of deliverance-acceptance compares with God's incarnation in Jesus Christ. In the fullness of time God came as the Logos, in the flesh of the person of a beloved Son. Jesus claimed among other amazing abilities and assignments and talents, to be the way and the truth and the life. Delivering the Gospel was so crucial to building the foundation of the Church that Jesus took painful steps toward guaranteeing that non-acceptance would not prove a stumbling block to the Church. By the time he was crucified he had trained twelve—one a failure—to use the guaranteed tools of deliverance-acceptance: preaching, teaching and healing. It worked.

No one was, at first encounter, more an obstacle to deliverance and acceptance than Saul of Tarsus. His behavior changed dramatically when Jesus met him in a vision on the road to Damascus and turned him around. Paul became the greatest missionary of the New Testament, and in fact, of all time. He introduced most of his Epistles, not with, "I decided to go out and preach," but "Paul, called to be an apostle by the will of God…." His motivation consisted, in part, to witness to his own dramatic salvation, and to couple his love of Christ with his love of proclaiming the message. He wrote in the Romans Epistle: "How are they to call on one in whom they have not believed? And how are they to believe in one of whom they have never heard? And how are they to hear without someone to proclaim him? And how are they to proclaim him unless they are sent?" (Romans 10:14-15.) Their voice must go out to all the earth, the Apostle determined. People must not die without someone planting the seed in them. The Church had been so commissioned by the Head. Who would deliver the treasure if the Church that had been entrusted with it did not?

After he had trained the Twelve and had won a multitude of followers, the task of deliverance had to be handed over to others. Surely they would hear the summons; surely they had sung, "How beautiful are the feet of those who bring good news!" (Isaiah 52:7 and Romans 10:15.) People gifted with the Gospel would surely want beautiful feet! Feet had begun to become more beautified on the first Pentecost after Jesus had risen and ascended back into heaven. On a day signaled by heavenly pyrotechnics such as the world had never witnessed before, and has not experienced since, the Holy Spirit moved into the Church, guaranteeing its equipping by God with the power and presence to vindicate God's sending the only begotten Son to save the world. God exploded out of total being-essence and from infinite-source to squeeze into a human body. After completing the intended and necessary work of redemption and inauguration of the Church with the Son on the Cross, the continuing work of deliverance-acceptance became the inheritance of the Holy Spirit. Jesus had promised the Apostles: "You will receive power when the Holy Spirit has come upon you; and you will be my witnesses in Jerusalem, in all Judea and Samaria, and to the ends of the earth." (Acts 1:8.) And so it happened, and keeps happening.

The Church has never had sufficient Paul's, in spite of God's promise:

> For as the rain and the snow come down from heaven,
> and do not return until they have watered the earth,
> Making it bring forth and sprout, giving seed to the sower,
> and bread to the eater.
> So shall my word be that goes out from my mouth;
> It shall not return to me empty,
> But it shall accomplish that which I purpose,
> and succeed in the thing for which I send it.
> (Isaiah 55.)

The preacher/evangelist always goes out with an assurance of acceptance. Paul had a glorious vision of the success of the Church, and he wrote, "...at the name of Jesus every knee should bend, in heaven and on earth and under the earth, and every tongue should confess that Jesus

Christ is Lord, to the glory of God the Father." (Philippians 2:10-11.) On the day of his ascension back to heaven forty days after his crucifixion, the deliverer gave his initial band of twelve—including the one who had replaced Judas Iscariot—their new Pentecostal commission: they had a global mission ahead of them, and as they delivered truth, people would accept their message. Most important, they would not be denied his company: "I am with you always, to the end of the age." (Matthew 28:20.)

As Paul discovered in the Church's earliest evangelism efforts, deliverance of the Gospel has not always gone out with, nor has acceptance resulted from, the purest of motives. The Apostle wrote to the Philippians, "Some proclaim Christ from envy and rivalry...others proclaim Christ out of selfish ambition, not sincerely but intending to increase my suffering in my imprisonment." (Philippians 1:15-17.) Paul would not submit to either disappointment or discouragement. He held so fervently to the values of walking in the way and the truth and the life of Jesus Christ, that he was amenable to compromise: "What does it matter? Just this, that Christ is proclaimed in every way, whether out of false motives or true; and in that I rejoice." (Vs. 18.) Wrong motives for preaching the Gospel may have small effect on its acceptance; wrong motives for acceptance, however, may quickly decay into hypocrisy, immorality, or abandonment. (Cf. Jesus' parable of the four soils, sometimes also known as the parable of the sower, Matthew 13:1-10.) The deliverance style he wanted the deliverers to practice was: deliver boldly, deliver simply, and deliver applicably. The acceptance wisdom was: expect results, ask for results, clarify results, recognize results, acknowledge results, and participate in results. However, do not count on acceptance as a quick process; or one that always has a happy ending. And remember this enduring truth of the kingdom of God, and preach it: God will one day judge you not so much by what you said, but by what you did.

The Church may take a lesson on endurance in deliverance from the following historical vignettes:

- a rich man wanting to know how to inherit eternal life, walking away sad after he was told to give away all his possessions;
- an Apostle betraying Jesus for thirty pieces of silver, and committing suicide after those who had purchased his infidelity would not take the money back;
- a German firebrand Reformer (Martin Luther), a French-turned-Swiss Scholar, John Calvin, and a Scott "firebrand" Theologian (John Knox), calling the Church to return to the authority of Scripture, and succeeding against the Roman distortions of the Gospel in Germany, Switzerland and Scotland, and eventually in Europe and the United States of America and then globally, through the movement known as "The Reformation;"
- a German Pastor who believed fervently enough in the assassination of evil persons, that he compromised his pacifism and joined in a plot to kill a Dictator who had created a Nazi following to commit the genocide of six million Jews in Europe;
- an Archbishop publicly assassinated in front of his cathedral in San Salvador for preaching justice and liberty for the oppressed;
- and an American Baptist Clergyman drawing 100,000 listeners to his "I Have a Dream" speech on the Capitol Mall in Washington, D.C., the greatest force in Civil Rights History in the United States, but later assassinated one night on the balcony of a Tennessee Motel.

These heroes of Church History, notably the martyrs, join the Biblical cast whose epitaph deserves the words from the Hebrews epistle: "Of whom the world was not worthy." They answered their opponents like Peter in Jerusalem when he—and John—were warned that they would be arrested again if they preached Christ in the Temple environs: "We must obey God rather than any human authority." (Acts 5:29.) These faithful deliverers of the Gospel had come to terms with the dangerous word.

Obituaries complement the witness of Pentecost and of the Early Church on acceptance of and victory over the threats one faces when unconditionally accepting the theology of a risen Christ. Sowing the seeds of proclamation, instruction and compassion produces fruit one hundredfold: obedience and evangelism, study and justice, the needy treated as if they were Jesus, righteousness and salvation (of individuals and society), love and justice, liberation and prosperity. The beneficiaries will once again say "amen" to Jesus' oft-repeated announcement, "The kingdom of God is among you."

The best of the good news in obituary theology locates in the words of these dead who had come to terms with a theology that was not simply spoken, but sacrificially done:

> "He was called into the presence of his Lord and Savior Jesus Christ on (date).... Services will be held in a Gospel Chapel."
>
> "(Her name)_____, age ___, Sunset on ___(Date). Services at Temple Baptist. (Date.)
>
> "(She) went to rest with our Lord on (date)...She devoted her life to studying God's word at Bible Study Fellowship...."
>
> "(Name), age 92, went to be with her heavenly Father on_____(date.)"

Theology has sometimes been called "The Queen of the Sciences." Who is the King? Jesus Christ surely takes that honor. His court consists of theologians, amateurs and professionals; saints, male and female, who acted in his name as humble servants; and on occasion, a traitor. Neither one has special favor with Jesus. The favored ask Jesus, "When did we do mercy to you?" (Cf. Matthew 25:37 et. al. His answer will be, "Certainly not because you are a learned systematic theologian, but because you saw the needs of the least, and you did it unto them." (Ibid.)

The Chapter closes with an obituary excerpt of a Presbyterian Clergy colleague. Marjorie and I first became acquainted with Pat during the two years we raised Church

Mission money in Buffalo, New York, 1988-90. She grew up with the Gospel, she accepted the Gospel, and she delivered the Gospel in word and deed. I suggest that before you read Pat's obituary excerpt, you find a Dictionary and look up the word "abstemious." If you are already duplicitous with the word, do not waste your time!

THE ABSTEMIUS REVEREND DOCTOR PAT: Pat wrote part of her own long obituary. Her words in places are humorously self-contradictory. She wanted to be remembered as: "Someone who has lots of fun, is full of life, intelligent, engaging, curious, easy to talk to, a loving mother, a loyal friend, a cherished Pastor, and always abstemious." Travels, education, seven children, including "steps", sports, professions and friendships proved immune to her "abstemiety." Born a Californian, and raised an "All Over American," Pat died a Washington State resident. She had attended numerous educational and theological institutions, and had obtained a Doctorate degree. Once a "frustrated" (her own words) ordained Episcopal Deacon, she eventually became an ordained Presbyterian Church (U.S.A.) clergy. Pat came to theological terms with dying when she had breast cancer, and ended near death. After two months in a respirator, she experienced a "miraculous recovery." She died in 2008, and her funeral took place in Seattle. She requested that her ashes be scattered "from a tall ship full sailing the turquoise waters off Virgin Gorda." Bon Voyage, dear abstemious Sister in Christ!

III.

Coming To Terms With Authority

"I believe in God the Father Almighty, …and in Jesus Christ his only son our Lord…I believe in the Holy Ghost…."

The Apostles' Creed

……….

FAMILY WISHES BIRTHDAY PEACE, WHILE WAITING: A family wished a deceased member a "Happy Birthday." They are convinced that he rests in peace while he waits for the rest of his family to join him. They expect to see him soon. They sound confident and hopeful.

HEAVENLY AIRSHOW PERFORMANCE: The family remembered him with a tribute on the anniversary of his leaving. Much of their comfort arises from their assurance that their former pilot husband and father flies with other air-show performers who had preceded him to the eternal skies, and those who arrived after him. "What a heavenly air-show it must be!"

……….

Jesus looked up to heaven and said, "Father, the hour has come; glorify your Son so that the Son may glorify you, since you have given him authority over all people, to give eternal life to all whom you have given him." (John 17:1-2.)

……….

The survivors of the deceased subjects in the excerpts that open Chapter III obviously had confidence. They both left trails of evidence of it, if not in their own statements, then in the obituary lines of the persons who had known them intimately. The comfort friends and mourners appear to be receiving at the moment echoes some of the benefits Jesus announced that his death would bring. One of the subjects is at peace. The other is peace active, happily performing in "heavenly air-shows." (Ed. Did he die in one? The obituary does not say.) Both obituaries hint at a deep love between deceased and survivors. Both also reflect an almost universal human longing: to live beyond their years on earth, in an existence that will reach its fullest expression and richest fulfillment when an anticipated reunion takes place with those with whom they had lived. The excerpts from their obituaries indicate that they had believed that another life awaited them beyond their present one. Authority is evident in their expressions of hope.

Faith in post-death survival centers in the Christian belief system. The dogma receives its weight from a multitude of sources. It results from a theology of acceptance. It evidences a coming to terms with authority, particularly the authority of theology. Some person whom the Subject had trusted had delivered a message with authority and the deceased had accepted it. In many instances, the family of the deceased had been the primary authority behind the confidence. Or perhaps a mystical experience that may be attributed to the Holy Spirit had opened your mind and heart to a position of hope. Faith conceives hope. "For who hopes for what is seen? But if we hope for what we do not see, we wait for it with patience." (Romans 8:24-5.) We take post-death survival on trustworthy authority. We have good support for our confidence. Paul reminded the Church: "So faith comes from what is heard, and what is heard comes through the word of Christ." (Romans 10:17.) In the passage quoted at the opening of the Chapter (Matthew 28:18) Jesus himself made an amazing claim: the sovereign God had given him "authority over all people."

Obituaries that contain information that *OT* regards as theological claim a base in authority. Its source has objectivity, that is, it does not arise out of the mind or experience of the deceased; it has verification in Scripture or Church Doctrine, and it postulates benefits and fortune that comes to persons both before and after they die. Whether the person obtained it there or not, or is aware of it, the confidence they have aligns with the Church's authority gained from the Bible and Church History; and—here the subjective dimension comes in—on the need for comfort and consolation. These statements receive their validity and credibility in part on the sources of authority, and on the reasonability and rationality of the statements. Chapter Three will examine coming to terms with authority in spiritual matters, particularly those related to dying and death.

The opening Chapter of the Church's *Form of Government* makes clear statements about the authority of Jesus Christ for the Church: "Christ is present with the Church in both Spirit and Word…Insofar as Christ's will for the Church is set forth in Scripture, it is to be obeyed…matters (of worship, service and government) of the Church are to be ordered according to the Word by reason and sound judgment under the guidance of the Holy Spirit." (G-1.0100.) The authority for these words is derived, in part, from the statement of Jesus quoted at the beginning of the Chapter, and found in John 17:2. These truths reflect Reformed Theology. Most Christian Churches also subscribe to them. Versions of them often find their way into obituaries.

In spite of his recognition of the authority of God, the Biblical Prophet, Job, leaves no doubt about his conviction that believers can take advantage of the propriety and opportunity to question God's authority. Admittedly Job came to this point in the midst of despair, and maybe not in the condition quoted in the previous paragraph about the role of reason and sound judgment in the discernment and use of authority. Job was on the threshold of losing his reasoning, therefore, good judgment. It took the Prophet some time, even with help—or hindrance, from objective counselors, more objective than perceptive or intelligent—

to advance beyond feeling sorry for himself, or thinking through his dilemma theologically. His despair at the loss of health, wealth, family and happiness turned into a contest between him and God, and proved a test not only of his own patience, but also of God's. When faced with God's ultimatum—"Put up, or Shut up!"—Job shifted to a different attitude, and softened in his submission to authority. He finally quit concentrating on his misfortune and began contemplating God's power in nature, and the evidence that the Creation gives of God's divine providence. Having arrived at that point in his thinking, the prophet humbly confessed, "I know that you can do all things, and that no purpose of yours can be thwarted….I had heard of you by the hearing of the ear, but now my eyes see you…. therefore I despise myself and repent in dust and ashes." (Job 42:5-6.) Full restoration for his loss, and reinvigoration of his physical condition followed the Prophet's contrition.

Obituaries frequently include theological statements or offer nuances that challenge Biblical authority; the statements can also be as orthodox as John 3:16. How do you measure them against or in comparison with reliable orthodoxy? How can you avoid being judgmental with obituary information that you believe trounces orthodoxy? Thinking critically does not give an individual the right to judge God; it challenges a challenger to look at several perspectives of an issue. If you are dissatisfied with a Reformed—or Episcopal or Methodist or Pentecostal authority system—check out others. In your grief, and any distortion of reason it may be responsible for, you may be able to come to a position where you cry and laugh and be angry with God. Begin to exercise your courage to explore God in depths that you have never penetrated before. Dying and death need not be grounds for a divorce from God. As Job came to discover, God is never other than the innocent party.

Reformation theology finds spiritual comfort with authority. One of its iconic slogans states: "Reformed, but always reforming." In other words, beware of arrivals; beware of swelled heads; beware of "final" words; beware of "never." Gospel Writer John reminded human beings of the necessity of treading humbly when walking through the mazes of theology. His first reminder may be found in John 16:13. Jesus told the disciples, "I have many things to say to you, but you cannot bear them now… When the Spirit of truth comes, he will guide you into all the truth; for he will not speak on his own, but will speak whatever he hears, and he will declare to you the things that are to come…he will take what is mine and declare it to you…." (*Ibid.*16:12-15, selected.).

The second example of Johannine wisdom may be found in his words about the volume of Jesus' words that never appeared in Biblical text. John believed dogmatically that no library in the world, (not even the amazing one in Alexandria?) could record all that Jesus did and said; there are so many "other things." John believed, "If every one of them were written I suppose that the world itself could not contain the books that would be written." (Ibid. 21-5.) (Ed. How about computers?) Checks and balances, some of them internal to the Bible itself, may be employed for establishing the basis of Jesus' authority. (John 28:18.)

Ever since the Reformation—Division and Reorganization—the Church has retained a spiritual commitment and sensitivity to coming to terms with authority. It has had no hesitancy in asserting the supremacy of Scripture, as Source. The Church claims to be built upon: "the apostles and prophets, with Christ Jesus himself as the corner stone….in whom you also are built together spiritually into a dwelling place of God in the Spirit." (Ephesians 2:21-2.) Theology—with authority—has a history full of refining from giants like Luther, Zwingli, Calvin, and all the Samson's who have followed behind them. Now, finally, women have joined the ranks, to the glory of God, and have deposited some needed feminization. (Obituaries will also come under consideration.)

Disagreements over authority have always risen in the Church. Probably the most memorable one in Church History happened in Jerusalem over the issue of circumcision. Some of the more conservative legalistic new Christians were spreading out in Asia Minor insisting, "Unless you are circumcised according to the custom of Moses, you cannot be saved." Missionaries Paul and Barnabas were in dissension with the conservatives. A meeting of the Council was called. Apostles and elders came to consider the matter. Peter gave a persuasive speech, followed by Paul and Barnabas. James presided. The final decision was to send out a letter about the essentials of the matter: "...that you abstain from what has been sacrificed to idols and from blood and from what is strangled and from fornication. If you keep yourselves from these, you will do well. Farewell." The recipients of the letter had a favorable response: "When its members read it, they rejoiced in the exhortation." (Acts 15:1-30.) If the subsequent history of the Church could only report such amicable solutions to questions over doctrine, practice and authority!

Church polities have resulted. Church divisions have taken place. The Church still quarrels over where authority centralizes: with a large representative group, a congregational body, a hierarchy, a democracy, or another configuration? Does it finally and ultimately rest on a pinnacle at the top, in one person, such as the Pope, or in a Cardinal or a Bishop? Or does an elected, ordained representative governing body, as in some Denominations a Council, a Consistory, a Classis, or a system of Governing Bodies (like Presbyterian) hold the reins of authority? The Reformers insisted that democratic decision-making, works best, especially when parity between laity and clergy prevails.

Church authority has currently become a critical consideration in issues that fall into the category of "Church and State Relations." One of the most serious conflicts currently resides in Denominations whose polity claims governing body ownership of property. Several congregations in disagreement with national church actions and legislation have declared an intention to leave the National Organization, and they insist on taking their properties with them. Episcopalians and Presbyterians are currently dealing with several congregations struggling with this dilemma. Money either invested in, or endemic to, valuable tracts of land exacerbates finding easy solutions. A search for a solution begins with searching the will of God in Jesus Christ, as revealed in authoritative Scripture, as sent from God his Father, and as co-sender of the third person of the trinity, the Holy Spirit. Church authority aims to discern the mind of Christ and apply it with love and charity and justice. As a Reformed body, the Presbyterian Church (U.S.A.) operates on the principle of shared power by its governing bodies (Session, Presbytery, Synod and General Assembly). Each higher governing body shares authority over the one below it. The system also calls for "continuity with and faithfulness to the heritage which lies behind the contemporary church. It calls equally for openness and faithfulness to the renewing activity of the God of history." ("Form of Government, G-4.0303.") (Ed. A recent decision in a civil court, May 2009, denied a departing Episcopal Congregation exclusive ownership of its church property.)

The authority claimed by Jesus Christ, noted in the Chapter Introduction as covering "everybody," goes broad and deep. Reformed doctrine holds that because of the special union that exists, not only between the persons of the Godhead, but also between Jesus and the creation—including human beings—and by virtue of his word in the Gospel and his death and resurrection in history, Jesus proved credible in making the claim. He had the right. Baptism commits believers to the claim; it also acts as the seal of it. Believers will be united to him, as he covenanted, in a death and resurrection like his. The anticipation of those events gives the Church the authority—and the duty—to speak confidently about him, and the Father and the Holy Spirit; and to write about them; and to ask for commitment to them. In fact, the first sign and seal of our calling to be a disciple of Jesus Christ and to walk in his way is the union that baptism creates with him. The union has a future tense, as well as a perfect and past tense: "Do you not know that all of us who have been baptized into Christ Jesus were baptized into his death…? If we have been united with him in a death like his, we will certainly be united with him in a resurrection like his."(Romans 6:1-6.) The other one of the two sacraments in Reformed Theology, the Eucharist of Holy Communion, also unites observers of union with him in his death. The Cup is served with these words from 1 Corinthians ll: "...he took the cup after supper saying, 'This cup is the new covenant in my blood. Do this, as often as you drink it, in remembrance of me. For as often as you eat this bread and drink the cup, you proclaim the Lord's death until he comes.'" (Vss. 23-26.) Praise God for the authority Jesus "sacramentalized" in water and bread and wine!

Obituary theology does not often rise to the level of dogmatic sophistication or illumination in the history just surveyed. Its features rank closer to literalism, subjectivism, conjecture, and even hubris. Its theology occasionally classifies as "works-righteousness." The results may be thought of as a pasteurization of sincerity, suffering, style and sympathy. Although the language may be Biblical, the theology may not conform to orthodox Reformed principles. Reformation dogma holds that authority about the Trinitarian God and about life and death resides in Jesus Christ, revealed in the Scripture the Church has declared "canonical," that is, official; and authority is sent from God, with Jesus as the sent and the Holy Spirit as the co-sent; and with Jesus Christ as the Head of the Church, as crucified, dead and buried, and risen and coming again at the close of the Ages. Obituary theology meets the standards that Paul put on Scripture: ".... inspired by God and useful for teaching, for reproof, for correction, and for training in righteousness." (2 Timothy 3:16.) Paul, of course, wrote those words about Scripture, not about obituaries.

Time has come to meet an author of an autobituary. I want to introduce you to a remarkable character, now dead, Virginia Sue "Ginna" MacKenzie, who lived in Lynchburg, Virginia. She died in the year 2008. She left behind an autobituary. It details Ginna's life and death, and theology.

By the time that Virginia ("Ginna") Sue Mackenzie of Lynchburg, Virginia had died from kidney failure (in 2008), she had composed the creative document about her life and theology and death. Although her literary skill and prophetic insight did not match or surpass the skills of Daniel or Mark or the John of either the Gospel or the Revelation, Ginna nevertheless evidenced a strong persona, and in spite of her debilitating illness, a strong sense of vocatio, or calling from God, to various enterprises. She wrote her own obituary with a flair for creativity and a flavor of humor. Her literary style could even classify as "simple apocalypticism," that is, employing the form that some Biblical authors had followed centuries before her time. Ginna's paragraphs stir the imagination, elicit sympathy, and create dramatic end scenes. Hers is a classic autobituary. It reflects her years of suffering kidney failure, and extensive dialysis. Her "autobituary" appeared in the October 07, 2008 of *The Lynchburg (VA) News and Advance.* Excerpts from her story are quoted, with permission from her Newspaper's Managing Editor.

Ginna's ability to express her feelings humorously—even when she must have been feeling dreadful—indicates a high level of intelligence and faith. Toward the end of her document, she said, "Well, I am gone/out-a-here/tootleloo, as of 5:15 A.M., Thursday, October 11, at Lynchburg General Hospital. I hope God is happy with what I have done because I certainly wanted my life to be different than it was. I don't mind having been so ill. I do, however, mind that no one would hire me. The whole point of having a transplant aims at restoring health to the point that patients can work and be productive….I was educated, receiving a BA and ME from Lynchburg College, had a reasonable amount of intellect, spent my life trying to grow and be better, and have never felt like I fit in anywhere. I am sorry about that; it wasn't fun for me either. Hence, my spiritual path became the most important thing in my life…."

Ginna's largess of spirit—charity and religious commitment and sensitivity—reflected in her request: "Please, no flowers. Send your money in thanks to the… Nephrology Clinic, in Lynchburg….Starting now, enjoy your lives. LOVE more than you ever have before and help others as much as you can. I wish I had understood that much sooner than I did. I want you to know, however, that in all my medical life I was NEVER, EVER, ONE TIME afraid. That was a God-thing....I will be cremated and a service of celebration will be held at a later date. For details call.... Those wishing to send an online condolence please visit..... (the site)....."[1]

Before her last breath, she continued to assure her family and friends that she was dying in faith, and it was based on traditional concepts of authority. It came across most of the time that her faith compared with that of many of the ailing people whom Jesus had cured. She had had times when she wished for a life beyond her earthly years, but she had not slipped into self-pitying hypochondria. Among other virtues, she revealed strong convictions and a self-assured approach to dying and death. She lived with positive expectations of herself, many of which had already come true. She gave evidence of being "Renaissance," an extraordinarily gifted and intelligent woman, with a variety of enviable skills and interests.

Then Ginna died. She was gone, gone from mortality, never to return to her kidney problems, never again to be saddled or overburdened with any of the handicaps that for several years had crippled her employment and a fuller enjoyment of life. Before she had died, Ginna left abundant evidence that she had come to terms with many issues surrounding death, especially how to deal with suffering. She could write frankly about death; she could, and she did, admonishing and encouraging others suffering similar maladies to be hopeful and faithful. She could even be blithely spirited, and humorous. She had the wisdom and spirit to advise persons in the midst of dying and death. You surely need to come to terms with both here and hereafter in order to survive as productively as Ginna did. She provided a remarkable testimony to the logo, "Thinking Critically, Living Faithfully." She lived and died, as she had written, with an appreciation for authority. She had observed and absorbed that standard through her relationship with the one who claimed to have authority because he had been sent from God, and after suffering crucifixion, would return to the place where he had originated.

Ginna's autobituary raises a question which only she could have answered, maybe did: do persons suffering like her, and like Job, rely and depend upon, and appreciate more, opinions from persons who can speak with more authority than a person who has occasional migraines or a tooth extraction? Do they demand more frequent, and fuller, "blow-by-blow" accounts of what is happening to them, and what can they expect as death draws nearer? The Kidney Dialysis Staff who worked with Ginna was skilled in making her feel realistically hopeful, as was Hospice. She found comforting companionship in human beings, as well as in her religion.

The reputed professional counselors who came to offer their services to the Biblical character, Job, when he was in his deepest psychological and spiritual pit, sounded like men of reputed authority. They kept treating the wise prophet like a child, addressing his child-like person with "Naughty Boy" analysis: "You have sinned, Job; just confess your sin, and all will be OK. You will receive an amazing compensation for all you have been going through. God knows what is going on, and God will pity you and have mercy on you." The therapy sessions must have bored the scabby, skinny, scared Prophet! His visitors lacked both the authority and skill of a psychologist or a psychiatrist, and especially, of a Pastor.

Before Job's recess at this juncture, an issue at the center of his story, and one often at the center of dying and death patients' odysseys, is known as "theodicy." Certain terminally ill patients make good candidates for theodicy research. Many of them are as righteous as Job, and if records could be sent from heaven, theirs would possibly be signed A+. They have sometimes died without satisfaction about why they had to die under such excruciating circumstances. Sufferers do not usually approach their physicians with philosophy or psychology, enquiring, "Why am I having to endure this pain so long?" The person who asks questions like that can most usually expect medical, but not theological, words for an answer—which, of course, fits physicians' expertise. Wait until your Pastor comes to see you; then discuss theodicy issues with her/him. Do not expect even deep philosophy from Oncologists, or Oncological Nurses. Not many Physicians study Metaphysics in Medical School, as far as I know. Increasingly the Institutions are teaching medical ethics. Care Facilities hold therapy sessions that concentrate on your illness, where you could possible go into theodicy. Physicians and nurses are authority persons, and we trust them with diagnoses and treatments and drugs and surgeries and conversation on the "What?" level. We will feel more comfortable talking to our Pastor or the Hospital Chaplain or a Psychologist about the "Why?" issues. Do not be surprised, however, if they prove no better with answers than Job's visitors. Some medical facilities are better equipped with philosophers than they were in the days of Dr. Elisabeth Kubler Ross, the reputed *On Dying and Death* author mentioned in Chapter I. You may have to settle on working out your inquisitiveness with the Authority in Highest Command. You may also receive the grace of an Epiphany about it. In the meantime, imitate Ginna. Or Job. Or Jesus.

In her autobituary, Ginna MacKenzie had some theodicy nostalgia when she lamented, "I certainly wanted life to be different than it was." First, she had longed for work; second, she had wished that she had had siblings: "I am an only child. They (Sic., her parents) are retired. We had a hard time of it." She had wanted to be "better off" financially. She appears to have had a desire to be married, and to become a mother. She had certainly hoped for more social acceptability; she wanted "fun." In spite of her handicaps and longings, Ginna had a sympathetic listener and faithful companion. She reported on the diversion from her problem that her part-time employment gave her. She confessed to being, "An artist of sorts. I loved the things that I know: logo design, and newsletter/ magazine layout." She did not die entirely without companionship. She listed among her survivors: "Leonardo Varallo, MY Most Main Man for

35 years....my brother by choice...(she also had enjoyed) numerous cousins, and various and sundry people "whom I have loved, and who have loved me."

Dying people who have come to terms with their enigmatic distress frequently qualify as teachers or trainers in endurance and patience and courage. If you were in need of an effective teacher on coping with fatal illness, you would be most fortunate if you could have a Ginna on the opposite end of your "McGuffey Learning Log." She could probably have given you better lessons on coming to terms with your dilemma than many healthy John Hopkins or Mayo Clinic graduates; or maybe even Yale Divinity School, or the Pittsburgh Presbyterian Theological Seminary. Persons of her ilk and experience have become expert in living toward death without crippling fear or nagging self-pity. They have learned how to energize the amazing resources that can make their remaining days even more valuable than the sum of all their previous ones. The teaching expertise has grown out of their suffering, and their skills at surviving.

Authority plays a significant role in the healing ministry performed by Biblical "faith healers." I call their methodology the "MnMnM Scheme of Healing: **M**iracle, **M**edical, and **M**ind." It could also go by the description, "The Elisha Specialty." (Read about it in 2 Kings 5:1-19.) Elisha's ministry was notable for its practice of "MnMnM." One of the prophet's most notable achievements occurred in connection with his miraculous healing of Naaman, top Commander of the Syrian Military Forces. The event had begun when the King of Assyria had asked the Prophet of YHWH to heal the idol-worshiping foreigner, his Army Commander. When Elisha consented, Naaman set off for Israel, loaded with money and gifts, and hope.

Prophet and Commander met. Elisha began with the same tactics he had used many times before with believers in YHWH. He introduced a couple of "spins" in dealing with Naaman. Elisha told the man of power to take a hike to the muddy brown Jordan River—the bathroom for both human and beast, the washing machine, the swimming pool, the teeth cleaner, the trough for animals to obtain a drink, the absorber of land runoff from the nearby Golan Heights, and the shallow pool to cool off in: that was the Jordan River to which Elisha sent Naaman, with the command, "Go and wash in the Jordan seven times…."

At first Naaman was intimidated. Back home they had clean rivers, like the Abana and the Pharpar. The Commander refused to humiliate himself, and "dunk" seven times in the Jordan. His soldiers disagreed with his decision, and they set out to reason with him: the request was such a small item for such a significant release from such a scurrilous disease. Naaman did not want to die, or spend the rest of his life wandering about with such scrofulous scars; he would lose his position, and probably his pension. The Commander changed his mind and headed for the River. He dipped seven times in the Jordan, and the miracle happened. A greater miracle was yet to take place, a spiritual one. He converted to believe in YHWH, the God of Elisha, and the God of Israel. (2 Kings 5:1-19.) Spiritual Authority, ironically, was one of the 3M's by which a Commander ended up a Convert. His belief and practice of Military and Political authority, as in one of Jesus' miracles (Matthew 8:1-13), might have disposed him to listen to his "Non-commissioned" officers. Many righteous Christians, for some inscrutable reason that may be connected with God's will, again as in the case of Jesus' healing the young man born blind (John 9), do not immediately—if ever—fare as well as some unbelievers, even idol-worshipers. Several cases in my ministry, (my Mother-in-law in particular, when she died from Amyotrophic Lateral Sclerosis) have offered testimony to the mystery of faith healing, and others have given their testimony through endurance possible through faith without healing, but with the resultant of increased faith.

In matters related to dying and death, coming to terms that can result in endurance may prove a chore, for reasons suggested by Dr. Kubler-Ross: "Death is neither frightening nor painful, but a peaceful cessation of the functioning of the body. Watching a peaceful death of a human being reminds us of a falling star: one of the million lights in a vast sky that flares up for a brief moment only to disappear into the endless night forever. Being a therapist to a dying patient makes us aware of the uniqueness of each individual in this vast sea of humanity. It makes us aware of our finiteness, our limited lifespan. Few of us live beyond our three score and ten years, and yet in that brief time most of us create and live a unique biography and weave ourselves into the fabric of human history."[2] (Kubler-Ross, p. 276.) Some patients have weaved more perfectly and beautifully than others; they have chosen the more perfect yarn: faith, hope and love, first of God, then of others, and finally of themselves.

Jesus weaved the most perfect faith fabric of all through his most perfect three-fold ministry: preaching, teaching and healing. His preaching and teaching required courage, intelligence, and audience sympathy and identification. He had a dangerous message. Its primary principles consisted of these a-priori dogmas: the New Empire was coming on earth as it is in heaven, and especially from one with claims of oneness with God; Caesar who was also regarded as Divine, would lose his front-runner rule. Jesus' analogies and metaphors were Palestinian, though they had universal application. His teaching was a new law, as anathematizing and threatening to Israel, as "New Empire" was to Rome. As troublesome as anything were the speed and enthusiasm with which his increasingly large gatherings were forming. Amazement and inspiration characterized his crowds' responses. They kept asking, especially those who knew of his having grown up in Nazareth, "Where did this man get this?" His reputation for being a son of a carpenter was well known. At the end of the "Sermon on the Mount," he was praised: "Now when Jesus had finished saying these things, the crowds were astonished at his teaching. For he taught them as one having authority, and not as their scribes." (Matthew 7:28-9.) The scribes taught Leviticus, or the "Midrash" (didactic commentary on passages of the Bible or the Tradition) as a final authority; many of them could quote pages of it from memory.

The miracles Jesus performed frequently resulted in one of three emotions: anger because he broke the Sabbath doing them; or amazement, or appreciation. When critics argued with Jesus that the Scripture prohibits work on the Sabbath, he either ignored them, or offered replies that stumped them: "It is lawful to do good on the Sabbath....If your donkey is in a ditch on the Sabbath, don't you go and help it out? Which, then, is easier, to say (to a cripple lame from birth), 'Your sins are forgiven?' Or, 'Stand up and walk?' But that you may know that the Son of man has the authority in earth to forgive sins, I say—(to the crippled man)—'Walk'" (And the man did, and the audience shushed.) Jesus added, "The Sabbath was made for humanity, not humanity for the Sabbath." And one more, "The Son of man is Lord of the Sabbath." (Luke 2:27-8; 6:5; 13:16; 14:3-5, etc.) These rebuttals convinced both the rich and the poor, the illiterate and the intelligent, the Jews and the Gentiles, that his ministry of preaching and teaching and healing had divine authority behind it. The audience response to his argument about "Which is easier?" makes an unequivocal statement about Jesus and coming to terms with authority: "The crowds saw it, they were filled with awe, and they glorified God, who had given such authority to human beings." (Matthew 9:8.) People who observed or received the benefits of Jesus' ministry enjoyed privileges no one before or after him has witnessed.

At the end of her life, Ginna, the Lynchburg, Virginia autobituary composer, known as a courageous woman, was praised by her parents as a person who not only knew that she was dying, but who had come to terms with her fate; and even more importantly, she had come to terms with Jesus' authority. Her mother and father had no recollection of Ginna's reporting a vision of Jesus when she was tortured with pain, but they guessed that she probably had. Their closing tribute to her was, "We love you so much, and we're all so very thankful to you for enriching our lives and touching our hearts in a way no other person could. Thank you for everything you are and for what you have given T.L and me. May you soar with eagles and sing with the angels until we meet again." The Prophet Isaiah would have applauded. (See Isaiah 40: 27-31.) Jesus could have been soaring through the clouds on an eagle, with Ginna holding on to the neck of the bird, and Jesus' tunic swishing around the tail!

The following obituary excerpts offer testimony from persons who, before they had died, had come to terms with Jesus' authority:

FAMILY ANTICIPATES A GRANDMA REUNION: The family wanted to inform their departed Grandma—by way of her obituary—that they miss her laughter and endless supply of love. They made a promise to go with her in spirit on the journey that her dying had initiated. They were anticipating a reunion when they would see each other again.

PRINCESS IN ROYAL COMPANY AT COURT: Her family was convinced that on a specified day, the day of the little girl's death, their little princess had taken her place in "The King's Court." She was committed to the King Jesus.

FAMILY BACK TOGETHER: A family member's death had consoled other family members that she had consummated a reunion in Heaven with her parents, and other close relatives. The group also included someone she called her "Friend, John." Her faith and her hope had hung on to the Scriptural dogma of heavenly re-connects.

WISH GRANTED: The obituary states the family's firm conviction that their loved one's wish—to come closer to Jesus—had been granted the day she died.

FACE-T0-FACE: When the devout Lutheran "passed" at almost ninety years of age, she had convinced her family on earth of a reunion in heaven, in the presence of Jesus. She had often sung: "Face to face with Christ my Savior.... I shall see him by and by."

LET THE CHILDREN COME: According to the obituary writer, a child ten years of age delighted in stories about Jesus. They are convinced that she is now safe in his arms, and is enjoying eternal pleasures. The Biblical support by which her family finds comfort appears in the report about Jesus chiding his obstructing Apostles when little children wanted to touch him: "Do not stop them. For it is to such as these that the kingdom of heaven belongs." (Matthew 19:14.)

Grief as wrenching as that occasioned by the loss of a child, especially a child baptized into the community of the Church's Redeemer and Lord, seeks authority from the most reliable source. How much more reliable can you find than the one who said, "Let the children come to me. For of such is the kingdom of God (heaven)?" (Mark 10:13.) However, a family grieving the recent loss of a child may have trouble hearing the voice of Jesus in the invitation. Their hearing may be impaired not only by the heaviness of their sorrow, but also possibly because they had never memorized the following verse that I memorized in grade school; or if they had, they had forgotten Alfred Lord Tennyson's lines from "In Memoriam:"

> "Strong son of God, immortal Love,
> Whom we, that have not seen thy face,
>   By faith, and faith alone, embrace,
> Believing where we cannot prove."
> (Quoted from Memory.)

Jesus' prosaic words to Thomas the second Sunday of Easter also endorsed the experience of believing what has not been seen—or proved: "Blessed are those who have not seen (Sic. or had proved to them) and yet have come to believe." (John 20: 29b.)

As literature composed in situations of extreme grief, especially if the composer is a family member or close friend, obituaries sometimes bear an apocalyptic semblance. The authors of that form of Bible record occasionally attribute their inspiration—that is, those who acknowledge it—to being caught up into higher levels of consciousness, caught up "in the Spirit," according to some apocalyptic writers. Revelation Author John commented: "I was in the Spirit on the Lord's Day, and I heard behind me a loud voice like a trumpet, saying, "Write in the book what you see…." (Revelation 1:10-11.) Obituary writers sometimes go out of this world sightseeing, and they find comfort in writing what they see; or what they imagine their deceased loved ones now see. Who is to question? How comforting apocalyptic Scripture can be to a family grieving a deceased child, especially when they find a comforting passage? Examples follow: Isaiah saw the vision of a place in the New Jerusalem safe enough for "Children to play over the holes of the asp?" (Isaiah 11:8-9.) John wrote of a New Jerusalem construction: "The holy city, the new Jerusalem, coming down out of heaven from God, prepared as a bride adorned for her husband." (Revelation 21: 2.) The city had been freed from the grief associated with mortality: "Death will be no more; mourning and crying and pain will be no more, for the first things have passed away." (Ibid. 21:4.) What an improvement over Sheol! Who is to judge that obituary inspiration cannot originate in mourners' desperation, resulting in apocalyptic literature? Some of the following excerpts stand on the threshold:

WISH TO WALTZ TO JESUS GRANTED: She died at age 89 of Alzheimer's. One of her most cherished wishes had been granted, her family believed: she had wanted her dying to take the form of a waltz to Jesus. The dance would also rejoin her with her deceased Pastor-husband. (She had apparently judged Jesus a better "waltzer." Maybe her husband's theology had regarded dancing as sinful.) He was believed to be there waiting for her, not wearing dancing shoes, but holding her gardening gloves, so that, when not dancing, the two of them could join in their second most-favored pastime: gardening. They would share the joy of sowing the first tomato plant of spring. (Ed. If my deceased gardener Mother had read the obituary, she might have repeated one of her famous phrases, "No rest for the wicked!" Or, "I would have told your dad to do the planting himself! I would be glad to process the produce!" They all might have laughed. And Father would probably have put on the gloves. Mother had come to terms with her rest in heaven.)

TRUE LOVE WAS DAD: "Angels took her back" expresses the belief of a family about their juvenile daughter's death. The snatch would have reunited her with her one true love, her deceased "Dad." He had been the loving authority figure in her life.

Presbyterian Church Officers—Ministers of Word and Sacrament, and Elders and Deacons, and certain commissioned lay professionals—come to terms with the sources of authority when they are ordained and installed into office. (The same holds true, I am certain, for other Denominations and Bodies of Christ's Body.) In the service that endows them with ecclesiastical authority, nominees are asked: "Do you accept the Scriptures of the Old and New Testaments, to be, by the Holy Spirit, the unique and authoritative witness to Jesus Christ in the Church universal, and God's word to you?" (*Constitution, The Book of Order,* Directory for Worship, W-44003.) If they say, "I do," their ordination proceeds with questions and vows about their adherence to the Presbyterian form of Government and matters related to their moral and spiritual habits. A final induction statement by a presiding Moderator follows prayer and the "laying on of hands" by the Ministers and Session Elders of the Church. Unless a church officer resigns the office, or is dismissed by the ordaining body for doctrinal or moral reasons, ordination is perpetual. Terms ordinarily run for three years, with a possible three additional successive years—if elected again. After six successive years in office, an officer has to be off the session or board of Deacons for at least one year before being eligible for re-election. Authority thus has a time to rest! Parity of voting by clergy or laity attaches as one of the gifts of the office. Clergy have privileged authority stipulated in the Constitution over certain ecclesiastical responsibilities.

Bible publication has benefited the case for the Bible as a reliable authority in matters religious. At the same time, it has increased respect for church authority. The year 1611 holds the distinction of being the year of publication of the King James Version of the Bible. Christians alive in that year felt as if they were living through a Biblical Jubilee. Appreciation for the King James Version of the Bible could not be expressed deeply or broadly enough. Commemoration upon its release burst out all over the British Empire, (or whatever political designation was given to the political configuration of the

British Isles at the time.) The excitement and purchase of KJV Bibles, when available, bore marks like those of the previous century Reformation. The excitement spread to English speaking entities in Europe. The King of England and Scotland was honored to have his name attached. James was King (Number VI of Scotland {1567-1603}, but Number I of Scotland-England (reigning 1603-25). Separation of Church and State: what is that? And at such a momentous period in the history of the English-speaking world, who cared? The tribute statement in the remarkable English of the period may still be found in most KJV Bibles:

"To the Most High and Mighty Prince James, King of Great Britain, France, and Ireland, Defender of the Faith."

Charming words and exultations follow: "Great and manifold (are) the blessings that the dread Sovereign, Almighty God, the Father of all mercies, has bestowed upon James and the Empire." The text continues: "But among all our joys, there was no one that has more filled our hearts than the blessed continuance of the preaching of God's sacred Word among us; which is that inestimable treasure, which excelleth all riches of the earth; because the fruit thereof extendeth itself, not only to the time spent in this translation, but directeth and disposeth men unto the eternal happiness which is above in heaven."[2] How simple and legal it was in the year 1611 to come to terms with the authority of Scripture!

If the Apostle Paul had been in the official governmental and ecclesiastical halls in London when the KJV Bible was first brought forth, and had attended the dedication ceremony, he might have easily and unashamedly been lifted out of his seat. And if an oversight in protocol had resulted in no role for the Apostle at the dedication, can't you imagine his volatile response?

> "Listen, I claim some authorship of the authority derived from that Bible; I sent the Gospel all around Asia and parts of Europe through my own proclamation, and through my young and brilliant student, Timothy. There was no confusion

> or question in the young pastor's or my own mind about the meaning of 'inspired.' I wrote it clearly in 2 Timothy 3:16, 'All Scripture is inspired....for every good word and work.' Please notice that inspiration is not described as 'literal,' or 'verbal,' or 'plenary'—just 'inspired.' Now a question: if the Bible is not all inspired, who determines what is and what isn't?"

After his speech, the Apostle might have sat down and shut up—if you can imagine it —while the Assembly applauded, none louder than King James. Other apologists might have desired to stand up and give a lecture or present a dissertation on Isaiah's theology about the Word accomplishing God's purposes; or about Jesus' assurance to the Apostles that they would have better understanding of the truth he taught them following his death and resurrection and Pentecost. By that point in Paul's speech, the Congregation would be ready to leave for Buckingham Palace for tea with the Queen. (That is, if Buckingham had been built by that date.)

Scholarship has supported, increased, and improved upon the Church's growing confidence in Biblical scholarship. Progress and improvements have been made in several areas: textual accuracy, archeological diligence, Criticism (Higher and Lower), parallel manuscript studies, contextual historical investigations, technology that guarantees accuracy as far as machines can accomplish that purpose, allowance for changes in cultures through the centuries, and intelligent application of many arts and sciences and technologies.

Early in the Twentieth Century, Biblical Scholar and Chicago Biblical Seminary developer, Evangelist Dwight L. Moody, became concerned about promoting the authority of Scripture. He advocated that authority is understood and conserved through effective, comprehensive reading. He included an introductory section to his version and called it, "BIBLE READERS' AIDS: HOW TO STUDY THE BIBLE." He summoned diligence in coming to, and reverence and care in handling, "so precious a Book of Books."

Another affirmation of Biblical authority appeared in a Version given the simple title, The Holy Bible. The World Publishing Company produced it in 1924. The "defense" page reads: "The Bible is a storehouse, of whose contents no one can afford to be ignorant. It repays reading and study whether it be approached merely because of its literary value, or its ethical teachings, or its practical bearing on energy and life....Those who come to the Bible in a devotional spirit, seeking to know more about God and His will regarding us, are the most blessed....I thank God there is in it a height I have never been able to reach, a depth I have never been able to fathom, a length and a breadth I know nothing about. It makes the book all the more fascinating AND PROVES IT DIVINE."[3] (Pp. 27-8.) (Note: according to communication with the co-publisher, because of its date of publication, permission is not necessary for quoting the sentences.)

Few summons to Biblical appreciation and authority ascend to such eloquence, or deliver such a superlative and commanding call. So, young person and elder and senior, "Go and read your Bible!" When you run into difficulty understanding it, then pray, talk to your Pastor, search out a "Commentary," read and re-read the passage, and trust that God will impress you with the profundity of its terms; or at least as much profundity as your mind can comprehend and use! Do not expect obituaries to offer deep scholarly insight; they are not written with that intention. Nor do their composers claim to be Biblical scholars!

The editors of the *Revised Standard Version* of the Bible, published in 1952, had high hopes that both the Church and the public would enthusiastically endorse and purchase their publication. Those that respect the scholarship required to complete such a monumental task would sacredly appreciate it, and they would not allow it to become a dust collector. The true Bible aficionado would possibly be so grateful as to be ready to imitate Moses' obedience when God commanded him: "Come no closer! Remove the sandals from your feet, for the place on which you are standing is holy ground." (Exodus 3: 5.) Moses surely obeyed. The record does not say. It does say, "And Moses hid his face, for he was afraid to look at God." (Vs. 6.) The labors of the RSV publishers testify to their Moses-like holy diligence that resulted in such a monumental accomplishment.[4]

The most scholarly successor to the *RSV* arrived at booksellers approximately forty years after the *RSV* had come out. It is entitled, *The Holy Bible, Containing the Old and New Testaments, New Revised Standard Version.* In an introductory expression of gratitude for previous publications, Professor Dr. Bruce M. Metzger paid this well-deserved and realistic honor to the *KJV*: "In the course of time, the *King James Version* came to be regarded as the *Authorized Version*. With good reason it has been given such accolades as, 'The noblest monument of English prose, ever,' and it has entered, as no other book has, in making a high quality of civil and personal character among its adherents, and creating first-class public institutions by, and among, English-speaking peoples. The World owes to it an incalculable debt. Yet the King James Version has serious defects."[5] Archeology, manuscript discovery, and scholarly "sweat" have corrected some of those shortcomings, to the point that newer translations can adopt the maxim: "The older the new, the better the old."

Besides helpful commentary on the Scripture, another scholarly section of the *New Interpreter's Study Bible* consists of a series of theological essays dealing with several aspects of Scriptural authority. Several authorities from major American theological institutions have made contributions. The list includes: Walter J. Harrelson, Phyllis Trible, Roger Gnuse, and John R. Donahue.

The first essay, written by Professor Harrelson, Distinguished Professor of Old Testament, Emeritus, The Divinity School, Vanderbilt University, Baltimore, Maryland, deals with the "Reliability of Scripture." "Original intent" plays a part in a claim for authority, the Professor maintains: "Debates raged within the churches with regard to the reliability of this (*NRSV*) biblical text in its various forms. For our purposes, the Bible can be said to be reliable if it can be reasonably claimed that its contents as preserved through the centuries are, in substance, what the original writers spoke and said....The consensus of biblical scholarship is that readers do indeed have reason to accept current translations of the Bible as close approximations to what the biblical authors said and wrote."[6]

Professor Trible, who teaches at Wake Forest University Divinity School, Winston Salem, North Carolina, contributed an article entitled, "Authority of the Bible." She stated: "The concept of authority overlaps with such concepts as reliability, inerrancy, inspiration, interpretation, and canonization.... In short, the phase, 'the authority of the Bible' lacks the authority of definition.... Traditionally the phrase has meant that the Bible is the word of God. For John Calvin authority did not lie in the words themselves but in the activity of the Holy Spirit at work both in the Scriptures and the Believers. .... Within the Bible the subject of authority receives no definitive treatment. It teems with ambiguities and uncertainties." Her list of "Seven Features of Authority," posits the following as the most convincing: "The persistence of the Bible witnesses to its formative and normative authority, and (places upon the reader) the responsibility to make the right choice.... And the Bible offers the right of discernment."[7]

Professor Robert Gnuse (Professor of Hebrew Scriptures, Loyola University, New Orleans, Louisiana) closed his article on the "Inspiration of Scripture" this way: "(Many assert that) the nature of inspiration is connected directly to the authority of the Bible, and thus becomes a serious issue of discussion. Many theologians, including this author, would suggest that the reason for the authority of the Bible lies elsewhere, perhaps with christological or existential religious arguments. Because it is then authoritative, the Bible subsequently may be characterized as inspired as well. Either viewpoint affirms the importance of the inspiration of the biblical text in some way."[8]

Father Donahue, S.J., (New Testament Professor, St. Mary's Seminary, Baltimore, Maryland), dealt with the role subjectivity plays in "textual determinations:" "Every reader brings cultural, social and personal perspectives to a text that influences interpretation." Fr. Donahue is convinced that Biblical scholarship proves most profitable in the issue of authority when these principles are followed: 1. Close reading of the text; 2. Knowledge of the genre or kind of literature being treated; 3. Awareness of the historical context; and, 4. Attention to the 'canonical' context. Attention must also be given to these Biblical disciplines: 1. Literary criticism; 2. Reader-response criticism; 3. Study of the social setting and culture out of which a document emerges; 4. Readings concerning Liberation. Since the "Enlightenment," and in view of other Biblical scholarship of the past two centuries, "The spectrum of Liberation concerns ranges from protest against massive social inequality through consciousness of the independence, rights, and dignity of women; to rejection of colonialism in all its forms; and emphasis on readings from different social locations."[9]

The Father raises issues about validating interpretation. Not every interpretation is acceptable, he offered. He suggested four validating criteria that literary criticism contributes to the process: a. respect for the text as it stands; b. interpretation consistent with itself that elucidates the whole text; c. interpretation that explains anomalies; d. an interpretation that is compatible with what is known from other sources. (Ed. These criteria may also assist in critiquing obituaries, though on a much different intellectual and emotional level.)

The preceding comments can be of significant help in coming to terms with authority. Be warned, however: not all the insights gained from the scholars may prove helpful or crucial in understanding or gaining spiritual knowledge from obituaries; in fact, one of the joys of obituaries is that little help besides basic childhood and youth instruction in the Bible is needed. Again, hold onto Jesus' teaching that a child's ability to understand mystery sometimes outpaces an adult's. The Psalmist made this contribution to the endeavor: "Out of the mouths of babes and infants you have founded a bulwark because of your foes, to silence the enemy and the avenger." (Psalm 8:2.)

Professor Dr. Bruce Metzger contributes a historical note and a cryptic comment to the discussion of authority.

He observed that the NRSV translation of the Bible received adoption by the National Council of Churches of Christ in the United States of America, in part, because the scholars most responsible for its publication had adopted this goal: "To introduce changes as are warranted on the basis of accuracy, clarity, euphony, and current English usage." An overarching principle dominated: "As literal as possible, as free as necessary."[10]

Scholarly effort on coming to terms with authority appears in a study authorized early in 2001 by the General Assembly of the Presbyterian Church (U.S.A.). The study grew out of the Church's conflict between progressive and conservative groups, expressed in polarizing over several issues, particularly gender and ordination. The General Assembly elected a Task Force charged with discerning "The peace, unity and purity of the Church." After five years of prayerful labor, the Group presented its report to the Assembly at its 2006 meeting in Birmingham, Alabama. The definitive document was entitled, "Peace, Unity and Purity: A Season of Discernment."[11] Coming to terms with authority figured prominently in the discerning process. Several Report paragraphs deal with the authority of the Bible. The following paragraphs relate most relevantly at this point in the discussion:

"*We are a people whose identity is expressed through the proclamation of the Word.* As Reformed Christians, we believe and confess the canonical Scriptures of the holy prophets and apostles of both Testaments to be the true Word of God, and to have sufficient authority of themselves, not of [human beings]." (Re.: *The Book of Confessions, The Second Helvetic Confession,* 5.001.) "The Scriptures, inspired and illumined by the Holy Spirit, form our identity and teach us who we are, whom we worship, and how we exist in the world as the body of believers."

"We acknowledge that there is heated debate over biblical interpretation among Presbyterians who honor the authority of Scripture. In the midst of these debates it is important to remember that the witness of Scripture to Jesus Christ binds the consciences of us all. Even as it is important to preserve freedom of conscience in the interpretation of Scripture, such freedom is subject to standards (*Book of Order*, G-6.0108a); and must be exercised within constitutional bounds." (*Book of Order*, G-6.0108b, G-6.0108, "Freedom of Conscience".)"

The Westminster Confession of Faith, one of the "Standards" the Task Force spent serious time studying, has guided Presbyterians in doctrinal systemization for more than half a millennium. The section, "Of Holy Scripture," maintains that we human beings in ourselves, relying on our own resources, lack sufficient ability to discover sufficient "knowledge of God, (and of the Divine will), necessary unto salvation." Human ignorance "maketh the Holy Scripture to be most necessary; those former ways of God revealing his will unto his people being now ceased."

Item Number Four of the Statement continues: "The authority of the Holy Scripture, for which it ought to be believed and obeyed, dependeth not upon the testimony of any man or church, but wholly upon God (who is truth itself), the author thereof, and therefore it is to be received, because it is the Word of God." Item Number Nine further elucidates the Confession's position on interpretation: "The infallible rule of interpretation of Scripture is the Scripture itself; when there is a question about the true and full sense of any scripture (which is not manifold, but one), it may be searched and known by other places (in Scripture) that speak more clearly." (Support for these statements may be found in Matthew 4:1-5; 12:1-7.)[12]

John Calvin's dogma about the knowledge of God (referred to in the previous Chapter) raised a concern about how human disobedience and innate moral deficiency frustrate processes for discerning what the Spirit says to the Church.[13] Imperfect expression, imprecise understanding, and abuse of authority result. Creation and its creatures are intended to lead humanity to know and give thanks to God—at least Paul seemed to think so from what he wrote in Romans 1:18-23. Calvin insisted, however, "We need another and better assistance, properly to direct us to the Creator of the world...Though the human mind is naturally endued with it (knowledge of the Creator), yet it is extinguished, partly by ignorance, partly by wickedness." Natural theology cannot compensate for the deficiency: "Though it (knowledge of God) shines there with the brightest evidence, testimonies of that kind, however plain, are, through our stupidity, wholly useless in us." The only hope of knowing God effectively, and infallibly making possible authoritative "human word about Divine Word" (Ed's words) is Scripture.

Calvin proceeded to write metaphorically about authority: "Scripture works like spectacles, collecting in our minds the otherwise confused notions of Deity, dispels the darkness, and gives us a clear view of the true God.... Scripture discovers God to us as the Creator of the world, and declares what sentiments we should form of him.... In order to enjoy the light of true religion, we ought to begin with the doctrine of heaven; and no man can have the least knowledge of true and sound doctrine, without having been a disciple of Scripture....obedience to Scripture is the source, not only of an absolutely perfect and complete faith, but of all right knowledge of God...."

"Scripture exhibits as clear evidence of its truth, as white and black things do of their colour (Sic.), or sweet and bitter things, of their taste.... The principal proof, therefore, of the Scriptures is everywhere derived from the character of the Divine Speaker—the secret testimony of the Spirit..., which is superior to all reason.... None but those to whom it is given, have any apprehension of the mysteries of God.... The force of truth in the sacred Scripture is too powerful to need the assurance of verbal art.... Scripture does not need foreign aid....The final verification of its authority depends on the Logos in tandem with the Holy Spirit." (The Institutes, Book 1, Chapters vi-viii.) Calvin's numerous Scriptures in support of his dogma may appear to slight Christology, but that dogma shows up almost everywhere in his writings, as in the often cited, "Christ died for us.'" (Cf. Romans 5:4.)

When he was on trial for heresy at the "Diet of Worms" (April 18, 1521), on charges of rejecting the office of the Pope and the authority of the Church, Martin Luther passionately, and defiantly, expressed his reliance on the primacy, not of a Primate, but of Scripture. Faith in Jesus Christ as attested to by the Word of God established the foundation of Luther's testimony before the Diet. Holding a Bible high, and probably waving it briskly, the Reformer pierced the intense eyeing of the Council, and bravely asserted: "Here I stand; I can do no other. God help me!"

Where may a grieving mortal, or a dying human, or a Presbyterian Reformation Pastor, or any believing Holy Catholic Christian, find firmer rock? As usual, Paul provides the best answer: "For no one can lay any foundation other than the one that has been laid; that foundation is Jesus Christ." (1 Corinthians 3:11.)

Excerpt

AUTHORITY WITH HUMOR: He lived a full ninety-two years. An authority in sand and gravel and ready-mix, gardening, Husky's Football and golf, he also managed his renal failure expertly the last three years of his life. His humor helped. "Where's the beef?" was one of his favorite and often-used introductory lines. Two weeks before he died he gave a smile to one of his nurses when she asked how he was. He replied that he would be better if she just stepped a little closer!

If besides the authority of his age, the man had had the authority of a Nurse or a Physician, he might have ordered her to—if he dared! Few gifts are more abused than authority. Few persons have been more accused of abuse than Jesus. Even fewer have died as a result.

Section II. "Events"

IV.

Last Breath

"I believe.... in Jesus Christ, his (God's) only Son, our Lord...who was conceived by the Holy Ghost, born of the virgin Mary, suffered under Pontius Pilate, was crucified, dead...."

The Apostles' Creed

....

HIS DEATH BREATH EASIER THAN HIS BIRTH GASP: Adam Adams of Pietsville, Washington died July 2 at his life-long home. He was seventy years old. During the last days of his struggle with prostate cancer, his family kept constant vigil. His daughter commented: "His last breath came easy." She continued: "Maybe it came easy because, as Mother has frequently told us, Dad's first breath caused anxiety. The Obstetrician had become alarmed. He finally gave Dad a whack on his bottom, and his chest started expanding, rising and falling rhythmically. Soon he was bawling lustily. His color changed from light blue to pink." The immediate family circle had heard Adam's birth story frequently. He lived three score and ten years. Shortly before he died, he remarked to his wife, Ann: "I have lived my Biblical quota." She smiled and responded, "Now, if I just live ten years more...!" And they both laughed.

Adam had been born into a Christian home. He had grown up in the Pietsville Presbyterian Church, where he had been baptized as an infant, and where he and his wife were married. In addition to his wife, his survivors include three sons, a daughter, and eight grandchildren. Funeral Services will be held July 5th at 2:00 P.M. at his Church, Pietsville Presbyterian. Memorial gifts may be made to the Church's Memorial Fund. *(Note:* Author Composed.)

LAST OF TOO FEW BREATHS: The infant's last breath, the obituary said, placed her into the loving arms of Jesus. The family bade her good-bye and best wishes as she ran and danced to heaven, to play "ring-around-the-rosie" with the angels. Her Grandmother commented at the hospital death scene that their little girl had had too few breaths.

DAYS' END: *The Birmingham* (Alabama) *News* obituary section gave her name and her age (48), and described her last breath, "Sunset."

DIED CHARGING: The Obituary, using the deceased's own words, said he had charged up the hill. He had had varied business interests, all successful. He requested no commemorative service; he anticipated that it would cause too much fuss.

JESUS' LAST BREATH (Luke's Version:) *"It was now about noon, and darkness came over the whole land until three in the afternoon, while the sun's light failed and the curtain of the temple was torn in two. Then Jesus, crying with a loud voice, said, 'Father, into your hands I commend my spirit.' Having said this, he breathed his last." (Luke 23:44-47.)* Mark's Version: *"Then Jesus gave a loud cry and breathed his last."* (Mark 15:37.)

....

Chapter One dealt with a process, dying. Chapter Four deals with the end result, death. While you're still living, while you're still breathing, while you seem still to have a body-soul union, you and your family share hope. When you have taken your last breath, your body becomes lifeless. Communication has ended. The living respond appropriately to the loss: mourning and crying and hoping for the best. If they are believers, they can count on receiving comfort. Scripture promises it: "Death will be no more … for the first things have passed away." (Revelation 21:4.) The challenge faced ahead by the mourners calls for endurance and patience—until the age of "New things" arrives. No one on earth knows when that will happen. Even Jesus, as the human being, could not divulge the secret: he did not know it.

Jesus had known, from all eternity, that he was going to die young and violently. He told his Apostles about it on at least three occasions. He lived with the consciousness that his end would probably come within three years from the beginning of his public ministry. Then the day for the process to result in the product had arrived. On the Friday of Passover Preparation, he breathed his last breath; he died as a falsely convicted criminal. He was accepting of his sentence. His apostles were still unclear about it. The predominant populist position was confusion. The people in power had ruled, "Guilty." Pilate had ambiguously complied with the populace. Some of the Calvary crowd were asking, "What happened?" A minority questioned, "What for?" If only they had heard Jesus praying in Gethsemane, they would have had a clue: "I have finished the work you gave me to do." (John 17:4.) Paul later offered the insight, which Reformed Theology zealously guards and fervently believes: "Christ died for our sins." Redemption, rescue, forgiveness, reconciliation, atonement and many more words of deep theological meaning answer the "What for?" of Jesus being "crucified, dead and buried."

So what? What does "What for?" mean for the Church? How do perceptions of "What for?" sound in obituaries? How do human beings deal with them? Widely differently, of course! Further examination of the two questions at hand deals with three issues. They also receive attention in obituaries, and feature prominently in the minds of survivors. The three issues are **circumstance, cause and consequence.** The three sometimes overlap, but each also has its own identity.

CIRCUMSTANCE

Although every death has issues in common with Jesus' last breathing, none exactly matches his death, or any other human being's, in either "what?" or "what for?" Nor has any other person's death accomplished as much. Certainly no other human being has ever died in such strange circumstances.

Unusual death circumstances prompted a recent ceremony—exemplary of how Reformed believers respond under similar situations—at the Renton, Washington, Mount Olivet Cemetery. The day was gray and chilly, a wet afternoon in late March 2009. The event had a compensatory circumstance attached: it compensated an honor that circumstance had denied several area residents—and strangers. Clergy, nurses, executives, an official of the King County Medical Examiner's office, formerly and currently homeless persons, and associates at the Pioneer Square Clinic in Seattle, joined several curious and sympathetic observers. The occasion inurned the cremains of two hundred nine persons.

A *Seattle Times* news story and photos told the story. The circumstances surrounding each individual's death are only sketchily known. "Some had been homeless; others lived alone; and when they passed away, no next of kin could be found, or no one stepped forward to claim their ashes." The news story continued: "The cremated remains were buried in a grave capped by a headstone reading: 'Gone but not forgotten, these people of Seattle.'" Some of the group had shared homelessness in downtown Seattle. One set of remains had been found on a sidewalk, simply marked "St. Vincent de Paul." One bore the title, "The Oregon Logger." He had occasionally visited the Clinic. One day he came carrying what a staff member described as "the biggest chain saw I've ever seen." He was homeless. A comment at the close of the ceremonies served as a charge to the mourners and to the City of Seattle—and readers of the Newspaper: "Every human being is important, and we need to remember that to solve homelessness." Homelessness is not a comfortable or honorary circumstance under which to die, but hopefully it will soon become one of death's disappearing misfortunes. Until then, sensitive people may learn of the circumstances and improve upon them.

Another obituary-like news story in a recent *Seattle Times* interestingly related circumstantial information about the death of a fisherman. It occurred during a tragic boating/

fishing accident that had taken several lives. The account noted that fellow sailors of the deceased had given the man his nickname, the "Alaska Ranger." The obituary opens with John Masefield's poetic line, "I must go down to the sea again…." The Ship's Captain had died tragically, trying to save his crew on the *Ranger*, tangling with a storm in the Bering Sea. (Ed. Observe that the poem was misquoted; "go" did not form part of Masefield's original composition. It reads, "I must down….")

A circumstantial issue centered in still another recent close-to-death *Times* news story. The article was about the death of the Mother of celebrity and actor, Kirk Douglas. A photo shows him sitting at her hospital bedside. She was experiencing troubled breathing. She was conscious enough, however, to perceive her son's agitation and discomfort. At one moment when the room was quiet, the Mother suddenly opened her eyes, perked up, looked about the room, leaned forward, turned to her bedside offspring, and let out, with a raspy voice, "Don't worry, son, it happens to everybody!"

Why when death happens to everybody do people sometimes hesitate to talk about it? When I was a curious child, I heard my Father say frequently, "Death is something we don't ever bring up; the same holds for religion and politics." (Ed. He never mentioned sex.) One reason for shy talk about death may be the "distaste" factor that Dr. Elizabeth Kubler-Ross addressed in her Book that has already entered into the discussion, *On Death and Dying*. You may remember that the Psychiatrist did in-depth studies of patients terminally ill with cancer.

Not many persons confront unusual "circumstances" surrounding a death, but every death is worth regarding as unusual. And whether expected, anticipated or quietly awaited, death still introduces unpleasantness. Dr. Kubler-Ross' "distasteful" statement referred to earlier, expanded into the following sentences: "…death has always been distasteful to man, and will probably always be. From a psychiatrist's point of view this is very understandable and can perhaps best be explained by our basic knowledge that in our unconscious, death is never possible to ourselves. It is inconceivable for our unconscious to imagine an actual ending of our own life; in our unconscious mind, we can only be killed. It is inconceivable to die of a natural cause or of old age. Therefore, death in itself is associated with a bad act, a frightening happening, something that calls for retribution and punishment."[1]

Of all the long-suffering saints in Scripture, few had more challenging circumstances to deal with than the "Prophet," Job. (Ed. As evidenced in the previous Chapter, Job ranks as one of the favorite subjects of *Obituary Theology*!) The way his life was going, the prophet was hoping it would end soon. He had trouble understanding why it continued. He exemplified the circumstances that tempt a person to cry out, "Why?" "Why shouldn't good luck be mine, instead of this hell I am living through? I have lived life holy; why am I suffering so badly?"

As hinted earlier, theology has a description for this kind of thinking: "Theodicy." "Why me? What did I do wrong to deserve this? Why do such distasteful circumstances come into the life of good people?" Some of Job's most poignant lines came out of his most desperate moments. Some of them seem almost blasphemous. Few people would advocate removal of his Book from Scripture, however. Too many sufferers find his situation comparable to theirs. Author G. K. Chesterton made a helpful observation about understanding Job: "The *Iliad* is a good book because life is a battle. The *Odyssey* is a good book because life is a journey. Job is a good book because life is a riddle." (Ed. Quoted from memory; the words do not appear in Bartlett's Familiar Quotations.) Triumph trumped tragedy for Job. He finally conceded to God, "I know that you can do all things." The last sentence of his Biblical obituary reads, "And Job died, old and full of days." (Job 42:17.) He had seemingly walked the "Lonesome valley all by himself," and the walk had been worth doing. At the end of the odyssey he received new insight into his circumstances, ceasing his rebellious attitude toward God, and double restoration of all that he had lost.

Jesus would have been most sympathetic—and probably was—regarding the circumstances surrounding the deaths of the subjects of the following excerpted obituaries:

ANGELS' WINGS IN EXCHANGE FOR PILOTS': The twenty-years-old Airman had achieved his goal of becoming an Air Force Crew Chief. Like more than four thousand other American young men and women, he was killed in Iraq. The family might have gained sympathy that his death circumstanced a "wing exchange"—from aluminum to angelic.

GOING HOME PHONE CALLS: The retired Coast Guard officer, upon learning that he had cancer, began to phone close friends with the news that he was "going home."

MIND REGAINED: Her writer believed that the woman's death had fulfilled her wish to see the face of Jesus. It surely also gave her back her mind: she had struggled with Alzheimer's. (Ed. A recent widow shared this anecdote. After her husband had succumbed to Alzheimer's Disease, one of her Granddaughters had adopted a mature Christian stance for the family's grieving: "Grandpa's got his mind back!" Grandma agreed.)

LAST BREATH RECLASSIFIED HIM: He was born in Belize with a Caribbean skin tone. He grew up with a "West Indian" accent. Upon coming to the United States, he was racially tagged black. Upon induction into military service, his race identification was white. His death certificate was stamped "Caucasian."

In summary, the circumstances that obituaries refer to most frequently come out like this (in some cases with an allusion to the cause): "She died peacefully at home, surrounded by her family.... he died peacefully in the arms of his wife.... the child died quietly at the Children's Hospital.... the Sergeant died in Iraq from gunfire in an ambush by the enemy—far away from his wife and three children."

Sometimes the circumstances are not known. At present the flight of a Brazilian Airlines plane that suddenly went down in the Atlantic Ocean about four hundred miles from the South American coast has raised many questions about the circumstances. So far one of the crucial Black Boxes has been retrieved from the Ocean Floor. It may be too late. At least one-fourth of the bodies has been found. (06/06/09.) More recently a plane from Paris bound for Yemen crashed in the Indian Ocean, and of the one hundred fifty-three passengers, a fourteen year-old girl was the sole survivor. Strange circumstances!

CAUSE

Obituaries ordinarily state more about the cause of death than about its circumstance, certainly much more than about its consequences—except for survivors. One in five Seattle media obituaries fails to mention cause. As already noted, cause and circumstance often interconnect, but more reader interest appears to settle on cause. In most cases, death comes, and it is perceived according to Dr. Kubler-Ross' previously quoted observation, as a "bad act." Some persons welcome death. The dying preceding it had been so distressful that last breath means relief, bringing a perceived long overdue reward, not only for the deceased, but also for the family as well: it ends suffering. Other matters rest in the hands of the invisible God, in the same way that many issues before the death had been.

Cause uses several nametags. "AID" will serve as an acronym for them: "A" will stand for aging, and related conditions, such as physical atrophy; "I" will track incidents, like accident, overdose, homicide, tragedy, etc.; and "D" will identify untimely or unusual disease.

Age dominates obituary listings as causes of death. When you read a statement that the Subject had reached a lifetime of high 80's or low 90's, or even 100 and had died of "natural causes," you can fairly accurately guess that the cause was attrition due to age. As some of the more acerbic and witty may say, "She lived too long." The United States has a growing percentage of its population approaching "Senior Status." China claims that more than seventy percent of its people fits that category; a large segment of China's population falls into the 16 to 20 years category. A curious sociologist may wonder, "Why do the Chinese live so long?" Is it more an environmental than an inheritance issue? Is it due to healthy, happy habits? Does their religion make a contribution?

Jesus certainly did not die of "A"—aging. Based on Luke's birth accounts, and a reference in Matthew, scholars have suggested that he was in his early thirties. One reference clarifies that he was no way near a half-century mark. The occasion was his attempt at explaining one of his enigmatic sayings. He was in the process of persuading his listeners of his authority as a Jewish prophet, thus placing him in the long tradition of Jewish covenant history. He had made the comment, "Whoever keeps my word will never die!" The statement aroused a question from one of his opponents: "Are you greater than our father Abraham, who died?" Jesus moved the conversation into his role of glorifying the Heavenly Father by his ministry, concluding, "Your ancestor Abraham rejoiced that he would see my day; he saw it and was glad." Still not penetrating the mystery, his angry rivals piqued the remark: "You are not yet fifty years old, and have you seen Abraham?" Jesus again approached the argument obliquely with an even more mysterious riddle: "Very truly, I tell you, before Abraham was, I am." That affirmation provoked the crowd to collect stones to throw at him. He quickly deserted the temple. (John 8: 48-59.) Jesus would not die from being old.

Paul's statement, "Christ died for our sins," of course penetrates to the theological heart of the cause of Christ's death, but does not totally satisfy a number of related cause questions. The Apostle expounded on the "for" issue by contrasting Jesus' death and Adam's. (Ed. That is, the Genesis "Adam," not "Adam Adams.") Publishers sometimes entitle the paragraph, "Adam and Christ." The premise of Paul's discussion states that humanity stands in desperate need: for atonement and justification by God, because: "Sin came into the world through one man, and death came through sin....so death spread to all because all have sinned...." (Romans 5:12.) Paul's argument advances from cause—Adam's sin— to cure: "If the many died through the one man's trespass, much more surely have the grace of God and the free gift in the grace of the one man, Jesus Christ, abounded for the many." (Vs. 15 b.) The conclusion is: "Just as one man's trespass led to condemnation for all, so one man's act of righteousness leads to justification and life for all. For just as by the one man's disobedience the many were made sinners, so by one man's obedience the many will be made righteousness." (Vss. 18-21, condensed.) The comment could encrypt to, "Adam killed Jesus." Another perspective along the same theological track is offered in the "famous" five-words statement, twenty-one less words than John 3:16! The same "Christ died…" statement appears in other writings of Paul, but much expanded.

The *Westminster Confession of Faith* lays out the simple and centuries-old Reformed Theological interpretation of death, the fatal human origin of death and the resultant consequence, the primordial "fall" of humanity: "They (Eve and Adam) being the root of all mankind, (are the means through whom) the guilt of this sin (resulting from subtle Satanic seduction) was imputed, and the same death in sin and corrupted nature conveyed to all posterity, descending from them by ordinary generation."[2] The final section of the same Chapter in the Westminster document defines sin as transgression of the righteous law of God, and adds that the consequences are fatal. Humanity has from soon after its beginning been fatally infected and doomed: sin "made (humanity) subject to death, with all its miseries, spiritual, temporal, and eternal." (Ibid.)

Unlike Jesus' beneficial death that atoned for human bad doing, sinful humanity has on occasion died from bad-doing of good. An instance occurred in 2008 when a gullible woman was seduced by the offer of an attractive prize for the person who could drink the most water in a given determination of time. The ruse started when a local radio station advertised an unusual event: a water-drinking contest. Contestants gathered in Sacramento, California. Seventeen applicants competed. They included a twenty-eight year-old mother. The attractive reward was a "Ninto

Wii" game console. Participants had to drink as much water as they could without having to urinate. Ms. Strange started drinking in the morning. She was dead by afternoon. Her death was ruled by a Coroner to have been due to "Water Intoxication," known scientifically as "hypotremia." The disorder results when sodium levels in the blood drop too low, leading to brain swelling, seizures, coma and death. The woman's ill-advised, unintentional, greed-induced suicide left three children for someone else to care for. Family and friends—and surviving fellow competitors—grieved the deceased's fatal lack of judgment. Several staff members at the radio station have been dismissed, and the sponsoring show is "off the air." Attorneys for the Strange family plan to file a wrongful-death lawsuit against the Station. Intemperate intake of too much of the good thing too quickly can cause death too early.

Homicide, genocide, suicide, murder, manslaughter and a host of other natural, human atrocities, all too frequently, due to intensity, timing, frequency, or, as in a hunger strike, inadequacy, cause death. Do not look for an obituary to reveal the information, however. A news story may appear and announce the circumstances, but the information will not appear in an obituary. Another death-intervention becoming more widely practiced, and more overtly admitted in obituaries, is "Death with Dignity"—as in the case of Lovelle Svart in Chapter I. A large segment of the American population still regards "Death with dignity" as an indignity, a sin or even a crime.

The Heidelberg Catechism makes this relevant comment on the Sixth of the Ten Commandments:

Question: 105. What does God require in the sixth commandment? ("Thou shalt not kill." Sic. *Newer Versions use "murder" for "kill.")* A. That I am not to abuse, hate, injure, or kill my neighbor, either with thought or by word or gesture, much less by deed, whether by myself or through another, but to lay aside all desire for revenge; and **that I do not harm myself or willfully expose myself to danger**. This is why authorities are armed with the means to prevent murder.[3]

In other words, do not commit suicide, either by a slow bad-habit process, or by a sudden atrocity.

The obverse of the sixth Commandment is "Glorify God with your body." Do all you can to make sure your lungs and all vital organs, and valuable senses, do not deteriorate because of abuse or neglect. Or if they do, or if you suspect a decaying process you can do something about, you will not follow the scenario currently being carried out by a Mother with her teenage Son. (05/20/09.) The lad has a malignant disease treatable by chemotherapy. He has already had one treatment, with a painful reaction; but with a reduction of the tumor size. The family holds to religious scruples about medical healing. Mother and Son disappeared for a short time, but finally returned home, reported to the authorities, and she, with the son's apparent cooperation, seems positive about continuing therapy treatment. No word has been broadly publicized as of this date, 07/05/09, if the treatment has been applied. If and when it is, the lad may breathe his last as a senior adult!

The Sixth Commandment could also be interpreted as, "You shall treat your depression, if that is your malady, with therapy and drugs, as necessary. Suicide usually results from a depressed mind." Evil always—consciously or unconsciously—comes from a wicked heart. You are more culpably accountable if you contribute to an untimely or premature death by not caring for your body—or for your mind and soul. Continued diet abuse, or home stress, or work-cheating and other bad habits can have the same effect.

Jesus once pointed out in a controversy with the Pharisees about oppressive, legalistic restrictions on food, and to some extent, drink: "What goes into the body" may have fatal potential. "What comes out" definitely does; it can destroy both your physical and spiritual being. (Cf. Matthew 15:11-20, and other parallel Gospels.) A caveat: Jesus taught this truth to Pharisees who were being meticulously oppressive over casuistries. He cautioned: beware of straining out a gnat and swallowing a camel. (Matthew 23:24.)

Sin trumped common sense, and the Biblical standard for human longevity, in another bizarre death featured recently in a *Seattle Times* news story. A man died after he had performed sex with a horse. (The Biblical code in the Book of Leviticus, 18:23, says, "You shall not have sexual relations with any animal…it is perversion.") In the man-horse case, voyeurs were illegally filming "beastiality" at a local farm. The beast attempted—and succeeded in—penetrating the man's body; the assault ruptured his colon. The injured man took his last breath before being transferred to a Seattle Hospital. The filming crew is being prosecuted.* They should have known better, and knowing, they should have acted with more common sense, taking seriously the Levitical prohibition: man and beast are not to copulate. The genitals and seminal discharge of both are not designed for sex between them. The sixth commandment applies equally to any human experimentation with unnatural behavior.

"D" stands for "disease, " as a cause of death. With women the figures are highest for cancer and accidents. Increasingly lung cancer is taking women's lives. The same syndrome, along with heart disease, is true of men. The younger generation succumbs more to alcohol-related accidents than any other cause. Suicide is also prevalent among younger adults. (Alcohol is singled out here because alcoholism ranks in human disorders as a disease.)

Obituary excerpts dealing with incidents and accidents and other external violence that have caused death follow:

PARKINSON'S: Anticipation of relief made the summons to die appealing. The obituary reported that the Lord called him to leave family and residence on earth, after a long siege with Parkinson's disease.

MOTORCYCLE: An accident killed him at age 47. He loved to ride his motorcycle. Knowing he died doing something he had always enjoyed relieved his family's discomfort over the death incident.

CAUSE?: He died at his house in San Francisco after a protracted pulmonary illness. Donations were suggested for the Bailey-Boushay House, which offers care for AIDS' victims and families.

---

*(The voyeurs have recently been arrested for similar crimes. 11/09)

BULLETS: A twenty-one year-old sailor died on active military duty. The family is convinced that now, having known Jesus, he seeks even more beautiful adventures in heaven.

HEART: The young man had served a stint in the U.S. Army Air Corps. He survived military service; he died of heart failure.

CAR: He was twenty-two years old when he was injured in a car accident. He was still alive when airlifted to a local Medical Center. The doctors worked for hours trying to "save" him. They did not succeed.

CONSEQUENCE

Of the three issues connected with death discussed in this Chapter, neither circumstance nor cause compares in theological significance with consequence. Consequence relates to the impact one's dying/death has on the Subject, as well as on the communal, civil, and psychological environment in which the Subject had lived. (Consequences due to God's judgment or related to life after death will not receive consideration: first, because of the danger to which Jesus said judging others exposes the judge; and second, because of a statement about the future that Jesus himself made: some of the events and judgments even he was not aware of, like on what date of which year at what time he would return.) Human judgment about the consequence of a death will be limited to phenomena that can be factually and socially or psychologically verified, in order to be credible.

The author of the Epistle to the Hebrews maintains that no trauma that an individual experiences in death compares in consequence, either to himself or to his followers, or to history, like Jesus' death: "He had to become like his brothers and sisters in every respect, so that he might be a merciful and faithful high priest in the service of God, to make a sacrifice of atonement for the sins of the people. Because he himself was tested by what he suffered, he is able to help those who are being tested." (Hebrews 2:17-18, quoted previously.)

The creeds of the Church address consequence, *The Apostles' Creed* in several clauses:

- "...dead, and buried;" (Chapter VI will expand on Jesus' burial.)
- "...he rose again from the dead...."—as he had promised he would;
- "...he ascended into heaven...."—again, as prophesied;
- "...and sitteth at the right hand of God the Father Almighty...."—where he belongs, until he returns to earth again;
- "...from thence he shall come to judge the quick and the dead;
- "...the Holy Catholic Church...." Which is the body that Jesus said he would build on the foundation of the apostles and prophets, himself as the chief cornerstone; and he would keep both residences and residents (ritually) clean;
- "...the communion of the saints...."—the fellowship he longs for all humanity to enjoy and for which his body was broken and his blood shed;
- "...the forgiveness of sins...."—what more can be said?
- "...the resurrection of the body,"—of which his resurrection is the first fruits;
- "...and the life everlasting."

Jesus spoke frequently and convincingly—with authority—about eternal life. A reminder: life everlasting begins on this side of heaven; it is an offer of life in "abundance, full of meaning and pleasure and challenge;" and it continues beyond death, into eternal life in heaven. To speak accurately of eternal life is to speak of life intensively and extensively and eternally. It is life that occasionally explodes into an extravagance of love, peace, joy, and satisfaction; and occasionally for some purpose in the mind of God, it stays sparse. But you need never worry again about sin or death, just accept that "it happens to everybody."

The *Westminster Confession of Faith* deals with consequences dualistically: "The bodies of men, after death, return to dust, and see corruption; but their souls (which neither die nor sleep), having an immortal subsistence, immediately return to God who gave them. The souls of the righteous, being then made perfect in holiness, are received into the highest heavens, where they behold the face of God in light and glory, waiting for the full redemption of their bodies; and the souls of the wicked are cast into hell, where they remain in torment and utter darkness, reserved to the judgment of the great day. Besides these two places for souls separated from their bodies, the Scripture acknowledgeth none."[4] Theological statements in other Denominational Creeds and Statements of Faith read similarly.

Knowing, studying, understanding, and saying (as a means of appropriating) the Creeds of the Church, plus being aware of the Biblical foundation for them, identify the pious exercises that make their truth effective. They also act the same when mortals swallow the "godawful" cup of death. Healthy grieving helps. Pursuing the pre-emptive comfort of God holds highest priority: "Blessed are those who mourn for they will be comforted." (Matthew 5:4.) Simultaneously seeking the listening ear of a neighbor or a counselor can also bring a peace that passes all understanding, as long as you fulfill the other requirements in Philippians 4:4-7: rejoice, and rejoice again; do not worry; make prayer supplications to God with thanksgiving. Pre-emptive dealing with sorrow, according to the suggestions made in the opening chapter on coming to terms with dying, ripens the fruit of comfort. Do not bury anger at God or the drunk driver—or yourself—in your subconscious. See a counselor, if necessary. And make sure you read the final Chapter of *OT*, "Knowhow."

Grief therapy offers one of the most satisfactory approaches to sorrow. As soon as possible after a death, become active in a grief group. Psychologist Bob Deits makes a case for therapy in his book, *"Life After Loss: A Personal Guide dealing with Death, Divorce, Job Change and Relocation."* Mr. Deits states in the Introduction: "Loss is painful beyond words." He strongly encourages individuals, in spite of their possible depression or other debilitating attendant weakness, to take an assertive initiative in rising above a tyrannical morass of mixed and complicated feelings. Force yourself, or engage an "enforcer" to help you cross the lonesome valley to the truth that there is "Life after Loss." Mr. Deits offers practical suggestions for Group Meetings: "The fundamental principles for a self-directed group are these: Feelings are neither right nor wrong.... The leader must be as accepting of anger and frustration as of hopefulness and joy.... It takes a long time to work through loss and grief." (P. 215.) The Author comments on "Recovery:" "The day will come when you will know deep inside that you have recovered your balance, completed your journey through grief, and are ready to get on with a good and full life. On that day, you will be a stronger person than you have ever been before." (P. 50.)[5]

John Calvin, the courageous, brilliant sharp-tongued Reformer, offers words of comfort to the grieving mourner: "The Scripture declares that Christ is present with them (the righteous dead) and receives them into paradise, where they enjoy consolation.... The souls of pious men, after finishing their laborious warfare, depart into a state of blessed rest, where they wait with joy and pleasure for the fruition of the promised glory. All things remain in suspense until Christ appears as the Redeemer."[6]

Calvin goes on to warn against harboring unfounded and mischievous, imaginative, and dangerous anxieties about the eternal consequences of your loved one's—or your own—death: "Over-curious inquiry respecting their (the dead's) intermediate state is neither lawful nor useful.... It is folly and presumptuous to push our inquiries on unknown things beyond what God permits us to know.... The question respecting place is equally senseless and futile; because we know that the soul has no dimensions like the body.... It is enough for us, at the close of this pilgrimage to be received by the Father of believers, and to participate with him in the fruit of his faith." Calvin believed that the righteous dead, in some form and location consistent with the spiritual status in which they had died, are peacefully waiting out the "intermediate" gap between death and resurrection. Since judgment has already been pre-determined, Calvin anathematizes purgatory.

The Westminster "Divines," Calvin also, had obviously not missed their Seminary New Testament class sessions the days their Professors lectured on Paul's letters to the Corinthians. The advice that the Apostle insisted on when teaching, preaching or writing about the Gospel in the context of death and resurrection can be summarized in five words: "Nothing beyond what is written." (I Corinthians 4:6.)

New Testament resurrection theology trumps Old Testament testimony—fortunately—on one of death's most depressing consequences: the consignment of the soul to Sheol. Recall the dire and dark and bland and cardboard-like existence in which the Old Testament writers had portrayed "Sheol?" The Church proclaims Christ, the light of the world, is alive and at the right hand of God. The soul of the dead may be asleep, but the sleep may consist of different degrees of unconsciousness from the slumber Paul writes of in 1 Thessalonians 4, and other places.

Recommendation: Survey the whole Scriptural landscape on the consequences of dying. The New Interpreter's Study Bible suggests that the older material on the hereafter, as in Psalm 139:7-12, serves exegetical purposes for dealing with death's profundities: "Mysteries attached to conceptions of death, future life, and Sheol in the book of Psalms allow for later interpretations of God's omnipresence, and the fate of those who no longer live."[7]

One of Jesus' parables interprets judgment surrounding the "sleep" of death under a rubric that may be called, "chasm theology." As it allegorizes death, "chasm" is a consequence word. (See Luke 16:19-31.) According to Luke's account, Lazarus, a poor man on earth, died and went to the comfort and wealth of Paradise. While on earth as a victim of extreme poverty, he had requested immediate first-aid help from a rich man, sometimes called "Dives." Dives had consistently refused to allow Lazarus even to eat the scraps left over from lavishly served banquets; he dumped them in the garbage containers.

Both men eventually died. Lazarus went "up," Dives went "down,"—in status, in wealth, in options and in accommodations, condemned to a dreary and uncomfortable existence in the compartment of Hades called "Hell." Lazarus was housed in Paradise. "Dives" sent a desperate message to Abraham (paraphrased): "Send Lazarus down to this hothouse with relief—as minimal as a finger dipped in cold water—and place it on my tongue." Abraham responded—now the parable will be quoted: "Child, remember that during your lifetime you received your good things, and Lazarus in like manner evil things; but now he is comforted here, and you are in agony. Besides all this, between you and us a great chasm has been fixed, so that those who might want to pass from here to you cannot do so, and no one can come from there to us." (Vss. 24-27.)

What good fortune for the Bible and for theology that understanding of the underworld matured into a compartmentalization paradigm. Sheol did not exactly end up in shambles, but it described life after death "in the underworld," in terms of places for the good and places for the bad. In terms of the Lazarus-poor man-parable, the good place, Paradise, is reserved for the citizenry who did compassion and justice in their lifetime. Withholding basic sustenance from persons who lack it merits residence in Hades. And between the two environments, as Jesus' parable insists, a great chasm has been fixed.

The situation may remind the reader of the current wall between the city and the West Bank in Jerusalem, necessary, the Israeli Government says, to protect Jews from Palestinian violence; unjust, the Palestinian Authorities say, first because it violates the terms of the settlement of the 1967 conflict, and second because it makes travel for Palestinians who work beyond the wall an almost insurmountable transversal obstacle. (The other non-obituary passage about post-death communication between mortals and immortals—Jesus' preaching mission to the dead—has already been exegeted. {1 Peter 3.})

Another curious consequence of death that drew the attention of Old Testament scholars and teachers of the Law—especially the Scribes—relates to contamination. Contact with the dead put a Jew in cultic jeopardy. Wisdom warned:

don't stare, don't glare, and, for God's sake and your own, don't touch a dead body! Don't you dare! If you do, "Don't brag, don't tell." Otherwise, you will not be allowed inside either the synagogue or the Jerusalem Temple; nor will you be able to return to normal business or social relations with fellow Jews. Hurry and immediately upon contact, set up an appointment with a religious authority about your shunning. Do not be surprised when you are compelled to go through a Levitical ritual for the cleansing of your profane condition; you are polluted. The contamination could result from several causes, many of them interpersonal: related to contacts with non-Jews, non-covenantal religions, and circumstances like death and disease or gender. The Book of Leviticus abounds in lists of them. Lepers, for instance, had to warn the public about their condition, by yelling "Leper!" when outside or in crowds. (The requirement calls to mind the Nazi requirement during World War II that Jews display a "Star of David" patch on their clothing.) Pollution in Biblical society condemned you to a lonely and shameful life; a "Star of David" condemned you to a concentration camp, and probable last breath.

Attempts at contact with the dead were also regarded as a profane—against cultic law—activity, which in turn resulted in spiritual pollution, which in part explains why the Medium (Witch) of Endor was hesitant when King Saul came to her, pleading that she exercise her profession in having Samuel brought back from the dead. (Of course, the King had decreed the practice illegal, upon threat of serious reprisals.) Saul would have done better if he had stayed on the battlefield and done war. Samuel's honoring the summons of the Medium resulted in bad news that consequently resulted in bad ends for the King and his sons, and his armor bearer. (I Samuel 28.)

One of the messages that the Medium/Witch-Saul-Samuel episode sends out clearly is: "Mess around with the consequences of death, and you may spoil both your life--and your death." Scholar Alan Richardson, former Professor of Theology at the University of Nottingham in England, in *A Theological Word Book of the Bible,* commented on intrusions on the underworld: "There is no biblical sanction whatever for spiritualistic experimentation, but rather an attitude of horror at the very suggestion of it, as an interference with the divinely appointed order of things."[8]

No Old Testament writer—not even Moses or Elijah or Isaiah or, especially, Qoheleth and Job—softened Old Testament theology on the consequences of death like the prophet Daniel; and Isaiah, to some extent. What a challenge Old Testament authors left to New Testament writers—and to the Church! And the Holy Spirit! But then, the Church had the advantages of the baptism with the Holy Spirit, and the death and resurrection of Jesus. During his ministry Jesus had frequently reminded his Twelve of the necessity of both—Spirit and resurrection—for the fuller understanding of the Gospel. Much ado about death and hope and consequences needed new insight and inspiration. Except for Daniel no other Old Testament dogmatic giant could, and none ever did, produce apocalyptic literature that compares with New Testament apocalypticism.

The nearest to it may be found in Sheol references, especially the references to the ambiance of the abode of the dead; and to the judgment, and even non-judgment, that sends and keeps you in post-death consignment. Every person who died went to Sheol, and some of them found it worse than others. Some rested, some were tormented. Along came Daniel with his innovative insight and remarkable literary skills, to challenge certain expressions of "human word about Divine Word." Before his prophecy, the universal family of the children of Abraham was challenged by the horror of Sheol to stay healthy and alive, and out of trouble as best you could. You reach that goal by knowing the Torah, and faithfully keeping it. You could joyfully sing, "I know that my redeemer lives…et. al." (Job 19:25.)

No New Testament thinker, author, instructor or theologian matches Paul as a base from which to write. Pauline brilliance combined with Pauline experience to create incomparable—until John's "Revelation"—statements about the theological, particularly eschatological, consequences of Jesus' death (and resurrection). Some of

Paul's sentences have already been covered in this chapter: "Christ died for us...."; and "If God is for us, who can be against us?....It is God who justifies. Who is to condemn? It is Christ Jesus, who died, yes, who was raised, who is at the right hand of God...." Paul's profoundly dogmatic theology about nothing being able to separate us from the love of God in Christ Jesus (Romans 8:31-9), clearly declares a transforming truth, which fortunate dying people may trust and hold onto; and living people may embrace as daily bread.

Consequence theology has inspired—I am self-confident enough to use "inspired"—an Easter hymn that I composed a few years ago, entitled, "Out." The last stanza offers these words:

"Resurrection power, stir us
With unrest with unbelief,
With impatience with injustice,
With compassion for relief!
Send the Church with food and funding,
Serum, counsel, cloak and bed;
'Till the world affirms our dogma:
Christ is Out, raised from the dead."
(Metered 8787D)

As the hymn reminds us, and as Jesus taught us, resurrection theology goes dormant—even dreadful—when not nurtured by neighborliness, kindness, sympathy and justice. While I am introducing Elgin liturgical creations, I will insert here my "mantra," original-composition, prayer. Theologically, the prayer declares that authentic spirituality bears belief in a Triune God, and witness in social action: "Father of Jesus, I receive your mercy, with thanksgiving in the Spirit, and with commitment to your kingdom." (I habitually pray the prayer in my Daily Prayer, usually following self-absolution after Confession of Sin; and at other times. Open your hands and pray it—now!)

Obituaries do not take readers into as deep and compelling theology of death's circumstances, causes and consequences as the foregoing discussion, but they frequently express sentiment and insight derivative of orthodoxy. Commitment is implied. They exult in the confidence embraced in Presbyterian Women's leader and song writer, Jane Parker Huber's "Live into Hope." It sings of the consequences the Church can anticipate because Jesus Christ "was crucified, dead and buried. The third day, he arose again from the dead...:"

> Live into hope of captives freed,
> Of sight restored, the end of greed.
> The oppressed shall be the first to see
> The year of God's own jubilee.
>
> ....
>
> Live into hope, the blind shall see
> With insight and with clarity,
> Removing shades of pride and fear
> __A vision of our God brought near."
>
> (*The Presbyterian Hymnal,* No. 332.)

Obituaries that follow speak of the consequences of death, sometimes more with Christian meaning than with Christian vocabulary or Reformed Theology. Paul might have said, "What difference does it make, as long as Christ is witnessed to as raised from the dead?" (Philippians 1:15.)

RECENT CONVERT JOINED THOSE "GONE BEFORE:" He died at age fifty-six, a recent convert to Christ. His family was grateful that as a consequence of his faith, he was guaranteed an eternity with the God of his personal Lord and Savior. They believe that, consequent upon his conversion, he has joined those with whom he had lived, and who had gone before him. His life had made such good impressions on those left behind, that he would remain forever in their hearts; he was "gone but never forgotten."

FAMILY REUNITED: Although death has separated her from her family, they are convinced that her spirit has not perished; it would have power to reunite the dead, continue to live on through her children, and keep unity in the family.

"CHILDREN, COME:" The little girl had memorized and recited, and was now into the fulfillment of, Jesus' invitation, "Let the children come to me." Her death, her family believed, had placed her in Jesus' heavenly presence. (This obituary has been noted in another context.)

CHANGE CHANNELS: Among other purposes, her obituary was published in order to alert God to have heavenly TV tuned into the right Channel (ESPN); the Political Activist was on her way. TV had played a huge roll in her political activism. Death would not destroy her TV addiction. (How about heavenly politics?)

The Church offers the best resources for dealing with the "it happens to everyone" consequences of death: a sympathetic Pastor, hopefully; a Board of Deacons; certainly, a loving and sympathetic Congregation, possibly; and a Grief Group, eventually. Two resources that a congregation, or a mourner, may take for granted, but which are frequently overlooked, are: 1. Worship, with a spiritual family, and hearing a message centered in the Gospel of Christ; taking part in the sacraments, particularly the Eucharist if offered; and, 2. Outreach services to the needy, including to the grieving. Christ comes to the heart and soul of the believer under, by, with, in, and through these rites—by grace. He invites, "Come unto me all you that are weary, and overburdened, and I will give you rest." (Matthew 11:28-30.) And Jesus promised, "Those who love me will keep my word, and my Father will love them, and we will come to them and make our home with them." (John 14:23.)

Remember to pray your prayers when you go to bed tonight, and if you haven't already prayed it in your morning prayers, include the Lord's Prayer. It could result in the last exercise of your last breath! However, do not let the prospect silence you! According to Calvin, your last exercise would identify you as one who died doing a Christian's "principal exercise."[9]

V.

Commemorated

"I believe in....Jesus Christ.... he was crucified, dead and buried...."

The Apostles' Creed

HONORED WITH WAHEGURU AND AKHAND PATH FUNERAL: A much beloved son left his family to be with Waheguru. Funeral services at a local Funeral Home followed three days of gathering of mourners at his house of worship for sacred readings of Akhand Path. Akhand Path assures the grieving family that their loved one rests with "Waheguru."

PARTY PRECEDED CHURCH MEMORIAL SERVICE: Several commemorations of her commitment to nursing—and her faith—preceded her death from terminal illness. Friends, neighbors, colleagues and cancer survivors observed a living "Pink Lady Day." Friends gathered on her front lawn, bearing pink balloons, flowers and plants. She kept insisting to her sympathizers that she was not afraid of the "End;" her regret was that the end was arriving sooner than she would have liked. A Church Memorial Service spiritually commemorated her. (*Tacoma News Tribune.)*

MASS: Friends of the deceased visited and "viewed" her at the City's Funeral and Cremation Center. A Mass was celebrated at Our Lady of Joy Church. In lieu of flowers, commemorative donations were designated for the local Parkinson's Chapter, the Children's Museum, a Trumpet

Chair of the Youth Symphony Orchestra, and the Greater City's Food Bank. (*Pittsburgh Post Gazette,*'07.)

....

Commemoration constitutes the second of the three major events consequent upon a person's dying; first comes death, last comes disposition of the body. Between the two, family or survivors memorialize or commemorate the life and accomplishments and career of the deceased. Increasingly, however, commemoration does not center in the funeral or in a memorial service; if it happens outside the family circle or environs, it takes the form of a social gathering or a party, sometimes a gala. Family and a few invited guests gather either at the home of a relative or friend of the deceased, at a social hall, or at a park or sports bar, and reminisce about the departed. Commemoration may also take the form of a private family social or religious gathering; or a pre-death event, like the early morning lawn assembly for a terminally ill lady shortly before she died; or an evening service of "Akhand Path" for an immigrant; or a country club reception by invitation only; or a back-yard family picnic; or a trek to a favorite outdoor spot where the deceased had enjoyed activities like hunting, bird watching, hiking, doing photography, or just relaxing. If a pastor accompanies the group, a Scripture may be read, a prayer may be offered, and reflective comments made.

Whatever the style, commemoration serves several purposes. It honors the deceased's achievements. It ameliorates the grief that family and neighbors are feeling, and sometimes balances conviviality and sorrow. Memorial services may also provide occasions for the acceptance of the reality of death. This Chapter will critique the procedures, practices, and habits of commemorations. Discernment from a Biblical and Reformed Theological profession and practice will be made from the limited data available as to how comforting and satisfying the gathering could have been.

Do you recall that one of Jesus' most admiring followers performed a commemoration for him? The Lord distinguished it by saying that the world— the believing world, that is—would never forget the woman who had done it. Mary, sister of the resurrected Lazarus, took oil and anointed his feet with her hair, and kissed them repeatedly. The event took place at a meal in their home. While not mentioned, it is probable that her sister Martha was also present, but from what we know about her on one of Jesus' previous visits, she was probably fussing about preparing a lavish meal. Other guests were present, including the disciple, Judas Iscariot. (Cf. John 12.)

Not everybody at the table was impressed with Mary's gesture. Jesus' future betrayer criticized the woman for being extravagantly wasteful. Jesus rebuked Judas for his hypocrisy. The meal seemed to have proceeded, nevertheless, and the place obviously smelled less of leeks and lamb, and more of perfume. Neither music nor eulogy attached to the service. It demonstrated more love in action, than a celebration in word. It ended up being one of the few commemorations Jesus would receive; the hour of his death precluded both pre and post-crucifixion ceremony.

Both Matthew (26:6-13) and Mark (14:3-7) record a commemoration without ceremony, performed on another occasion and in a different setting, this time at the home of Simon the leper. Were the two the same event? Differences in their recording could have been due to one of the writers lacking information about the details. Scholars are not in agreement about Jesus' commemoration. An unnamed woman anointed Jesus—at Simon's—applying expensive nard to his head. No mention is made of her using her hair. When criticism arose over her extravagance, including a personal scolding of the woman—again by Judas—Jesus made the same rebuke he had done at Lazarus' home: "Let her alone...She has performed a good service for me. She has anointed my body beforehand for its burial. Truly I tell you, wherever the good news is proclaimed in the whole world, what she has done will be told in remembrance of her." (Ed. Scholars have speculated that "she" could have been Mary Magdalene.)

Commemoration while Jesus was dying could have been omitted out of fear that such attention was inappropriate—and dangerous. It could have been withheld because he had already had two "services." Or it could have been that some of his disciples and followers were doing rememberances verbally and surreptitiously. One observer, and that one a "foreigner," a Roman Army Officer, was so impressed by Jesus' dying that he looked toward the pitiful creature on the center beam, and "Praised God and said, 'Certainly this man was innocent.'" (Luke 27:45.) Any other commemoration, private or social, could not have been carried out more sincerely.

The Presbyterian Church (U.S.A.), like most Christian units, honors the gesture Mary performed and Judas condemned. The Presbyterian *Book of Order*, the "Directory for Worship," prescribes that upon breathing their last, the dead are to be honored on a timely schedule with an orderly procedure, by a final commemorative "act," or several "acts." (No expensive perfume or nard is required, but neither is it prohibited.) Recognition takes place, regardless of whether the body is to be buried, interred, inurned, donated, or otherwise legally and reverently disposed of, regardless of whether it has been naturally or tragically disfigured or dissembled. Whatever the case, commemoration order calls for thoughtful and reverent protocol. Although not legislated by ecclesiastical fiat as crucial, or necessary, physical, emotional, financial, cultural and personal matters related to the process are nevertheless to be given reverent consideration, including decisions about the difference a venue can make.

The commemorative treatment of Christ in his last days and hours has benefited and influenced the Church in appropriately expressing last minute tribute. The guidance has assisted in dealing with questions like: Why arrange for such a service? When to have it? Where to hold it? Who, along with, or aside from a Pastor, should help a family or survivors most appropriately to organize a fitting tribute to a loved one? How to publicize it? Should the service be personal or private, or should an open invitation to attend be extended? How important are the wishes of the deceased, if known? Should the pre-death stipulations of the dead that there be "No service" be honored or ignored, and under what conditions? And how do you "cap" the gathering—by food, drink, or similar hospitalities? How appropriate is it to offer alcohol, or, as in some cases, hold the event at a Bar or Sports Club? These issues will be discussed.

The obituary excerpts that follow relate some of the ways commemoration happens in the Pacific Northwest:

MEDIA COMMEMORATION: A notation in the local Paper, with a photo of the handsome youth, constituted the family's tribute in honor of the Fifth Anniversary of the death of a sixteen-year-old. The text expressed that his survivors, possibly because of the lad's seemingly untimely death, still perceive his passing as a "moment ago" memory.

TO RECALL HIS LAUGH AND EXTEND HIM PEACE: The Family arranged for a private burial and memorial service. His obituary concluded with the sentiment that they would miss laughing with him. Wishes of eternal peace accompanied him to where they presumed he was headed. He was "at rest."

BOOK MEMORIALS: A family still holds tender feelings in their hearts. A commemorative suggestion was made: if any chose to honor their daughter's memory further, they could donate children's books to a school of their choice, making school libraries another place of commemoration of her short life.

HAPPY BIRTHDAY: A memorial was submitted to the *Obituary* Section of the paper on the date of the deceased's death. The narrative indicated that his loved ones continue regularly to celebrate his memory with joyful gestures: laughter, cooking, music, and the joy of living.

DEATH DAY ANNIVERSARY: She had died in her twenties. A blessing of God was wished for her on the first anniversary of her death. The family finds comfort in the assurance that she continues her post-earth life journey with God. Many of her surviving loved ones expressed this sentiment: part of our world slid into the sea with her passing and scattering.

As the Presbyterian *Book of Order* intimates and ecclesiastically legislates, commemorative rites offer more meaning, represent more appreciation, and more effectively assuage grief when venues and content and service style receive careful attention. The recommendations are: hold the services in a holy place; plan them carefully and properly, possibly enlisting family members and friends both in the preparation of the service and in participation by taking an active part; treat the memory of the deceased humanely and with dignity. Every human being has, or has had, unique character formation, as was part of the Creator's original design. Read Genesis 2.

A Pastor or a Church Secretary or Administrative Assistant may also help you with critical commemoration decisions. Presbyterians have numerous resources available, as most denominations have. The Presbyterian Church (U.S.A.) *Book of Order* offers specific guidance, like the following statement on time and place: "(A) Service on the occasion of death ordinarily should be held in the usual place of worship, in order to join this service to the community's continuing life and witness to the resurrection ....The service may be observed before or after the committal of the body...." (W-4.10003.)[1]

In addition to helping with grieving, commemorations may also serve less profound functions. For example, they may launder the life of the deceased. A person with a publicly reputed and displayed despicable character, and possibly judgmentally considered reprobate by some more conservative family members or neighbors, may receive non-judgmental credibility and social restoration through personal tributes or similar "Praise and Promotion" exercises. Too many accolades, however, may demand patience and politeness to sit through non-judgmentally, especially if you have knowledge that the person being posthumously puffed up had lived the life of a "deadbeat," a spouse-assaulter, a child-abuser, or a business "wheeler-dealer"—namely, a hypocrite. Clean-up can be thwarted by too much praise.

"Exploitive" or "imperialistic" evangelism at funerals and memorial services is inappropriate e.g., enthusiastic, Billy Graham style "invitations"—no suggestion inferred that Dr. Graham would preach for conversion at a funeral or offer an "altar call." But to submit to the temptation to "try to save" at a funeral those in the congregation whom you perceive as "lost" is not only spiritually tasteless, but also socially tactless. (The Reverend Billy Graham, I am certain, would disapprove; he would vouch for reserving evangelistic preaching for more appropriate circumstances.) Some funeral guests have shared that they felt as if they had been perceived as "Easter Sunday" and "Christmas Eve" Christians. Some funeral attendees have "given up" on the Church, often over a disagreement with a fellow family member, or with the Preacher, and have not been to worship lately, but they show up for funerals. The judgment is made—and sometimes passed on to the Pastor ahead of time—that some of the attendees have never heard the Gospel, or had heard it so long ago that they have forgotten it. It is doubtful that a funeral homily, especially for a family whose pastor is not the officiant, will effect reconciliation. Those matters have to be dealt with more personally, and under less emotional strain.

Exceptions arise. One occurred when I officiated a service for a young church-member who had committed suicide. As a child and early adolescent, he had been active in Sunday School and youth Activities. When Charlie died (Ed. Charlie's Mother has granted permission for this anecdote), and as the family and I were planning his service, they requested inviting a prominent national preacher to participate: The Reverend William Sloan Coffin—Preacher, Scholar, Chaplain, and at that time, Pastor of the Riverside Church in New York City. "Though dead, yet Bill speaketh!" He became widely known, not only through his reputation as a Chaplain, but also because of his writing and his national reputation for preaching and lecturing. I had had a closer relationship with him during a ten-days' study leave at Yale University. He was the Chaplain there at the time. The relationship grew deeper when my wife and I spent a sabbatical semester at the Union Theological Seminary in New York, and we worshiped regularly at the Riverside Church. Bill, and the suicide victim's parents, shared neighborhood summer-home properties in Vermont.

Pastor Doctor Coffin had credentials for being asked to help with the young man's service, besides the neighbor connections and his own competence as a pastor to younger generations. His son had recently slammed into a wall in New York while riding his motorcycle. The young man in our Parish had died of asphyxiation in his car, ironically parked on the basketball court outside the Church Office windows. He was apparently not trying to hide anything.

Dr. Coffin was contacted. He was available and would be honored to come and assist in the service. The commemoration transpired into one of the best attended and most memorable in the history of the Church, and in the experience of many mourners and Charlie's Pastor. A young quartette from the Church sang "Blessed Assurance." Giving his homily, Bill was at his inimitable and personable and consoling best. Several of Charlie's best friends who had been at the party at his house the night he had taken his own life, attended the funeral, sitting in the pews behind the family. At one point in his homily, Bill addressed them. He raised issues like careless motorcycle riding, drinking while driving, drug abuse, and irresponsible wild partying. He might also have included a point or two about "designated drivers." The family listened carefully, and the young men paid serious attention. Two or three of them held handkerchiefs over their eyes. Conversation between Bill and the "guys" resumed at a post-service reception in the Church Fellowship Hall. I venture the bold opinion that God was pleased with the Pastor-youth attraction, and that some young men might have left the funeral planning life changes. (*Ed.* I saw Charlie's Mother recently, and she expressed appreciation that I was recalling the event.)

The "Charlie" situation may compare with one that the renowned United Methodist Bishop William H. Willimon recounted recently. The Bishop has been recovering from a serious chain-saw accident. He and a purple-haired young man recuperating from a skateboard mishap were exchanging anecdotes about their misfortunes. The lad reported that it hurt him to stay off the skateboard for several months. In addition, he was still hurting from "a sore tail." But he had expressed some religion during the episode. He related that he had promised Jesus, "Get me out of this and I'll never skate again." The Bishop asked, "Did you keep your promise?" The reply was, "Naw…all I learned was--next time, be more careful about making any promises to Jesus."[3]

The increasing custom, "No Services, " raises concerns about both grieving and the impact of commemoration events. Who is responsible for the event? Has it been made thoughtfully, that is, by family, neighbors or friends? Obituaries that announce "No Services Planned" frequently add, "at the deceased's request." They indicate that the Subject had settled the issue before death. When I have had the opportunity to know about the plan before publication of the obituary, I have on occasion asked questions of the bereaved: "Have you considered how commemorating the deceased can assist you with your grief? Have you thought that perhaps the decision had been made without thoroughly thinking it through, or at a time when the deceased's mind was skewed by extreme suffering or other emotional pressures? While respect for the deceased's wishes is civil, your loved one will never know if you had complied with their request—until it is too late to make a difference, either for you or them or in your relations with each other! Wouldn't you like to re-consider your 'No Services' decision?" I ask. I continue, "You know, 'It is easier to obtain forgiveness, than to get permission.' And have you considered how many persons, even outside your family, would benefit from attending a commemoration? Besides, when persons have decided to attend a service, contrary to the expressed wish of the deceased, or of the survivors, they have frequently reported that the event had proved a blessing. And no one has ever reported residual guilt over the decision."

Availability of the desired venue for commemoration events has sometimes created a problem. Some churches deny their facilities for services for inactive, or non-members, and persons of questionable reputation; possibly, for good reason, related to the Church's policies or the Pastor's scruples. The disappointed mourner often expresses surprise, and becomes defensive: "I was raised in this Church…. I belonged to this church all my life….My parents are active members….My wife and I were married in this Church…. We send our kids to this church….I read the Bible….I am not an atheist….I come here every Easter Sunday, and often on Christmas Eve, and I always put something in the offering plate…" After a litany like this, I ask the defender where he worshiped God last Sunday, or why she has deserted Christ and/or the Church. I listen carefully to their answers to this question—that is, if there are further comments! I try to be as pastoral as I can, without causing alienation or intimidation. As I receive excuse upon excuse, I process them: *Remember also that these folk have tender souls at the moment; they are in deep mourning. Jesus sometimes made allowances—for foreigners, uncircumcised adult males, promiscuous women, Sabbath non-observers, etc. And so should you!* On occasion I have entered into discussion with some of the "defenders," and at times have felt I made some progress with them spiritually. As John Calvin asserted, sow the seed and let the soil and the Savior reap the harvest. Contrite promises are sometimes made. Are they kept? Maybe some of them should have been broken. I close conversations like these with a prayer that hearts would be changed and relationships restored. On a rare occasion, I have had an on-the-spot conversion!

A discomfort with large public gatherings has been offered as a reason to avoid a church funeral. "Too much fuss and trouble," one person remarked. Some families, church members, friends, or neighbors may need a quiet, more intimate small group for family commemorations. Large congregations, rather than being a channel of comfort, become too intimidating or detracting for certain people. For some it creates hypochondria, and funeral home Staff has been sought out for "smelling salts," or a glass of cold water. In one of the congregations I served, a parishioner attended every funeral—large or small. She expressed that as a member of the congregation she felt she should show her support for grieving families. I had judgmentally decided that she enjoyed the food at the receptions following the services. When questions about deserving the church funeral arise, I keep reminding myself—and others—that funerals or commemorations are for the living, and only in memory of the dead.

Funeral or memorial commemoration style order for Presbyterians requires that consideration be given to the role the Church plays in your value system, in your family and business relations, and in your personal devotional or spiritual life. If you are a believer and church member, and currently have or have had—in the case of the deceased—membership, and a life of worship and service in a church, you should arrange for your funeral or memorial there. On occasion individuals have opted for a different venue—most of the time for legitimate reasons. Perhaps a larger attendance than can be accommodated in their regular house of worship is anticipated. Others, usually of flimsy or minimal church connections, hold to the opinion that, other factors being reasonable, almost any place of beauty, solemnity or reverence can serve satisfactorily for commemorating. (And even in places without a whiff of "spirits" anywhere!) My experience is that when family and friends gather at a Country Club or public dining room, the service becomes more personal and social than theological. Some mourners regard cocktails as a helpful palliative for grief. That person needs a reminder: that liquored soothing may offer more burden than relief, and it slowly, and deceptively non-addictively, demands dangerous repetition. Other social factors like the spirituality of the deceased or of the survivors may influence the choice of commemoration place.

Churches and Funeral Homes still take priority as commemorative locations. One practical benefit to whichever receives the honor is that the advertising is free. Sometimes churches take precedence over other places in order to launder character, a matter written about earlier. Although not frequently chosen today, a private-home funeral, if the house is spacious and comfortable enough to accommodate the number expected to attend, deserves re-thinking. Painful memories may attach to your "home" church, and psychologically rule it out as appropriate for commemoration. People "get mad" at the Church or at the leadership. Some have more serious objections: a Pastor had abused you, or a member of your family, during childhood. Some of the same effects may mitigate against a home funeral. Other reasons may persuade families to avoid the home church, or the "home" preacher. A disgruntled member of our congregation once confronted me, first, with his gripes against the church; and second, with his threat: "I'll take my business elsewhere." Yes, in many respects both funerals and churches are businesses.

A comment that has come to me three or four times in my career is: "I just can't bring myself to come back to the Church. Ever since Mother's funeral there, I cry as soon as I come in the door. I am so embarrassed." I politely suggested that perhaps we could cooperate on starting a grief group in the congregation. "Oh, no," she replied immediately, "I could never do that." I persevered and suggested she investigate a grief group somewhere in the community, or perhaps she and I could discuss the matter sometime; or I could suggest a good counselor to help her work through the problem. She said, "I will think about it." She has taken a long time to think about it!

A sad situation that took place in our Church several years ago created a family of counselors willing to assist others connected with funeral phobias. A beautiful wedding was held at the Church on a Saturday. The Bride's funeral transpired the following Saturday. Following their wedding the handsome couple left on their honeymoon. A tragic accident occurred on the first or second day of their trip, and the bride was killed. Both had just graduated from the University. The groom survived with minor injuries. The Church facility had been crowded for their wedding. The Church filled again the following Saturday for Judy's funeral. The family had decided that the Church was the place to which to return for commemorating her life. More than half the congregation felt the same way; they attended both ceremonies. Judy was clothed in her wedding dress. The funeral homily took on a different tone from the wedding sermon, but both proclaimed the Gospel. The service had an uplifting feeling, the Gospel of Jesus Christ receiving all the credit. The joy of the wedding weekend merged into the joy of Judy's victory over death in Jesus Christ. The family received considerable support from the humble, at times even awkward, but simple efforts at expressing Christian sympathy.

The Presbyterian *Book of Order*, as pointed out earlier in the Chapter, stipulates with regard to commemoration: "Funerals should be held where the deceased had worshiped, for good spiritual reasons, but primarily to witness to Christ's resurrection." Besides familiarity with the setting where the worshiper met God and God drew near to the worshiper, the most significant reason for arranging for the service at your "home" church is: "In order to join the service to the community's continuing life and witness to the resurrection." (W-4.10003.)[3] In other words, the service serves the mystical function of evangelism and proclamation, and maybe conviction. It lifts up the greatest comforting hope the Church can offer a grieving community. If one member suffers, all suffer together, Scripture says; and if one is comforted, all ought to be comforted. The perfect Comforter is Jesus Christ, and comfort is dispersed through the preaching of his rising.

Commemorative Service styles and visitation-viewing customs have changed, but a customary schedule still prevails, both in villages, small towns and metropolitan areas. They abide by this calendar, unless body disposition happens as soon as the arrangements can be made with venue, cemetery or scattering location, and needed personnel is available; or unless family members may be out of the country and cannot be present three days following a death:

- Day 1, Death Day: the Funeral Home coach picks up the body, and the embalming, cremating, or other preparations for final disposition of the body are begun;
- Day 2: Visitation-Viewing—if the corpse is available, and the family chooses, at the funeral home;

- Day 3: Commemoration, perhaps viewing in the morning if the funeral or service is in the afternoon or evening, as close to 2:00 P.M. as possible.

In recent years commemoration and burial services have "divorced," particularly in the Pacific Northwest; and I perceive, in the Northeast, and even in some cases, in the more conservative regions of the Nation. Burial, inurnment, donation, and other disposition plans increasingly disregard the time and place of the Funeral or Memorial. The family, and perhaps with some invited close friends, gathers at the graveside, with the Pastor or officiant. Survivors are also planning smaller family services on a date when scattered families can conveniently convene; or as soon after the death and preparation of the corpse allows, often not publicly announced, and therefore "closed." A more intimate venue is chosen.

A cultural custom observed in western Pennsylvania—maybe still instituted—called for the placing of a wreath of flowers on the front door of the home of the deceased as soon after the death as possible. Blinds and curtains were pulled or closed, and as soon as it was ready, the corpse was brought "home" and located in the parlor. Floral decorations surrounded the bier, and the Funeral Director brought special floor lamps, a lectern for a Guest Book, and, as soon as printed in a nearby small city, memorial pamphlets. Funerals occasionally took place in the home. At the time of the service, or following if it were held in the home—front-door wreaths were removed and taken to the church or the cemetery. The two days' of visitation-viewing turned into two Christian Sabbaths. Our one-street town—where almost everybody knew almost everybody else—itself seemed to be quieter and more solemn following a death. As a young boy, if I had to walk past a home that had a wreath on the front door, I pulled the "Good Samaritan" trick: I crossed to the other side. No taverns were open in our town, or dance halls, so there were no business closings: unless the deceased happened to be part of a prominent business family. Services never had to go to the High School gymnasium. On rare occasions did attendees have to stand through a service held at the larger Methodist or First Presbyterian Churches; that capacity did not hold true for the smaller Presbyterian Church of which I was a member. Pamphlets were handed out at the funeral home, the family home, or the Church where the service was observed. Obituaries were carefully prepared, carefully distributed and thoughtfully saved. Many of these customs have changed. However, the Scripture from another context applied to small towns—and possibly to urban and suburban neighborhoods as well—that (paraphrased), "When one member suffers, all town folk suffer together."

During the almost two years that I was an Interim Pastor in 2002-4 in San Juan, Puerto Rico, I participated in a local tradition of meeting with the families at the Funeral Home or the home of the deceased, the night before the regular service for a "Protestant Wake." A songfest and a mini-funeral took place. We sang some of the same songs and read some of the same Scripture the next day, either at the "regular" funeral at the Funeral Home, or at the Church.

Take a leap of imagination now from the Tropics to the Arctic North Pole. In 1991 I attended a service at the Presbyterian Church in Barrow, Alaska. A Caucasian Policeman on the streets of the village the afternoon of New Year's Eve had shot a young Native American Indian-Eskimo Christian lad. The twenty-one year-old man—half Tlingit and half Inupiat—by his walk and erratic behavior had given the impression that he was intoxicated. Besides, he was brandishing a gun.

The service was held at the Presbyterian Church in the early twilight of the midnight sun, 2:00 o'clock P.M. A full-house congregation of town folk and family showed up for the commemoration. The temperature ranged from five to ten degrees Fahrenheit below zero; a warm day because of a break in the Bering Sea. The pastor, the Reverend Willa Roghair, presided, assisted by a well known, long-time Presbyterian Eskimo Pastor. Commemorating went on for two and one-half hours, mainly because of "specials"—poems, hymns, duets and quartettes by peers of the deceased: sermonettes, and tributes from family and friends of the young man, family members, and finally the Pastors. (The two of them, of course, spoke the most lengthily.) After several tributes, the other Barrow Pastor, husband of the woman presiding, announced: "We have no more time for 'specials,' except from those who have requested time." The paternal Tlingit Grandpa (from Southeast Alaska) gave the younger peer commemorators a lecture about living a sober life. Darkness settled in; the hour was 4:30 P.M. The service had finally concluded. The congregants started heading for the cemetery, walking or driving their own cars, the motors having run during the service in order to assure their functioning. A pickup truck took the casket to the nearby cemetery. Several of us walked.

Following Committal liturgies at the graveside, gravediggers loosened the frozen tundra, and the divorced parents and their spouses, family and friends and townsfolk took turns tossing the first spades of ground and frozen rocks into the grave. The commemoration continued that night at the lad's family home; it followed the tradition of a "Sing." Several prayers and solos were offered; the Tlingit Grandpa had located a guitar, and led in several hymns. On my way back to the Husband/Wife Pastors' Church Manse, I had one recurring reflection: Upik Eskimos and Tlingit Indians sure know the fine art of Christian commemoration. I was comforted by participating, as I perceived the community had been. Barrow, at least at a time of grief, reflects a village-family ambiance.

By the time I became an ordained Presbyterian Pastor, my commemoration education had not advanced far beyond a primary level. The death of my Grandma, when I was five years old, however, had significantly impressed me. Grandma had died of cancer. As long as I could remember she had been sick and had not been able to fulfill a grandmother role very energetically or frequently, even though she and Grandpa lived only two miles from us, "in the country." I had many questions about what was happening to Grandma in preparation for a service. My "Mum" told me that our Cousin Plum, the Undertaker, had gone to their home, and with the help of a neighbor—the midwife at the births of myself and my siblings—had washed and dressed Grandma in the upstairs bedroom where she had died. After she had her makeup applied, she was ready for viewing. Plum and Grandpa and Midwife Ellie carried Grandma's body downstairs and placed it in the casket waiting in the parlor. Floral bouquets were placed around her. Plum put his usual two black lamps at either end of the coffin. The wreath, of course, hung on the front door.

We went as a family to "see Grandma" as soon as "she was ready," and I was impressed. She looked the most beautiful that I had ever seen her, her body draped in the lavender lace that she had bought to sew a dress, but never had had the energy or time to finish. I think her obituary showed up in a local paper. Her service was held at Grandma and Grandpa's home. The families of my Uncle and two Aunts and Mother gathered in the upstairs bedrooms. Uncle Frank had ten children, so he and his family occupied the largest room. Our Pastor stood at the foot of the stairs to conduct the service. I heard a few of his words, especially ones that were becoming familiar to me, about the Shepherd doing everything you wanted! Following the service we traveled the two miles to the cemetery, Uncle Frank and his family in Plum's new black Buick, we in our Chevrolet. Daddy helped carry Grandma's casket to the grave. The preacher read the Bible and prayed. More tears were shed. We finally made our way to our cars, and headed back to Grandpa's for leftovers from the meal the Women's Missionary Society of our Church had fixed for lunch.

When I went to bed that night, I had trouble sleeping; I kept wondering if Grandma were cold— wrapped only in net. My Mother said, "No way. Grandma is dead, and her casket is covered over, and now six feet under. And she doesn't know what cold or hot is anymore. She is with God!" I said my "Now I lay me down to sleep" prayer, and when I came to "If I should die..." I began to cry. I began to shiver. My mother comforted me, and the next awareness I had was of sunshine, and being called to come to breakfast. As I poured my Wheaties, I asked "Mum": "What do you suppose Grandma is having for breakfast." My six-years-old sister had the answer: "Angel food cake!" We laughed, and started spooning our cereal.

I proceeded into middle-school commemoration education when I was twelve years old. One of my best friends, Pat, the son of the teacher in our one-room school house in the country, and one of the five boys in our seventh-grade class, was struck by a car and killed while riding his bike to school. Someone came to the school—since Pat had not shown up on time for the opening prayer and ten verses from the Bible, (Pennsylvania Law at the time)—and called Teacher Jessie outside to report the tragedy. The deliverer of the bad news—maybe Undertaker Cousin Plum—came inside and told the school, all eight grades of us. Jessie immediately "fell apart," and classes were suspended. We students picked up our lunch buckets and began our walks home. Fortunately, the weather was spring-like. The whole school was sad. Pat was a good-looking boy, and a fun guy. We grieved for our teacher, although none of us shed tears over having two or three days' vacation. I think I grieved over Pat.

His funeral was scheduled the third day after the accident, at the First Presbyterian Church, next door to our United Presbyterian Church. Highlights of Pat's commemoration that I remember are:

- At Pat's home: we seventh and eighth grade boys, the pall-bearers, all of us dressed in suits, some of us having to borrow one for the day, arrived at the family country home for lunch. After eating, we put on our white shiny gloves that Plum had handed us—Fred whispered "sissy," and we all struggled to keep from snickering. Jessie and a man we did not know—we soon learned it was Pat's formerly unknown to-us Father—put Pat's trumpet, Hershey's kisses, and other paraphernalia in beside him. The lid went down, and we carried Pat to the funeral coach, loaded ourselves into Plum's Buick, and headed out on the dirt road for the ten minutes' drive to the church.
- At the Church: the place was packed, the service was long, the family was noisy with their weeping, and

everybody went to Pat's casket for a last look, his Mother and Absentee Dad last. (A big mystery had been solved!) Plum finally persuaded Jessie that the casket had to be closed, and we had to head for the cemetery. We boys had never taken off our gloves. In fact, once during the service, Fred caught my eye and lip-synced "Sissy." I strained to keep my giggle girdled. We carried Pat to the black coach, and a long string of cars headed for the cemetery, all the headlights turned on.

- At the cemetery: you never saw twelve year-old boys as cautious as we were on the edge of the grave, trying to get Pat's casket square on the canvas straps. We made it without anyone falling into the grave. Then began what turned out to be a mini-funeral. The casket had to be opened again. The parting ritual was loud and sad. I might have even had a tear or two. I would miss the jokes Pat used to tell behind the boys' outdoor toilet.
- At Parting: We boys were told to walk by the casket once more. Jessie was calming down. Plum finally pulled her away from Pat, the lid was let down, and we headed back to the Church to meet our folks. Plum said we could keep the gloves. Fred looked at me and formed "sissy" on his lips again. I ran to my folk's Chevrolet, and convulsed. It took me a few minutes to assure my parents that I was not being irreverent. I had trouble sleeping that night, and I refused to say my "Now I lay me down to sleep" prayer. (I was still doing it at age twelve!)

"Sissy" passed among us boys when school finally reopened. Teacher Jessie never found out why. Remembrance of Pat's death at morning Bible Reading and prayer continued for a few weeks. Sometimes it brought tears to my eyes, until I whispered, "Sissy!" Teacher Jessie had occasional "fits" (as we called them) of crying. She would head out the door toward the girls' toilet, and no one misbehaved while she was gone. (She had her internal spies, and we all knew who they were, but as far as I know, Jessie never knew that we knew.) One day at Sunday dinner when I imitated Jessie's crying, my Mother stopped me short with, "Now how would you feel if you were Pat and I was Jessie?" I shrugged, but under my breath I gave a "smart-aleck" answer: "Depends on the day!" Sadness returned, and I ran for our outdoor "privy!")

Commemoration style has improved—at least, changed—since the days of Grandma's and my school mate's services. People behave differently, it seems; they do not show emotions as expressively. In fact, emotions have become a source of embarrassment—especially when they come from males. More people participate in the events, especially when an "Open Mike" opportunity is offered, or an invitation is extended to eulogize the deceased. In fact, services in many cases seem incomplete if friends of the dead are not offered the opportunity "to say a few words." The opportunity makes way for reverent—most of the time—levity.

A Funeral Director at a service I was officiating—he also happened to be the owner of the Funeral Home—received quiet soft laughs on an occasion when he offered a short eulogy for his "twenty-something" Stepson. The young man had been killed in a motorcycle crash. The Director asked me if he could say a few words during the service. Of course, he could. At one point, looking toward the casket, and with a sardonic smirk, Bud spit out an admonishing: "Now, if you had just stayed off that damned motorcycle!" A brief chuckle went through the congregation. The interjection seemed neither inappropriate nor irreverent. The man spoke the language of his stepson and several in the crowd. Heavy funerals sometimes benefit from that kind of touch. Humor in reverent taste has often proved to offer grief relief. "For everything there is a season, and a time for every matter under heaven…." (Ecclesiastes 3:1.) Levity occasionally finds its season at funerals.

The statement Jesus made to the Samaritan Woman on the occasion when they met and conversed at Jacob's well may be relevant when a family is considering an appropriate service venue. After they had become accustomed to the cultural mores they had broken—Jesus initiating the break by asking a drink of her, a woman, and then boldly venturing into her morals—the subjects of Messiah and religion arose. Jews thought of Samaritans as hybrid Hebrews, and the Samaritans seemingly "could care less." She decided he was a prophet, and she had a burning religious question to ask him. The subject concerned a disagreement between the two approaches to their one-time in the past, common dogma. The issue concerned worship venues. Samaritans worshiped on Mt. Gerizim, which the two of them could look at behind them; Jews worshiped on Mount Zion, which you had to go to Jerusalem to see. The Temple, of course, was the historical and cultural worship icon of true Hebrews. Jesus had a prophetic answer for the woman, which is what she had asked for. In essence he said: 'Which Mountain you worship on is of little consequence!' The answer was neither that the event makes the place holy, nor the place makes the event holy. Now comes the answer, via the real text: "True worshipers will worship the Father in spirit and truth, for the Father seeks such as these to worship him. God is spirit, and those who worship him must worship in spirit and truth." Spirit trumps location! Persons of good heart and spiritual motivation trump both event and place. The woman was smart; the answer turned her evangelistic. (See the account in John 4.)

Commemorations can be holy gatherings in a variety of settings, but are more holy when they follow the guidelines already cited from Presbyterian polity. In brief, as noted earlier, the guides advise: "Go to your Church." In that setting, you may come more quickly and more fully into fellowship with God and the Son Jesus Christ, in the Spirit. You practice good habits in that ambiance; it is the place where you customarily enjoy deep spiritual fellowship, where you customarily open your heart, and as promised, Jesus and the Father come and make themselves at home. If circumstances make it inconvenient to hold services at your own Church, or if it is not available, find another location, and do whatever you need to do, to make it a "Holy of Holies."

In view of the many pages of material you have just read, examine the obituaries before you now in terms of the message they may have for you:

POLICE MOTORCADE, CATHEDRAL MASS, MEMORIAL AND COMMITTAL SERVICES (Note: Previously cited, but not for the same purpose.) A private memorial mass for a Seattle Police Officer—one of the first in a series of commemoratives—was held at The Cathedral. Following the religious service, a Police Motorcade led several cars from the Cathedral to the University of Washington's Sports Pavilion. The *Memorial* there ran from noon until after 1:30 P.M. A committal service followed at Memorial Park. A Public invitation was extended to a Reception at 4:30 P.M. at the venue printed in the bulletin.

OPEN HOUSE: No formal services were held, at her request. The family shared "Open House" and honored and remembered her at her home.

FULL MILITARY HONORS AT ARLINGTON: Interment took place in Arlington National Cemetery, with full military honors, following a service in (a) Chapel.

MUSEUM OF FLIGHT MEMORIAL: A Memorial Service was held at the Museum of Flight. Commemorative "remembrances" could be sent to the Museum Foundation.

CHURCH, THEN TAHOMA MILITARY SERVICES, AND BACK TO CHURCH FOR LUNCH AND KITE FLYING: A Memorial Service was held at his Church. Private Services, with Interment, took place at Tahoma National Cemetery. Following the Church Service and lunch, kite flying was enjoyed on the Church lawn. Kite flying had been a favorite hobby of the deceased. (Ed. The deceased was an active worshiper of the Church with whom our household worships. We were out of town at the time of his services, or we would have attended. Fellow church folk commented on how the joy of resurrection faith abounded at the Church, the Cemetery and the Church Yard.)

LOVED ONE PEEKING THROUGH STARS: A celebration was held at the Funeral Home. The family poeticized that the stars in the sky may be thought of as openings where loved ones shine down, so grieving survivors may commemorate where the deceased has gone, and be consoled.

FLAGSHIP "REI" STORE SCENE OF COMMEMORATION: He died in a climbing accident. A Memorial Service was held at the REI Flagship Store in Seattle.

SOUND MARINA CELEBRATION: A celebration of his life took place at the Ballard Mill Marina commercial dock area. The venue fit his interests and enjoyments.

LIVING ROSE: A Service of Celebration and Thanksgiving was held to remember her. Her husband remarked that she had swept into his life like a rose emerging and blooming where one had never before been planted. He further honored her for challenging others to do like her: show numerous random acts of kindness, and though sad, your Commemoration will be positive.

CHURCH ROSARY AND MASS COMMEMORATION: An evening Rosary gathered mourners to her church, where a Funeral Mass was held the next day.

COMMEMORATED POETICALLY: Claiming his late "love" had been an Incurable Romantic, a follower of Christ, and a "Pre-posterous-millennialist," he commemorated her poetically. Verses formed part of her obituary.

DOWNTOWN STREET-INTERSECTION CANDLELIGHT VIGIL FOR A CYCLIST: A candlelight vigil in honor of the deceased cycle enthusiast was held one evening at the intersection of two major streets in Downtown Seattle. Cyclists met at 5:00 P.M. to memorialize her with their monthly "Critical Mass Ride." The deceased belonged to the "Critical Mass" group, and had been killed on one of their rides. A Memorial Service was held. Her "spunk" was celebrated at the gathering.

HAWAIIAN SHIRTS APPROPRIATE APPAREL FOR ROSARY MEMORIAL: The deceased loved life, and most importantly, her family declared, she loved Jesus Christ. Rosary was held at her Church. Her request: wear brightly colored Hawaiian shirts.

ALCOHOL-FREE CHURCH POTLUCK: A Celebration to honor her life was held at her Church. No alcohol would be served. A favorite dish for a potluck meal would be appreciated; casual dress would be appropriate.

Family requests for commemoration participation by fraternal organizations, social or special-interest groups, fraternities or sororities, lodges, or even quasi-religious organizations, happen frequently in the Pacific Northwest, the location of Fort Lewis, the Washington National Guard, McCord Air Base and the Madigan Military Hospital. One result is a significant military residency, and therefore in terms of commemoration services, frequent requests for participation in services with military protocol. Both Base Chapel and Pastors' "Service Books" offer guidance. The data can both raise conflict, or settle it. Presbyterian order stipulates: "The service shall be complete in itself, and any fraternal, civic, or military rites, should be conducted separately."[4]

"Separately," while intended to clarify the policy, sometimes ends up confusing or complicating it. Nevertheless, the statement is helpful: for both the Pastor and the family or the organization involved. The Pastor sometimes, to forestall further grief, has to compromise or adjust to procedures, which in her/his estimation, arise from a lower authority. The decision becomes more critical when it involves the Benediction. Military personnel want the gun salute and the presentation of the American Flag to be the "benediction." On occasions when I have been persistently stubborn, I have been accused of being "un-American," anti-social, even bigoted. I remind my accusers that I have had cadet military training at the Virginia Polytechnic Institute, and I have served in the United States Army Air Corps, which makes me a World War II Veteran. If I perceive that my tenacity is creating an uncomfortable scene, I may compromise my position, especially in services for highly decorated veterans, and for those who have been killed in Iraq or Afghanistan.

A "Living Memorial Service" has the potential to personalize and innovate commemoration—and comfort loved ones—in a way that a later church or funeral home gathering may not. Creativity becomes necessary for creating a reverent ambiance. Because of its advantages and the minimal but not insurmountable disadvantages, and after consulting with the principal persons involved, I once recommended to our local Kiwanis Club that we hold a commemorative Kiwanis Club meeting at the home of Club Member, Ed, who was terminally ill; and his wife, Fran. The Club Executive Officers gave unanimous encouragement. I offered to make homemade ice cream, and some of the men said they would bring cookies. Ed had been suffering from cancer, and had only a few weeks yet to live.

Meeting night arrived. It was a beautiful summer evening, and the Lake on which the Couple lived was serene and inspirational. The attendance was large; it reached an almost "perfect" count. Seating was comfortable, with Ed and Fran on the front "pew"—couch. I opened the meeting in a slightly different manner from usual: with Scripture and prayer. We conducted our Club business, and then we "did" Ed. Several Kiwanians spoke emotionally about our Brother—and about Fran. Tears of joy and grief added to the solemnity of the memorial. Prayer ended it. We shared ice cream and cookies and coffee, and bade each other "Good Night." Ed died a few weeks later. Kiwanian members attended his Church commemoration and sat in pews as a group. A member offered this analogy: "The Kiwanis commemoration at the Burk's home baked the cake; his Church Memorial Service frosted it."

Another of the more creative commemorative events I officiated featured special music provided by the deceased. A member of the Church I was pastor of, an Army Pediatrician at the local Madigan Hospital, Ron had several hobbies, including playing the piano and composing hymns. In his early fifties the Officer-Doctor had become ill with cancer. He was retired from the Service. During the last months of his battle with the disease, he had created several spiritual songs, and he had played the piano as he sang them. His family requested our playing a tape of some of his signing and self-accompanying during his service. Of course, we complied. The offering turned his service into a stunning tribute to a faithful Christian man. His voice sounded pleasant, his renditions were life-like, his pitch was accurate, and his piano technique so impressive that you had little trouble looking down toward the church piano and discovering that Dick was not sitting there. Tears flowed—especially from his teenage son and daughter; noses ran, hands held, the congregation was wrapped in a holy spirit. I avoided eye contact with any of his first-pew loved ones. Comments following the service flowed from family and friends like: "I have never participated in a more personal spiritual experience at a funeral." And, "My tears were more of appreciation than of lamentation." A commemoration congregation had never been more reverent. The event might have approached the reverence attached to Mary's anointing Jesus with expensive perfume in her brother's house a few days before his crucifixion. Commemorative services of this type leave more a "Hasta Luega" comfort, than an "Adios" closure.

The Oak Grove Presbyterian Church of Bloomington, Minnesota, formerly under the leadership of The Reverend Dr. Mark Bayert, (now Honorably Retired) has prepared a manual to guide planning for deceased believers' commemorations. *(Mark died suddenly in 12/09). (The Church has granted permission for quoting and referencing the publication in *Obituary Theology,* and has offered to make copies available by request. Local Presbyterian Churches may be contacted for an address.) Some of the material has already found its way into this Book, the main reason being that the Manual relies heavily on Presbyterian Order for authority on policies and rituals. Highlights treat of several essential matters that commemoration services should deal with:

- The most appropriate venue for commemoration is a Church Sanctuary or a similarly solemn temple setting, in order to testify to Reformed Doctrine, i.e., "The resurrection is a central doctrine of the Christian Faith, and shapes Christians' attitudes and responses to the event of death. Death brings loss, sorrow and grief to all. In the face of death, *Christians affirm with tears and joy the hope of the Gospel*. Christians do not bear bereavement in isolation, but are sustained by the power of the Spirit and the community of faith. The Church offers a ministry of love and hope to all who grieve." A service at the deceased's "sanctuary of habit" unites the worshipers with the saints—those in heaven and those on earth—in the communion that the *Apostles' Creed* highlights.

- Worship should be designed so that it offers family and friends the opportunity to grieve the death of their loved one, to give thanks to God for the life of that person, and to find comfort and hope in the Gospel of Jesus Christ's death and resurrection. Arrangements are to be made with the Pastor or officiating clergy. If the family desires a presiding Pastor other than the Church's, a consultation will be held with the on-site Pastor before an invitation goes elsewhere. Worship bulletin information and production, lighting and sound equipment, must be planned for. Congregational singing is encouraged; first consideration in regard to an Accompanist should be given to the already employed, or contracted church music staff. Ushers are important; if strangers, they will receive orientation regarding seating of the congregation.
- Disposition of the body, whether by "burial, cremation or donation for medical purposes" shall be a matter of Pastor-family sharing.
- Viewing or Visitation Schedules, and locations for such; Casket, Container, or Urn placement during the services; family activities immediately preceding and following a service, and protocol for the seating of family members, relatives and special guests; music recommendations, with suggestions for appropriate music will be considered and agreed upon.
- The Officiant's remuneration will depend on the services performed, if beyond the "standard."
- Special tributes, invited eulogists, and persons who may want to offer spontaneous comments or testimonies, other than the Pastor's eulogy or homily, need discussing. Pastoral coordination is necessary.
- Matters such as sanctuary or chancel furniture reloca-

tion, if necessary, are reviewed. Will the administration of the Sacrament of the Lord's Supper, prove meaningful or "comfortable" or appropriate, taking into consideration the congregation anticipated being in attendance? Floral and other arrangements, Power Point Presentations, photo displays, cassette tape playing, or screen projections on the life of the deceased, require special technician administration.

- Other administrative details are covered. Behavior such as emotional responses or interruptions during the services will be anticipated. Receptions or meals at the Church before or after the services will need arranging. Families may have special concerns that may need consultation and planning. Fairness policies and participation in the service by non-Christians may be an issue. Sacramental and other rites, especially if the congregation has an "ordered" policy based on Presbyterian polity, require approval. For instance, the Minnesota Church has an "Open Table" policy for participation in the Eucharist or Communion. The protocol both serves justice and complies with Biblical teaching, as Reformed Doctrine understands it.

The thoughtful and helpful information from the Oak Grove Church's Manual serves as a lead-in to the last section of excerpts connected with Commemoration.

FAMILY ACCOLADES: No Commemoration Services were held for the capable and Pioneering *Seattle Times* Reporter. Her obituary abounded in family tributes and friends' accolades. Her husband extolled her: "A very hard-working, determined, tough person." Others said: "Her greatest joys were her twin granddaughters." Upon being diagnosed with cancer, "She was unafraid to talk about it," a colleague said, "and she realized the fact that she was surviving was a source of hope for other people." Her son, Doug, a Senior Manager for Boeing, commended his Mother for insisting that his twin daughters, "Her greatest joys," use appropriate English in family conversation. She had banned "actually" from family vocabulary; it was unnecessary. Commemorative memorials were designated for a special Foundation, Hospice, and others.

RESTAURANT RECEPTION FOLLOWING FAMILY GATHERING: A private family service commemorated the deceased, following which Friends were invited to join the family at a well-known Seattle Restaurant, and share memories.

PARK MEMORIAL, FOLLOWED BY NATIONAL CEMETERY SERVICE: A Memorial was held at the Point Defiance Park Lodge, followed by a Military Service at Tahoma National Cemetery.

LIVELY SINGING, FAVORITE FOODS, GOOD STORIES, BUT NO RELIGIOUS SERVICE: She died at Ninety-Five. She had been married seventy years to her surviving husband. At her request, no formal service was held. Close family and friends gathered to share her life and celebrate her memory. The family believed that she had gone ahead to save a place in Heaven for her husband and children.

The Commemoration Chapter concludes with a grid on several changes in patterns of services since the year 1952—the year of my ordination to the Ministry of Word and Sacrament. Topics have been chosen from the standpoint of those customs that have been most affected by the innovations.

SERVICE STYLE: Then: A Funeral Service, Body Present, and Frequently Open Casket, followed by a Graveside Committal Service. *Current*— Funerals, Memorial Mass, Rosary, and others; increasingly, "No Service" to be held, usually at the deceased's request (and usually so stated in the obituary); "Celebration of Life," Informal Gatherings, Party, Graveside only; and others.

VENUE: Then: Funeral Home, the Deceased's Home (as mentioned earlier in the Chapter, already decorated with a swag of flowers on the front door), Church, Temple, Synagogue, or at a Family Member's home. *Current*—Funeral Home, Church, Park, Social Club House, Membership Organization Building, Restaurant, Graveside, Boat, Home Patio or Backyard; Marina; Scenic Location, or a Venue frequently visited, or having served like, or actually served as, a second home, and enjoyed by the Deceased, or reinforcing other emotional attachments. An obituary included elsewhere extended an invitation to come to a Pub to celebrate the deceased's life.

SERVICE ORDER: Then: Simple or Semi-Formal (Presbyterian); or Formal-Liturgical if services take place in Traditionally Liturgical Churches; *Current*—Many similar procedures, with both commemoration and burial, but more liturgical, even at Funeral Homes. Services often postponed beyond the customary "three days after death" tradition, scheduled at times most family and friends can participate. Number of Church Funerals increasing, in part to accommodate the Crowd; often including congregational singing, prepared remarks by family, friends, or colleagues; more cremations, with urns occasionally located in front of the congregation; power-point presentations, CD's and well-arranged photo displays; graveside ceremonies and committal services often before the funeral, sometimes days or weeks before, and primarily a family affair; attendance at Funeral, Memorial, or special Service, sometimes is "By Invitation only."

OFFICIANT: Then: Family or Church Pastor, Priest or Rabbi, Church or a Religious Affiliated Elder or Leader or Officer in a Church in correspondence with the Reformed Tradition; occasionally assisted by friends of the deceased, or colleagues or family members; a Funeral Director has been known to conduct the service when the Clergy forgot, or was delayed in arriving. *Current*—Leadership usually depends on the venue. Most Church funerals are officiated by Clergy or ecclesiastical officers. Elsewhere a clergy may officiate, if invited and approved by the Pastor on site, and if the person had been a church member or active church participant; laypersons, usually close friends of the deceased, may preside, if ecclesiastically licensed.

RECEPTIONS, MEMORIAL GATHERINGS, AND OTHERS: Then: Reception in the Church "Basement" or Social Rooms, or at the home of a Family or close friend of the deceased; occasionally at a Fraternal Organization Hall, or venue of a club or institution the deceased had belonged to.

Sometimes at a School Gymnasium, Auditorium or Cafeteria. Weather Permitting, outside. Informal comments may be welcomed, using an "open mike" forum; commemorative statements are informal, but numerous. Traditionally the Church or another family-connected group provided a meal. *Current*—Usually "Open" receptions following the funeral or memorial, occasionally by invitation only. At the Church Social Hall or Fellowship area, or a Funeral Home Social Room, either with a Church group like a Board of Deacons, a Women's Organization, or neighbors, or on occasion, the Funeral Home, providing food; a public catering venue, or a friend's home; "Open Bar" observed, and wine, sometimes hard liquor, is served. (Many churches prohibit wine service, more because of addiction than moral compunction.) Photographic displays may be located around the room, and on occasion, other memorabilia. A CD or video or Power Point presentation, if not already used during the formal service. At a recent reception, a family made available hundreds of valuable used Christmas Tree ornaments. Ginny had been collecting and displaying them at Christmas Parties over a number of years. Many of the guests at her funeral had also been guests at her seasonal parties. At the reception a member of the family encouraged friends to "Help yourself" to as many of the ornaments as you wanted. Few were left behind.

An extraordinary British commemorative ceremony took place recently in London at the Hoo St. Werburgh Parish Church. The article was compiled from the Associated Press and *The Washington Post.* The headline read, "After 700 Years Teen Gets Funeral." (The teen had already had a burial.) According to the article, two hundred people showed up on Saturday, March 14, 2009 at the Hoo St. Werburgh Parish Church. One purpose of the service was to make apologetic and spiritual amends for a botched "gruesome medieval ritual." The event also vindicated Scripture by, among other ways, performing an act of justice.

The honoree had obviously not lived the life of a teenage Jezebel, all the more reason that her memory should receive the dignity that had apparently been denied her.

Archeologists had found the girl's body in unconsecrated ground contiguous to the Church. Her head was lying beside her, as was not uncommon in medieval burial practices. The Church's current Vicar, the Reverend Andy Harding, justified the religious ritual: "Everyone deserves a dignified and respectable funeral." The Vicar knew his Bible, and proceeded with a commemoration service ordinarily conducted for devoted and compassionate Anglicans; his mode was Christian, his motive reverence, and his guidance Biblical.[5] (Note: Material approved for insertion by the *Seattle Times* reporter.)

On an earlier occasion the disciples had witnessed a prefigurement of the commemoration that would follow Jesus' rising from the dead. It happened following a demonstration by Jesus of his power over demonic evil: he had cured a boy so severely under the spell of demons that when he would be overcome with a "fit" he would slip into self-destructive convulsions. One day the father brought the boy to Jesus with the plea, "Teacher, I beg you to look at my son." The father went on to describe the lad's torment. Jesus said to the man, "Bring your son here." The man went for his boy, and as the two of them were coming to Jesus, the boy slipped into one of his fits: "The demon dashed him to the ground in convulsions." Jesus took care of the problem, and returned the cured boy to his father. The crowd was amazed: "All were astounded at the greatness of God." A short time later the disciple John reported to Jesus, "Master, we saw someone casting out demons in your name, and we tried to stop him, because he does not follow us." Jesus surprised the group with this startling command: "Do not stop him, for whoever is not against you is for you." (John 9:37-43; and 49-50.).

The Apostle Paul was not present at any of those commemorative moments. Several years later, however, after Jesus had been dead and had risen and returned to heaven, Paul commemorated the Lord with these resurrection credits:

God also highly exalted him,
and gave him the name

that is above every name,
so that at the name of Jesus
every knee should bend,
in heaven and on earth and under the earth,
and every tongue should confess,
that Jesus Christ is Lord,
to the glory of God the Father.
(Philippians 2:9-11.)

Before closing this Chapter, notice will be taken of another surprising and amazing commemoration of Jesus. An uncircumcised, idol-worshiping Roman did it. His tribute was offered during the earthquake that happened at the time of Jesus' crucifixion. The creditor was probably not circumcised and was probably an idol worshiper. He had an amazing conversion at the Cross. The Biblical record of the drama reads: "Now when the centurion and those with him, who were keeping watch over Jesus, saw the earthquake and what took place, they were terrified and said, 'Truly this man was God's Son.'" (Matthew 27:54.) The non-Christian, probably non-baptized, Centurion's judgment rests with God. His commemoration deserves the longevity and piety that Jesus had earlier said would attach to the woman's commemoration. Time has honored Jesus' prophecy; and the Psalmist's, "Out of the mouths of babes and infants, you have found a bulwark…" (8:2.) An aura of prayer, by Jesus, also surrounds the event. Jesus once prayed thanksgiving for God's revelation wisdom: "I thank you, Father, Lord of heaven and earth, because you have hidden these things from the wise and the intelligent and have revealed them to infants; yes, Father, for such was your gracious will." (Matthew 11:25-6.) What more valuable tribute exists for the likes of the Centurion than the laud the author of the Hebrews "Epistle" paid the persons cited in his roster of the great heroes of the faith: they were saints "of whom the world was not worthy." The world still isn't!

VI.

Buried, Cremated, Donated, Hydrolysized

"I believe...in Jesus Christ...crucified, dead and buried...."

The Apostles' Creed

BURIED

PACKER'S CAP SHARES CASKET WITH "CHEESE-HEAD": He had been addicted to football; his Green Bay Packer's cap was buried with him. He had also been addicted to jazz; he had organized "The Puget Sound Traditional Jazz Society." (West Coast Jazz mixes two trumpets, a banjo and a tuba.) For their honeymoon the football-jazz aficionado took his Wife to the grave of legendary Bix Beidercke. He had also been addicted to cheese; his friends gave him the nickname popular in the Wisconsin sports scene, "Cheesehead."

CREMATED

URN IN NATIONAL CEMETERY: A World War II veteran, he had served in the Army Corps of Engineers; he died at age 88. Inurnment took place at Willamette National Cemetery.

DONATED

FAMILY COMFORTED BY HER BODY "LEGACY": She died at age 80; she had lived the past twenty years in California. She loved living by the ocean, and golfing. She donated her body to the Willed Body Program at UCI School of Medicine. Her family finds comfort in knowing that her legacy of benefiting humanity will continue.

HYDROLYSIZED
(News Article, not an Obituary Excerpt.)

BODIES HYDROLYSIZED--Alkaline Hydrolysis has been increasingly claiming business connected with the disposing of dead bodies, particularly cadavers. The process currently remains legally limited, but hydrolysis is becoming more attractive as a viable human body disposition method, especially with universities that have a backlog of cadavers no longer needed. No obituary data available; do not look for a newspaper printing any soon, unless you live in Maine or New Hampshire. *(The St. Joseph [Missouri] News Press, May 9, 2008, Permission from both the Associated Press and the St. Joseph News Press.)*

"…I handed on to you what I in turn had received: that Christ died for our sins in accordance with the scriptures, and that he was buried…." (1 Corinthians 15: 3.)

Rosalia Lombardo died of pneumonia in 1920 in Palermo, Sicily; her preserved body lies there in the Capuchin Monastery. She does not lie alone. Two thousand mummies keep her company. Their bones had once housed righteous parish adherents who have been dead for hundreds of years. Rosalia looks as if death had taken her only yesterday and as if she were only a breath away from tomorrow. Her father grieved so deeply when she was gone that he contracted with a noted embalmer, Alfredo Salafia, to preserve her. His skill has worked well. Rosalia's story features in an article in the February 2009 issue of *National Geographic,* entitled, "Where the Dead Don't Sleep." 1

The little girl's photo gives the impression, that, as she sleeps, she may be dozing on the way home from a party. She rests under a filthy brown sheet. Unlike many of the other stained and dried mummies around her, she has her own hair; it hangs in doll-like blond curls over her yellow forehead, tied up with a yellow silk bow. Her eyes are closed, the eyelashes perfectly preserved. If the grinning skulls and dust and rot of the place did not surround her, a visitor to the tombs could be convinced that Rosalie could have been a future Sicilian beauty queen, or the wife of an Italian "Don." The *Geographic* article ends with: "In Palermo Rosalia is mentioned as a sort of semi-deity, a magic little angel. Drivers taxiing Palermo visitors to the airport invariably ask, 'Did you see Rosalia? Bella!'"

Following commemoration services for the deceased—if held, or previous to a service—disposition is made of the person's corpse. Three traditional dispositions include burial, cremation, and donation. In recent years a newer, more controversial, and not yet universally legal process known as "alkaline hydrolysis," has entered the disposition scene.

Use of hydrolysis has accelerated in the past sixteen years. The somewhat arcane method of body disposition that began as a modest necessity—to dispose of excess cadavers—has suddenly become an exigency. As cemeteries use up burial or inurnment spaces, hydrolysis may be called into service as a conservative measure. It had been instigated to do away with animal carcasses. At present, the medical industry uses it. The technique works as follows: licensed funeral professionals first wrap the body in lye and lay it in a large steel casket-shaped cylinder; three hundred degrees of heat and sixty pounds of pressure per square inch of material surface cause the body to dissolve. Attendees bottle the brown resultant oil-like liquid for final disposition, or delivery to claimers. (The *St. Joseph Missouri Press* account did not report how long the redaction takes, which of course could introduce an unfeasible burden, and possibly an environmental concern.)

Regard for and use of hydrolysis remains conservative, because, among other reasons, it has not yet been determined if it could prove environmentally harmless. Professional practitioners contend that the technique may be less harmful to the environment than the carbon dioxide resulting from cremation. They claim that the coffee colored "left-overs" are sterile. You may flush them down a sewer. Although judged by some as socially undignified, and by others as blatantly irreligious, the treatment has been declared legal in Maine and New Hampshire. Its proponents insist that it augurs well as a viable and economical option for future dead-body disposition. As far as is known, funeral homes are not currently practicing it. Some Funeral Industry leaders, however, foresee its emergence as popular and legal. More economical?

Law regulates the disposition of deceased bodies; methodology is still mostly laissez faire. The law requires that the party in closest relationship to the person who has died bears the disposition responsibility. If no "closest of kin" is available, the state names another party. The method, insists the Funeral Industry, must satisfy funeral protocol.

The protocol has been changing, however, as practice in the State of Washington testifies. The State does not publish statistics on the issue; therefore they are not available for examination by the public. Funeral Directors report that cremating—and to a lesser degree, donating—is becoming increasingly competitive with burying, and in some areas surpassing it. The practice of hydrolysis is so recent and the figures so negligible that so far it has had little effect on burying, cremating, or donating.

Newspaper obituaries occasionally clarify or offer tell-tale information on their Subject's body disposition. Of the thirty-five notices in a February 2007 edition of the Seattle Times, two obituaries used the word "burial;" four spoke of public or private graveside services, and the other twenty-nine were "disposition silent," or ambiguous. The excerpt that opens this chapter stood by itself as the single mention of donation in that edition. (A Funeral Director suggested that more cadavers may be donated for medical technology than are recorded.)

Biblical and Church Literature and classical theological documents speak more specifically on body disposition, and almost without exception they report burial. Jews and Christians, according to the Bible, buried their dead. Donation, if it happened in Biblical times, failed to be reported, with one or two exceptions. Medical technology for cremation did not exist when the New Testament canon closed—near the end of the first Christian Century. The lack of diversity in disposition practice, other than burial, can undoubtedly be attributed to primitive medical technology, rather than theological or psychological scruples. Times and methods are changing.

As just hinted, a Biblical allusion to cadaver volunteerism-donation appears in 1 Corinthians 13:3. In a pericope which newer translations of Scripture entitle, "The Gift (or "The Hymn") of Love," the Apostle Paul wrote: "If I give away all my possessions, and if I give my body to be burned, but do not have love, I gain nothing." (Vs. 3.) Martyrdom was undoubtedly paramount in the Apostle's mind. Giving up one's body in faith in a cruel or religious persecution—including fiery immolation—could be regarded, however, as volunteerism; hence "donation" would be a permissible classification. The contribution could also have constituted a spiritual "sacrifice," but hardly a selfless, self-chosen, or medical contribution, as donations are today.

A current practice of specifying a donation of body organs on your Driver's License (at least in Washington State) may account for the slight growth in the number of voluntary cadavers for study in medical schools. After the cadavers have served their social and medical purpose, responsible or designated persons may legally dispose of the parts left over.

Two donation obituary excerpts follow:

BRAIN, SPINAL CORD LEFT FOR RESEARCH: A Memorial Service was announced for a man who had arranged to donate his brain and spinal cord to medical research. One of his stated purposes was facilitating finding a cure for ALS (commonly called "Lou Gehrig's Disease.") Donations in the deceased's memory could be made to the ALS or the Muscular Dystrophy Association, and earmarked for research,

BODY WILLED TO CREATION: He was not afraid of death. Rather, he looked forward to becoming part of the elements: earth, water, fire, and air, thus nourishing the trees. Further, death would set him free to soar with the birds he loved. He stipulated the disposition of his body as a means to that goal.

Three Old Testament passages relate to donation. They all deal with death in war or by violence. The disposition decision was hardly reached voluntarily. Cremation might have happened for honor or altruism, but not from personal choice. Vengeance was involved in each of the situations. The cases are found in 1 Samuel 31, 2 Samuel 21, and Amos 6:8. (It is recommended that if you are not familiar with the passages, you review them before continuing with the text.) The Samuel passages deal with attempts by King Saul to obtain advice on military strategy from the deceased—and presumed Sheol resident—Samuel. Saul had already ruled the practice of contacting the dead illegal, but he was desperate. He finally persuaded a "medium" from the village of Endor, to help him. After extracting a promise from the King that she would not be executed for trying, she proceeded; she succeeded in rousing the Prophet. Saul would later regret that he had gone to the effort. (No record exists as to how much the King paid the commoner, if anything.) Samuel appeared, and soon learned why he had been summoned. He suddenly received a prophetic perspective. He had tragic news: Israel would be defeated. His mission accomplished, Samuel returned to his underground rest. Saul went into battle. The medium stayed home.

The battle with the Philistines ensued. The tide turned in the enemy's favor. When King Saul realized that his artillery was inferior to the enemy's, rather than die at the hand of an uncircumcised Philistine, he commanded his armor bearer to stab him. The officer refused. Still determined not to remain prey for the enemy, Saul unsheathed his sword, and forced his body down on it. The Royal Armor-bearer and Saul's three sons immediately followed suit. Their bodies fell on the spot. The Philistines took advantage of the celebrity suicides, and impaled their bodies on the city walls. They followed up with multiple indignities: they burned the bodies, making the royal family—recall that Saul had been Israel's first King, and his sons the first Princes—the first national cremations. "Incinerations" may be the more proper term. The cremation post-script ended with more honor than could have been anticipated. Saul's successor, King David, retrieved the scarred and scorched royal "cremains," and ordered them presently and properly buried.

The Amos cremation differed significantly from the King Saul-Medium-Prophet-Samuel episode. A feature common to the two incidents was military disadvantage. Israel appeared on the verge of suffering disastrous casualties in its current military engagement. The Prophet, Amos, had prophesied that a "relative"—also translatable as "one who burns the dead" or "one who does a burning, as a neighbor 'favor'"—would prove so violent and mercilessly retaliatory against Israel's enemies, that the follow-up cover-up would guarantee that everybody had died; a relative would shout back into a ransacked house about to be torched, "Is anyone else with you?" If a voice gave indication of human occupation, death by fire followed. (Amos 6:10.) Not exactly a cozy, or environmentally healthy immolation! The practice civilizes slightly with the knowledge that the remains received burial. That respect, however, benefited only the rich and the famous.

Cremation as a proper and efficient, and usually personally selected, disposition of corpses came into vogue in post-Biblical times; in one sense, it may be considered "modern." The practice has become extremely popular in the twentieth and twenty-first centuries—both with "Bible Believers," and nonbelievers. It is particularly "popular" in the Pacific Northwest, and the Northeast. One reason may be the current consciousness of the citizenry about "Green," or environmental conscientiousness. Cremation currently outnumbers burial by at least two to one in those regions. In other areas of the United States, the statistics are probably reversed.

Another demographic factor relates to the practice of disposition. The number of acres in cemeteries for burial or inurnment far outweighs the number in public parks. Some countries deal with land conservation and body disposition by "layering;" that is, placing more than one body in a grave, without casket liners and steel burial vaults. Will future population growth increase layering? Space for growing enough food for the world's population is increasingly a problem. Another concern: what about the fuel required by cremation and the cost of producing non-renewable energy? Is strict government regulation of dead-body "disposition" coming? The opening excerpts body-donation example pleased her family. They hope that her charity will encourage "imitatio" by other family members, and by future sufferers with her disease. It could also save some of the earth.

Responsible and non-toxic dead-body disposition, without embalming—which is my preference at this point—could benefit the Planet's population. It would significantly reduce the contaminants absorbed by soil and water. (Earth's efficiency so far performs humanity and the whole creation a remarkable decontamination favor. How long can it continue?) Green burial practice could eventually prove even more economically and ecologically beneficial than cremation. If hydrolysis ever becomes legal and universally available—and economically practical—and disposing of the remaining "coffee-colored brown liquid" more sanitized, it could also become environmentally friendly.

A recent Seattle Times edition printed a photo-story about an unusual disposition problem at a local Funeral Home: a surplus of urns. The photo showed the Funeral Home Owner in a room filled with 3,000 of them. Several had been left at the Establishment for years. A moral problem has developed for the owner: what to do respectfully with the "left behind" vessels? No person has made an effort to claim any of them, and attempts to contact the survivors have failed. Did the persons, or descendants, who held the rights to the urn or the ashes, not have the money to pay the funeral establishment? Or did they want to show more respect for the cremated person, but they could not afford a burial? Some of the deserted cremains have no valid identity; they have resulted from indigents' deaths. Their tags read "Anonymous." The State or the Funeral Industry may have to take action.

The two excerpts on cremation that follow indicate both a traditional custom—including the increasingly popular "no-services" decision; and a somewhat non-traditional plan for financing the disposition:

TOGETHER IN CREMATION: At the deceased's request, no services were held. Her cremated remains are to be placed beside her late husband's.

FAMILY SOLICITATION FOR ASSISTANCE WITH CREMATION, AND OTHER COSTS: The Obituary included three photos of a beautiful woman: first, as a young wife, then as a middle-aged mother, and finally, as a "Senior," just before her death. A "mother, grandmother and Nanny," she had left this world, her obituary composer wrote, to be in heaven with God and with her other loved ones. At the end of the obituary, a survivor-daughter remarked that, even though she found the request difficult to make, she felt compelled to include a special request with the obituary. She was facing so many heavy financial burdens, particularly ones connected with the dying and death and cremation of her loved one, that any financial help would be appreciated! Another factor that had led to the request was the example of the deceased's giving record. Her generosity had included donations to all sorts of charity: money, clothes, furniture, and food, whatever she could spare to assist the needy. A further comment stated that a check donation would be appreciated more than flowers. Gratitude was expressed, and the blessing of God extended. The obituary text stated that the document was being published in lieu of a service of commemoration. (If Jesus had been alive, he might have featured the obituary writer in one of his parables.)

As happens frequently when a need is perceived, entrepreneurs quickly "come out of the woodwork." Scattering of ashes offers an example. David Twiddy of the "Associated Press" wrote about the practice in an article in the "Close Up" Section of a 2007 edition of the *Seattle Times*.[2] (Permission to comment on the article was granted by Mr. Twiddy.) The sub-caption reads, "Rest in peace nearly anywhere." The text continued under the title, "A Boom in Scattering." ("The International Scattering Society" and the

"Atlantis Society" provided Data.) The dead are not content just to sit on the mantel anymore, so the article maintained. As cremation has increased, so has the demand for businesses that can help make sure that loved ones' remains spend eternity where the individual had wanted—no matter how expensive, how exotic, or how distant the locale.

Increases in Cremation, mentioned earlier, must excite the "Scattering Industry." The latest Scattering Society statistics (slightly different from an earlier figure) report that thirty-two percent of U.S. deaths led to cremation in 2005, compared with twenty-one percent in 1996. (Regional comparisons were not provided, but as noted above, the information available, alongside the judgment of Funeral Directors, supports professional claims that the Pacific Northwest leads other regions in the United States in the number of cremations.) A Twiddy prophecy was made that scattering will grow larger in the year or two ahead, by 21.7 percent.

Joanie West of Crystal River, Florida has introduced innovations into the business of scattering, according to Twiddy. Her company, "The Eternal Ascent Society" started ten years ago. Ms. West's procedure places the ashes inside a large helium-filled balloon. She then sends it aloft. Once it reaches a height of five miles, the balloon pops, distributing the ashes to the wind. The charge for the services amounts from $995 to $1,500.

Chapters of Scattering Societies are popping up all over the United States. Pilots are using private planes, or are chartering flight and watercraft for the chore. Bill Metzger flies his Piper Cherokee over Southern California; he charges $300 to $500 per scatter. Other institutions are increasingly joining the growing trend "of providing or assisting loved ones (to) find 'sleeping places' for the ashes and bones of their (deceased)." Chapman University in Orange, CA. has built a Columbarium, a honeycomb shaped edifice, and decorated it with sky-blue marble. It is designed to house the cremated remains of "alumni, faculty, partners, or pets." No mention is made of the eligibility of current students, families or University Board members!

The University of Notre Dame will soon unveil two limestone-and-brick mausoleums laced with full-body crypts. Spaces will sell for up to $11,000. The School has teamed up with "Trappist.Caskets.com," which advertises for an Iowa religious Brothers Order that crafts burial containers out of trees that grow on their six hundred acres of forest. USC is planning a columbarium as part of its projected $20 million Chapel on Campus. Companies are taking cremains overseas for scattering. Kelly Murtaugh, President of the "International Scattering Society," was quoted on the practice: "I think it's a way of cherishing the memory of that (deceased) person. Maybe they (the deceased or the survivor?) feel that they have a connection with that particular area." In another context Ms. Murtaugh commented on the comfort the "business" may offer: "It gives (loved ones) some closure; that's all we need." (Reformed theologians would insert that in the situation described, a bit, or a lot more, than expedient closure may be needed. Obituaries support the claim.)

One obituary reporting a disposition of cremains offers no information on whether the scattering was done professionally. In view of information on family connections in Hawaii, one could guess that the family performed the gesture: "KANA SCATTERING, NO MEMORIAL SERVICES." The sea, rather than a volcano crator or mountains or beaches, provided the depository. Remembrances were designated for the American Cancer Society.

Another disposition-related *Seattle Times* article (02/09/07) bore the headline, "Who wants to spend eternity in a dark old urn? These days you can turn your loved one's ashes into art, thanks to containers for cremains." (The article author is staff reporter, Jack Broom, with photography by "Funeria, Everlasting Memories and Ineternis.") Photographs of artistic urns decorate the piece. They bear the names, "Holy Smoke"—the urn is in the shape of a cigar humidor and it bears the inscription, "La Vida Buena." (Ed. Three members of my family did not die with "Vida Buena;" they died of lung cancer, and one remaining sister has complications from addiction to smoking. Except for our father, they have all had cremation, and the Sister plans on it. Each of them has chosen a more traditional urn.) The "Biker Heaven" urn is crowned with a helmet. (It looks very much like the one I wear when I bike.) "Wheel of Life," and "Final Pillow" are the captions of two other designs. Costs run from $55 to $4,500. Mr. Broom reports that nearly two-thirds of Washington deaths result in cremation.

As stated at the beginning of the Chapter, "burial" dominates the body-disposition method of most—almost all—Biblical and theological literature. The swing of the pendulum in Western States away from burial and toward cremation reflects an advancing secularism in the region. Increasing individualism in society has also challenged traditional institutional and family influences on the practice. In addition, spiritual sentiment has lost some of the force it once exercised. Finances may be the final determinant. "No Services" and "No Viewing" make disposition a less expensive option.

Biblical accounts of the disposition of dead bodies reveal meticulous care, human respect, and engagement in religious ceremony. Art and décor enter centrally into the process. Expense seems not to have been an issue. The record is impressive:

- **Adam and Eve:** His death is reported, but not hers. Nothing is said about disposition: "Thus all the days that Adam lived were nine hundred thirty years; and he died." (Genesis 5:5.)
- **Abraham (and Sarah):** The patriarchal couple pioneered in burial elegance. Abraham might have set that standard as a goal when he became the designated father of a covenanted spiritual family. Following Sarah's giving Abraham permission to have a baby by her slave, Hagar, she was reward for her generosity with a surprise pregnancy. As they aged, Abraham became both more fecund and death-conscious. He took action when Sarah died at age one hundred and twenty seven: he bought a burial cave called "Machpelah," meaning spiraling or winding. It is located near winding trails and hills in

the southern city of Hebron. The day for the "Father of Many" to die arrived: "Abraham breathed his last and died in a good old age, an old man and full of years, and was gathered to his people. His sons Isaac and Ishmael buried him in the cave of Macpelah." (Genesis 25:7-9.)

- **Rachel**, the second, and favored, wife of Jacob, and Grand-daughter-in-law of Sarah and Abraham, through Isaac and his wife Rebekkah, died bearing Jacob's child. The family was traveling at the time when she began to have trouble with her pregnancy. She died in childbirth and was buried near Bethlehem. It is written about Rachel's death and burial: "Rachel died, and was buried....and Jacob set up a pillar at her grave; it is the pillar of Rachel's tomb, which is there to this day." An indication of the ancient importance of Rachel's burial location may be found in (Genesis 35:19-20.) (I can testify that it is true: I have visited Rachel's Tomb several times.) An indication of its prominence in Old Testament times may be found in 1 Samuel 10. The Prophet Samuel had just anointed Saul at the request of the Israelites for a King; they wanted political identity, like the nations around them. Samuel decided it was a mistake, but he set out on a king search. He came upon the handsome and tall Saul, and it was revealed to him that his search had ended. Saul was honored. He had been out on a search for straying donkeys. Samuel had helped him locate them. After anointing him with oil and kissing him, he ordered Saul on his way, to return home so his father, Kish, would not worry about the donkeys, or his son. The prophet said: "When you depart from me today, you will meet two men by Rachel's tomb in the territory of Benjamin at Zelah. They will say to you, 'The donkeys that you went out to seek are found, and now your father has stopped worrying about them, and is worried about you.'" (1 Samuel 10:2.) Recall that Samuel would later be summoned from Sheol for a meeting with Saul to give the King advice about military strategy; and Saul would commit suicide shortly after. No kissing is recorded.

- **Jacob,** the Grandson (as noted) of Abraham, became the father of the twelve tribes, and he was also known as "Israel." He died on a drought-survival visit to Egypt. Before his demise, he had requested that he be taken home for burial. Pharaoh granted the family permission. Scripture records: "They carried him to Canaan and buried him in the cave of the field of Machpelah, the field near Mamre, which Abraham had bought…" It was a long way from Rachel's burial site. (Genesis 50:13.) Years later, **JOSEPH,** widely acknowledged as Jacob's favorite son, whom he almost lost because his ten older brothers had sold him to Midianite traders, ended up back in Israel, in the tomb with his ancestors.
- **Moses,** born "ex-pat" in Egypt, and rescued from Pharaoh's genocide of Hebrew infants, became the renowned leader of Israel out of the bondage of Egypt. He received the Ten Commandments along the way. Like Jacob, he succeeded well in the Egyptian government. He died while the twelve tribes were on their way to "the promised land." He was valley-buried, but without a headstone. The words have been recorded starkly: "Then Moses went up from the plains of Moab to Mount Nebo, to the top of Pisgah, which is opposite Jericho, and the Lord showed him the whole land….The Lord said, 'This is the land of which I swore to Abraham, to Isaac, and to Jacob, saying, "I will give it to your descendants….you shall not cross over there."'" And Moses didn't. He died and he was mourned for thirty days. His burial spot on Mt. Pisgah is both unmarked and unknown, an irony in view of his importance in the history of Israel: "Never since has there been a prophet like Moses, whom the Lord knew face to face. He was unequaled for all the signs and wonders that the Lord had sent him to perform in the land of Egypt, against Pharaoh and all his servants, and his entire land; and for all the mighty deeds and all the terrifying displays of power that Moses performed in the sight of all Israel." (Deuteronomy 34:1-12, selected.)

- **Queen Jezebel**, wicked idolatrous wife of wicked idolatrous King Ahab, imprinted her bloody mark—real blood—on both the innocent and the guilty. Her burial ended ignominiously. She was dressed like a prostitute when King Jehu entered the city of Jezreel. Thinking that she really was a tramp, he ordered her to be shoved off the window ledge. Her body splattered on the pavement, and the town curs started feasting on her. Her archenemy, the prophet, Elijah, had predicted it. Jehu proved compassionate. He commanded his soldiers: "See to that cursed woman and bury her, for she is a King's daughter." (She happened also to be a King's Wife, and a King's Mother.) Her burial ran into obstacles: "...when they went to bury her, they found no more of her than the skull and the feet and the palms of her hands." The King's command was carried out, nevertheless. (Cf. 2 Kings 9:30-37.)

These Old Testament "obituary" accounts cover only a few of the burial customs that would one day culminate with a similar disposition of a Savior King in a hillside cave, in a borrowed tomb, on Calvary, in the "City of David."

Burial according to Old Testament theology meant more than putting a dead body in the ground; it signified the beginning of the journey of the soul to the underworld residence of the dead, Sheol. The dead were doomed to journey to an existence in the dark. Sheol was conceived of as a barren, dismal place. Hebrew people dreaded it so much, that in their lyrical literature they begged God to keep them alive, even if they were living in misery. Bargaining was entered into, as in Psalm Six: "Turn, O Lord, save my life; deliver me for the sake of your steadfast love. For in death, there is no remembrance of you; in Sheol who can give you praise?" Early Old Testament Scripture was ambiguous about God's connection with the "place." Psalm 139:8b offered one ray of hope: "If I make my bed in Sheol, thou art there." The theology of Old Testament burial, in spite of the dismal Sheol destiny, occasionally offered hints of something better ahead for the righteous. However, it was best to stay alive and healthy as long as possible.

Jesus' death would radically alter the Old Testament theology of "dead and buried." His fate bears no mention of, nor connection with Sheol, unless Peter's words in 1 Peter 3 about Christ's journey during the "three days" between his death and resurrection to spend time with the "spirits in prison" implies that the visit was to Sheol. (1 Peter 3: 18-22.)

Regardless of the mysteries about post-death and pre-resurrection, or perhaps because of them, the Church sings our "alleluias" in honor of Machpelah and Jesus' Garden burial, and in mockery of Sheol and the Grave:

> "Death in vain forbids him rise,
> Christ has opened Paradise;
>
> ....
>
> Lives again our glorious King,
> Where, O Death, is now your sting?
> Jesus died our souls to save,
> Where your victory, O Grave? Alleluia."
>
> (From the *Presbyterian Hymnal,* No 113.)

The Church sings these hymns because, for among other reasons, we confess the theology of Paul: "Christ died for us," (Romans 5:8.) The Apostle expands his crucifixion theology with: "Just as sin exercised dominion in death (Sic. the Adam plot), so grace might also exercise dominion through justification leading to eternal life through Jesus Christ our Lord." (Ibid. Vs. 21.) Paul climaxed his doctrine with: "He was raised on the third day." (1 Corinthians 15:5.) The almost last words of the last Book of the Bible almost repeat Paul: "Death will be no more; mourning and crying and pain will be no more, for the first things have passed away." (Revelation 21:1-5.)

Death and funeral homes and caskets and urns and crematoria and lime will be among the first of the "first things" to be done away with when Christ returns. Burial, creation, donation and hydrolysis—and their effects—will have suffered redundancy. Christians are convinced of it:

"I believe...in Jesus Christ, God's only Son our Lord, who was....dead and buried; on the third day He rose...." The brevity of the Creed's words belies the eternity, catholicity and certainty of the Church's hope.

Some of the obituary excerpts that you are about to be introduced to can say what they do because of what Paul said Christ did: Christ's resurrection has increased human appreciation for the comfort we survivors have received when we have buried our loved ones in hope.

PIPED FOR, AND MILITARIZED AT GRAVESIDE: He was (figuratively) "piped over the side" during Memorial Services with full military honors...at Tahoma National Cemetery. (A Sailor, probably retired Navy.)

FOREST LAWN MILITARY SERVICES: Full military services were held at Forest Lawn Memorial Park, followed by burial.

LAID TO REST: The young slain Peace Officer (who has been referred to before) was "Laid to rest" at a Seattle area Cemetery. His sacrifice was also honored by a graveside ceremony.

ROYALTY BURIED TWICE: A Czarist Matriarch's body was buried twice. Empress Maria Fyodorvona, the Danish-born mother of Russia's last Czar, upon her death in Russia in the early twentieth century, was buried in Denmark. Two years ago, her twentieth century burial was undone, and the corpse was returned to Russia for reburial. Her body now lies next to her son and her husband in the Romanov family crypt in St. Petersburg. Nearly eight decades had passed since her death in exile.

KISSING FROM THE GRAVE: She blew kisses "up" from the grave for all those who had loved her, and had put up with her, even when, as she said, "I was a pain in the 'patootz.'"

BURIAL MASS FOLLOWD BY ENTOMBMENT: Mass of Christian burial was celebrated. Entombment services were held the next day.

PITTSBURGH MASS BEFORE BURIAL: Mass was held in Pittsburgh's "Our Lady of Joy Church," followed by Burial. (*Pittsburgh Post Gazette.*)

The expeditious, cautious, courageous and honorable burial of Jesus' body, while not dictating that burial exclusively demands Christian obedience as far as disposition of the dead body is concerned, nevertheless teaches object lessons about body disposition. Besides the example given by those who did the burial—which will be recounted in more detail at the end of the Chapter—burial receives strong support from both Scripture and theology. Lessons are learned from the women who came to the tomb early Sunday morning to tend to the perfuming of Jesus' body. What a surprise, and a puzzle: his body was not there. Then the stranger in white became visible and declared: "Do not be afraid…he has been raised!" He had further words for them: "Go and tell his disciples and Peter that he is going ahead of you to Galilee; there you will see him, just as he told you." (Mark 16:6-7.) They did not tarry; they fled the tomb. "My Lord, what a morning!" Nothing like it had ever happened. The women headed out to share the good news with the Apostles. Easter had given burial a new meaning.

Burial, or one of the other acceptable and reasonable body-disposition practices—but particularly burial, according to Calvin—testifies to the body as a creation of God, and a temple of the Holy Spirit. Besides the opportunity to prove the disposer a conscientious steward, the method certifies other Biblical truths: the resurrection, for instance. When a Christian puts away the body or ashes or physical remains of a Christian, they are symbolically anticipating that the body or reconstituted remains will emerge from the ground. Your sleep, according to the Apostle Paul, has ended.

The Church's theology on body disposition, until recent years, has almost unanimously favored burial. It is the position I hold as of this writing. I subscribe both intellectually and spiritually to the theology of Question Number 41, and the Answer, in the Heidelberg Catechism: Q. "Why was he (Christ) buried?" A. *"To confirm the fact that he was really dead."*[3] Not much of a search is required to find Scriptural support for the Catechism. The death and burial of Jesus is the place to begin: "Since it was the day of preparation, the Jews did not want their bodies left on the cross during the Sabbath, especially because the Sabbath was a day of great solemnity. So they asked Pilate to have the legs of the crucified men broken and the bodies removed." (Luke 23: 31.) According to Luke, as Jesus was dying he cried out, "I am thirsty." In response a sponge was dipped into sour wine and held to his lips. "When Jesus had received the wine, he said, 'It is finished.' Then he bowed his head and gave up his spirit." (Ibid. vs. 30.) And Scripture had been fulfilled: "None of his bones shall be broken." (Ibid. vs. 35.) The Scripture is found in both Exodus and Numbers. It refers to the treatment of the Passover Lamb that would be eaten when the Sabbath began (Saturday evening, at 6:00 P.M.) Psalm 34:29 offers another "broken-bones" passage: "He keeps all of their bones; not one of them will be broken." Jesus' naked and vulnerable side bore the breaks.

The Second Helvetic Confession supports the theology of the Heidelberg Catechism regarding the purpose of Jesus' burial: "To confirm the fact that he was really dead." *The Confession* (Circa 1563) instructs the Church in Chapter XXVI, dealing with the "Care to be shown the Dead: "As the bodies of the faithful are the temples of the Holy Spirit which we truly believe will rise again at the Last Day, Scriptures command that they be honorably and without superstition committed to the earth, and also that honorable mention be made of those saints who have fallen asleep in the Lord, and that all duties of familial piety be shown to those left behind, their widows and orphans."[4]

Until recent years, the Church's liturgical resources—and many of those supplied by Funeral Homes—have revealed a burial bias. A comprehensive and helpful liturgy may be found in the Presbyterian Church (U.S.A.) *BOOK OF COMMON WORSHIP: Pastoral Edition.*[5] (P. 224-233.) Appropriate liturgical outlines may be located in the same resource, e.g., in the case of cremation; or of burial of a body at some other approved place than the cemetery; and the same service adapts to donating a body.

The Apostle Paul's disposition theology obviously reflected burial consciousness. He softened the grief attendant upon disposing of a corpse, not only by the metaphor of sleep (1 Thessalonians 4:13-8), but by other teachings about resurrection: the "further clothing" analogy written about in 2 Corinthians 5, in spite of mixed metaphors—wardrobes and camping and construction.

Stewardship needs to be taken under advisement when making the decision about the method of body disposition. If burial prices were comparable today with 1939 when my paternal Grandfather was buried, it would strongly influence families to think little about the decision. This thought struck me recently when a copy of Grandfather's burial costs surfaced as I was sorting papers connected with organizing my late Sister's estate. Part of my curiosity stemmed from the fact that I was twelve years old when he died. I recall vivid details from his service—at the family home—followed by the burial in our local cemetery, and then a return to his house for the reading of the will. We older children were allowed to listen. The setting was the parlor where his body had lain in state for two days before the funeral. The itemization of Grandpa's death and burial costs follows:

- Casket and Personal Supervision, $165.00;
- Embalming, $25;
- Hearse for Funeral, $7.50;
- Tent and Grave Dressing, $15.00;
- Steel Vault, $85.00;
- Shirt and Tie, $1.70;
- Cemetery Charges for Internment, $15.00;
- Floral Tribute, $5.00;
- Telephone Messages, $2.50.

And the Total came to, $319.20. The sum does not quite match the entries, does it? A charge of $2.50 was lost. Maybe more telephone messages. Regardless, find a bargain like that today!

Theology takes precedence over finances in a Christian's consideration of body disposition. Consider the theological insight of a British scholar of the mid-twentieth century, Alan Richardson. Richardson was dealing with burial and the resurrection. Commenting on the mystery, he used the words "essence and form" to describe the "change" between the corpse that is buried and the body that will be raised. His exposition compares with Paul's in 1 Corinthians 15. The resurrected body, Richardson asserts, will bear both continuity with, and alteration from, the body of flesh; the result will be, "an identity of essence, a distinction of form."[6] John Calvin expressed a similar position, but much more literally: "We shall rise again with the same bodies we have now, as to the substance, but the quality will be different." The new body will be "more excellent;" it will have superior qualities, abilities and features," and be more ready and fit to participate in the pleasures that last forevermore. Most important of all, mortality will have been discarded.[7] How much are you willing and able to pay for the exchange?

Nothing testifies to stewardship dictation of disposition method like organ donation. Donation sanctifies and glorifies the conviction that the human body is a temple of the Holy Spirit. Rather than denigrating a body's value, willing your organs to a needy person honors it, sanctifies it, and makes it more holy—even more so if you have just celebrated your eighty-second birthday. The gift may also transform the body of the recipient of your organ into a "holy of holies." Another person whose death could have been imminent unless you had given one of your lungs, testicles or kidneys, or half of your liver or pancreas, has become a holier, healthier functioning temple through receiving your sacrifice. God not only approves, I am convinced, but also applauds. You have expressed your faith in God your maker, thanksgiving to God your keeper, and hope in God your protector. Burial or cremation is irrelevant in the matter; your temple has been vacated. Like foreclosing your home for a move to a furniture-furnished retirement facility, you have lost your need for so many household goods. Someone else's need has expanded: someone else has moved into new accommodations, some young Christian couple has married, and their needs are significant, but their finances are limited.

"Trafficking in body parts—as selling human organs is sometimes called—deserves approbation and demands legal action. Commercializing and giving away your living organs, whether for specious gain or serious need—whether for you or your family's survival, or to nurture your greed—demeans and denies God's wisdom and foresight in giving them to you. In the beginning, God so arranged the body parts—organs and systems—that their efficient functioning enables our living productively, if not profitably. Paul had this insight about the human body which also held for the Body of Christ, the Church: "God arranged the members of the body, each one of them, as he chose…giving the greater honor to the inferior member, that there may be no dissension within the body, but that the members may have the same care for one another." (1 Corinthians 12: 18 and selected.)

A nickname for a building connected with the Medical School at the University in Barranquilla, COLOMBIA resulted from human body trafficking. (The University is located next to the Colegio Americano Presbiteriano, which I visited in 2000 on a weekend trip while I was a volunteer in mission teaching at the Colegio Presbiteriano Americano in Bogotá.) I occasionally walked from the Barranquilla Colegio to the Apartment of my hostess. Concerned about my safety, she informed me of the University's nickname, in case I ever became lost. Find someone on the street with whom you can communicate, and enquire, "Donde es La Clava?" or "Where is The Club?" Pedestrians in the area would know immediately that I was not asking for directions to a cocktail lounge or a dance hall. I was talking academically, historically, and neighborly. And criminally!

The Medical School had gained a reputation several years previously as "La Clava" when cadavers were going cheap. Criminals and other indigents would stalk the neighborhood in daylight or dark, and return to the area after dark. They would stop behind the Colegio trees in search of a heavy tree branch. An opportunity to turn the club into a moneymaker presented itself when an alcoholic swaggered to the Bus Stop, or a crippled indigent or tottering senior citizen passed by. The club wielder attacked the innocent, vulnerable passerby, and swung the club into action. The murderer would then toss the club over the fence, and show up at the Medical School Morgue with a body, and collect a few days' wages. No questions were asked; none was necessary. The business became lucrative. The Police intensified surveillance, the City installed more street lighting, and the neighborhood exercised more caution. As far as the Colegio is now aware, body "trafficking" has ceased. The University obtains its cadavers legitimately—and no doubt, at a greater cost! At the same time, "La Clava" still serves as an efficient location signal.

Before this Chapter closes, I am moved by guilt, shame, regret, anger, a sense of justice, and a host of other emotions, to share a "burial sin." I became both a witness to, and an ancillary silencer of, a casket switch. I have had trouble forgiving myself for a lack of aggressiveness in resolving the issue sooner, but when you learn the circumstances, you may sympathize with my impotence in the situation. You may conclude that you also would have settled for the option I chose. Tell me, "What more could I have done?"

The principal victims of the crime included a dead man and his widow—call them Alice and Homer--and to some extent, me, their Pastor. Alice had not only lost her husband by death, she lost money in his burial by robbery. I lost respect for close Funeral Home Staff friends, and a minuscule bit for myself. How could they have behaved as if the widow and the clergy both were stupid, or blind? How could they have perceived me as a dunce?

When Homer died, Alice honored his wish—and hers also—"burial back home." Home was a drive several miles from where they had moved some years previously. I officiated Homer's funeral at a local funeral home, probably three days after he had died. My officiating role physically placed me at the side of Homer's beautiful cherry wood, brass or other metallic handles, open casket. Homer was dressed, as I had never seen him before: in a suit and shirt and tie, if I remember. Several bouquets of flowers beautified the setting.

Alice had assured me when planning the funeral that it was not necessary for me to make the burial trip just to conduct a brief graveside service. She had a nephew back home who could arrange that detail. I insisted that I wanted to be with her for the closure. In addition, we had friends we wanted to spend some time with following the service. We would drive to the cemetery early the next morning, and return home the next day.

The day after the funeral Marjorie and I headed out in wintry weather for the burial. Driving proceeded with caution. The roads were slippery in spots, but passable. We made good time. All parties arrived at the cemetery promptly—including nephews, and a few friends. By the time Marjorie and I arrived, the coffin had been stationed over the grave, and opened. Several folk were talking with Alice, and "viewing." Upon a signal from one of the two funeral staff present, I began the brief committal service, consisting of scripture, short comments, and concluding with a personal commendation of Homer to God, and Alice to her friends. I pronounced the benediction, greeted the friends and relatives, and said goodbye to Alice. She seemed to hold on to me. I asked her if everything were all right. She insisted it was, and suggested we "take to the road." It was snowing again. I moved to the casket, touched Homer's hand, and quietly said, "Farewell." Something about Alice's behavior did not seem right, but I attributed her actions to the cold, the closure with Homer, and the grief of leaving to return home. Homer would not be there. Alice said she would be back in our town in a couple days.

As I entered our car, I observed Alice and the two Funeral Directors beside the casket, having a discussion. I decided that they were probably settling on whether any jewelry should be left with Homer, sharing of the flowers, or other matters. As Marjorie and I drove away, I had a slight seizure of sadness—Alice and Homer had always been so kind to us, giving us rhubarb and produce and other amenities. As I took the last pass of the grave, a thought flashed through my mind, something like, "Hmm, a cloth-covered casket, and wood handles; Alice could have done better." Then I felt guilty for being judgmental. However, I had to concentrate on driving. No contradiction with the ambiance of the day before disturbed my thought. We headed for our friends' house.

We arrived home a day later. Two or three days after, Alice's nephew brought her back. The Funeral Home staff person, who had not gone on the committal trip, stopped by to see her. I phoned her.

A day later I went to visit Alice, to check up on how she was doing, and to hear about her trip home. She was happy to see me, but she also seemed distracted. We chatted softly and quietly. I read a few verses of Scripture, and started to leave. I hugged her and said good-bye. Alice asked if I could spare a few more minutes. I told her, "Of course," and I sat back down. She began to weep. She cleared her throat, blew her nose, and choked out a few words. She began, "They switched caskets on Homer." I was silent, and muttered, "Oh?" She continued. She had first noticed at the graveside that the casket interior did not have the silky and ruffled effect that Homer had lain in at the Funeral Home, the casket she had probably already paid for. The casket exterior was not the shiny wood that Homer had requested. Alice felt embarrassed by the one he was in at the gravesite.

At Alice's recital of contrast, my mind started a memory search. The search suddenly produced what she and I were both looking for, and what she had already become assured of. I rehearsed the scenes. Standing beside Homer as I officiated his funeral at the Funeral Home, I recall my glances at the shiny red wood, and the attractive brass or silver handles on the casket. I recalled being impressed: "Alice, you 'done' well!" Alice continued relating her graveside conversation. She had called the attention of the staff to the differences between what Homer was lying in at his grave, and the ruffles of his casket at the Funeral Home. (So it wasn't jewelry that I had perceived as the subject of the graveside conversation!) The Funeral Directors' stumbled on a response, something like: "Alice, in the dark tent and on a cold winter day, when you are shivering and grieving, things look different." (And the two men were probably thinking, "And when you are a weeping old lady, things look crazy—if you aren't too blind to see them!") Alice concluded—in tears—that the men had reassured her that she was receiving the service she had paid for. And that Homer looked so peaceful.

Alice opened a couple of other issues with the professionals at the burial site, but she received no more satisfaction about them, than she had about the ruffles. Deciding that her protests were futile, and glancing at how Homer seemed so at rest, she came to the conclusion that she would take no further action. She joined her two nephews, and headed toward the car. She was going to spend the night with them. (I do not recall if they had been apprised of the "switch" conversation.) I needed no further convincing that a crime had been committed. I muttered, "If only I had waited five more minutes before leaving the grave site." Alice comforted me, "That's all right, Pastor."

As Alice completed her tale of being robbed, my peace began to unravel. Two epiphanies revisited me, and a clash—almost a crash—exploded in my brain: I plainly and carefully recalled my observations about the casket at the Funeral Home, and my criticism at the grave. I recalled the red wood, and pink ruffles at the funeral; then I reflected on the cloth exterior, and the and plain interior at the burial. I shared my observations with Alice, and she listened intently. I convinced her that I was convinced that she had been cheated, which I recall calling "robbed." She believed me. She appreciated my support. I asked the grieving woman, "What are we going to do?" I offered my help. Alice blew her nose again, wiped her eyes, and said slowly, "Oh, Pastor Elgin, I don't want to disturb Homer's rest. So I have decided to do nothing." I told her that the decision was hers, and that I was standing by to help her in case she changed her mind. We kissed good-bye.

Going out Alice's front door into the cold winter afternoon, I was inclined to head immediately for the Funeral Home; or the Police Station. I reflected on Alice's words, "Homer's rest." I decided that all I could do at the moment was to pray. Pastors are also to act, or "do" as Jesus said. What did Jesus want of me at this moment? I felt at the moment that he wanted me to be quiet for the time being.

Sometime a breakthrough opportunity would arrive, and justice could be sought. There was little I could do at the moment. Questions arose. How can I live with myself if I allowed somebody to get by assaulting an elderly woman's grief and stealing her money? How often had the Funeral Home cheated other clientele by a casket switch?

Alice and Homer had plenty of money, but now she was alone, and she had been made to feel like a stupid and decaying old woman, a victim of a robbery by young professional people, active in the Church. I struggled painfully with the issue—for several days. I felt helpless. I prayed, and I wept, and I flailed, beating the air foolishly. I finally settled on supporting Alice's wanting Homer's rest. I would suspend my anger and personal feeling of also being psychologically assaulted by the affair, and I would wait in case Alice may some day change her mind. As the days and weeks passed, she seemed to be moving toward grief recovery, but seeming never fully to arrive at peace. At worship, her face was drawn. Her social re-entry was slow. Homer might have been at peace, but Alice wasn't. I recurrently asked her—for one last time, I finally decided—if she still wanted to abide by her earlier decision. Her answer left no doubt in my mind: not disturbing Homer's rest was more crucial to her than initiating a criminal case by digging him up.

On one of my last funerals before answering a call to another Church, I received an opportunity to revisit the regretful incident—with the owner of the Funeral Home. Following a service at his establishment, I rode with him in the funeral coach to and from the cemetery; providentially, I decided later. As we traveled one of the lanes out of the cemetery, our route took us past a family plot with the same surname as Homer and Alice's. I decided to "prime the pump." I said to the Director, "Oh, there is a family with the same name as Alice and Homer. I wonder if they are related?" The Director immediately came out, "Vernon, you won't believe this..." And he related Alice's accusation. He kept on talking for the two or three minutes it took to arrive at the Funeral Home. He talked the whole time. He concluded, as we arrived, "That old lady accused my men of making a casket switch on her." I was thinking, "Wait a minute; you are talking about one of my flock." He paused. I said, "Hmmm." He went on: "Can you imagine such a ridiculous idea? We've been in business here for years. We would never pull a trick like that...!" And he mumbled a few more words. I let him go on defensively. I said nothing, except, "Good-bye." I walked across the street to the Church, swung by Alice's door, asked if she were OK. I prayed and started home, quoting to myself Shakespeare's lines from one of his guilty characters—quoted several pages back: "Me thinks the man doth protest too much!" I shed tears as I kept trying to vindicate myself, muttering while I walked back home, "I made a promise." And like Argentina's Evita, "I kept my promise." May Alice and Homer now both rest in peace. And may the Funeral Staff have asked for, and received, forgiveness.

To summarize: As long as it meets Christian standards of reverence to God, respect for the death and temporary burial of Jesus Christ, appreciation for the environment, regard for the wishes of the deceased, attention to stewardship principles, and avoidance of ostentation and procrastination, the disposition of a corpse may be carried out without regard to the fact that burial has been the standard most adhered to in the Christian Church. Cremation and donation are free of stigma, and are certainly not subject to moral culpability; in fact, both practices can claim positive values, including stewardship of money and the environment. Donation may benefit society and individuals who may receive a cadaver's organs or "body parts." Hydrolysis may become a viable option as long as it does not prove environmentally invasive or socially reprehensible or divisive in a family body-disposition decision. It is also recommended that the procedure be done with prayer and an act of committal of the loved one to the Maker and Savior of the world.

Disposition decisions are frequently made ahead of the death event. The State of Washington has adopted legislation on the procedures: RCW 68.50.160. The provisions apply to whatever body disposition method is selected:

- A valid written document expressing the decedent's wishes regarding the place or method of disposition of his or her remains, signed by the descendent in the presence of a witness;
- Pre-arrangements may be prepaid, or filed with a licensed funeral establishment or cemetery authority. Under most conditions, they are not subject to cancellation, or substantial revision by survivors.
- In case a person has not pre-arranged details for a service, the hierarchy of authority for such responsibility follows this order: the surviving spouse; surviving adult children of the decedent; surviving parents of the decedent; surviving siblings of the decedent; a person acting as a representative of the decedent, under the signed authorization of the decedent;

The decision about a receptacle for your own or your loved one's remains, cremains, "donations" in case of cremation, or hydrolysis, should follow the procedures and guidelines already in place. Standards that meet Christian teaching are summarized in this way: as moderate as possible and affordable, and as consistent with the lifestyle of the deceased as advisable. If you plan on scattering, pay attention to "Green!' Care for the environment stands not only as a Biblical stewardship principle about God's creation; it also shows respect for the deceased, for humanity, and for the planet. Do not transform your living room into a macabre mausoleum. Law prohibits you from a Sicilian Rosalia practice in your downstairs Family Room. Plan ahead, and pay ahead, and your plan should be carried out. No dead human body, nor any parts of it, should end up as stray-dog food, or as blood for painting Main Street graffiti; or be publicly reduced to a skull and a few other bones and skin patches, as in the case of Jezebel and her cohorts. Human beings are better human beings when they have the sensitivity King Jehu expressed about why Queen Jezebel's remains should be buried.

The Chapter on corpse disposition with its introduction about Jesus' being "crucified, dead and buried" will conclude with a re-introduction of the two persons most responsible for his burial, Joseph of Arimathea and Nicodemus. (Nicodemus bore a reputation as "The man who had come to Jesus by night." John 4:1ff.) Joseph had not yet appeared in the narrative. The two men had witnessed the Crucifixion. Joseph suddenly became aware of the need of a place to put Jesus' body, in a hurry because of the imminent beginning of Passover. He had recently hewed a tomb of his own from a large boulder on the edge of Jerusalem. Without much forethought, it appears, he requested Pilate's permission to take the body down from the cross and put it there. Pilate granted the request. Joseph then summoned Nicodemus to assist him. Fortunately, Nicodemus had purchased the traditional myrrh and aloes to anoint the body; they weighed a hundred pounds. The two of them managed to remove Jesus, hastily prepare him, and place his body in the cave. John emphasized the temporary nature of their deed, not because the men believed that a miracle would happen in three days, but because of the law: "It was the Jewish day of preparation, and the tomb was near by." (Vs. 42.) And labor ceased at 6:00 P.M.

Both men had made previous commitments to Jesus. Their financial and political situation contrasted with most converts: they were both rich, and they were members of the elite Jewish establishment. Nicodemus had proved stealthy when he had earlier come to Jesus "by night" for a personal interview that turned into a discussion about "birth from above," (Greek "anothen.") Nevertheless, he had either come to the interview, or he left it, converted to discipleship. Gospel Writer John knew of both Nicodemus' and Joseph's caution; he described Joseph's attraction to Jesus as, "a secret one because of his fear of the Jews." (20:38.)

The two men must have felt good about their opportunity to bury Jesus; first, because they had the financial and ceremonial resources to do it; and, second, because at least Joseph had the courage to "come out of closeted discipleship," far and long enough to request the responsibility. And Nicodemus's commitment to birth from above had strengthened to the point that he was bold enough to offer to help. Their courage takes on even more admiration with the realization that their public display of posthumous devotion to Jesus probably jeopardized their seats on the Council. They deserve a unique share in the Church's privilege of confessing, "He was buried."

Burials and inurnments, possibly also donations and hydrolyses, occasionally move mourners, as they are leaving the scene, to gesture toward the body, or the container of its remains, and say, "Good-bye." Joseph and Nicodemus left the tomb—possibly to wash up. If they had offered a last "Good-bye," I would have delighted if I had had the opportunity to coach them on how to say it best in the Spanish language. As alluded to earlier, they had two choices: "Adios" and "Hasta Luego." One would have been more appropriate than the other on Friday evening. "Adios" applies when you do not expect to see the other person in the near future, or maybe ever again; "Hasta Luego" has a temporary connotation, "Until we see you later."

As Nicodemus and Joseph left the tomb where they had laid Jesus' dead body their more appropriate farewell would have been, "Hasta Luego."

Section III. "Identities and Pragmatics"

VII.

Vocatio Et Persona

> *"I believe in God the Father Almighty, maker of heaven and earth; and in Jesus Christ his only Son, our Lord, who... was crucified, dead and buried.... He descended into hell....he rose... he ascended into heaven.... he shall come to judge...."*
>
> The Apostles' Creed

WIFE, MOTHER, GRANDMOTHER, GREAT-GRANDMOTHER, ACCOUNTANT, JOKER, and STRAY CAT BOARDER: She lived to be 95. She had enjoyed a remarkable business career with Boeing. She had also found pleasure in joking, traveling, family relationships, and adopting stray cats. She loved good jokes. She was also gifted in making strangers feel cared for and appreciated. The Family/Career/Joker/Animal Lover enjoyed several hobbies: crocheting, gardening and travel. Her household at the time of her death had embraced three cats that she had adopted, and to which she had become fondly attached. Over the years she had tended to several other stray felines. Her commemoration took the form of a graveside service.

RELIABLE NEIGHBOR, INVENTOR: Neighbors appreciated his reliability. He was highly regarded by his family and friends for his simple, frugal and trustworthy character. A creative inventor, he was known for being totally unselfish and optimistic. He held several U.S. Patents. He had no biases and kept no grudges. His obituary records that he lived for others, especially for his Lord and his family; he kept his eyes upon Jesus. His family was convinced that on the day he died, at age 81, he had met Jesus instantly and intimately.

....

Excerpts of persons who impressively expressed "vocatio" and "persona" open Chapter VII. Vocatio relates to one's calling (from God), work, profession, "bread," "sweat," income making, volunteering, and even retirement. "Et" translates as "and." Persona deals with the psyche, front, character or façade an individual exposes. The characteristics will be dealt with in Latinized shorthand forms.

The first excerpt introduces a woman who filled multi-vocatio roles, and she apparently lived all of them well. She also contributed remarkably to her family and home life. She was obviously endowed with impressive parenting and grand parenting and other personal relational skills, challenging her spouse and offspring to imitate her.

The introductory persona excerpt stages a remarkable man. Described as a simple person endowed with ingenuity, selflessness and a deep religious faith, the inventor credited his character and accomplishments in a large measure to his faith in Jesus Christ. His record is truly a theological obituary.

Both the woman and the man reflected the strong vocatio sense that Jesus' ministry perfectly expressed. The man gave Jesus significant credit for his accomplishments. Both testimonies validate the truth declared in the Gospel Jesus Christ delivered in word and deed, and example: persons modeling superior vocatio and persona model the kind of person you would want as a member of your family or as a neighbor.

Jesus came from heaven enviously endowed with superior—Divine and human—gifts for his accomplishments. He was a super normal male, and an incomparable son, brother, friend, teacher and redeemer. He stayed celibate—though possibly with frequent assaults of passion, and occasional twitches of conscience. He appears to have been self-employed; he worked in carpentry. He chose persons of similar vocational status for membership in "The Twelve." They were probably able to grasp the meaning of his most esoteric parables. Though he might never have been invited as a guest performer, or an after-dinner program speaker or entertainer, he at times included humor in his lessons. He would probably never have classified as a "stand-up Comic." He probably never dated, wrestled, or boxed, except when a younger competitor invited him. He might have participated in the Nazareth intramurals. He probably traveled only domestically, and took his turn in the family's occasional visits south to Jerusalem, or down to the Galilean Sea. While mainly local in his outlook and culture, and a citizen of a small nation, Jesus was a unique human being, a person of, from, and with whom no other human being has ever compared closely; or ever will. He was either born with or achieved qualifications for his profession as a teacher, with which he also combined the work of preacher and healer.

Although neither an obituary nor a biography, *The Apostles' Creed* makes several helpful "vocatio" (work-related) and "persona" (character-assumed, and expressed) comments about Jesus Christ. His name itself endowed him with a calling. He was "Jesus Christ," Christ signifying a special anointing for a special accomplishment, implying but not imputing Divinity. (Though he was!) Some scholarly interpretations of his maturing, incarnating "Messianic Consciousness" raise questions about the weight of Jewish expectations on his self-understanding and public ministries. Regardless, he pursued his work congruently, convinced that his roles had been ordained in heaven, and that he had arrived on earth both conscious of them and committed to fulfilling them. In the Gospel of John he insistently claims his mission was of one who had been "sent." He felt compelled, for his own peace and the world's well being, to serve humanity, not only as a fellow human being, but also as a special Son of God. He was, in Greek "monogeneis," translated into English as "only beloved;" and he was as the Jewish long-gone wise men had prophesied, "the coming one." Messiah arrived in a stable in Bethlehem, home to the "Messiah," and, because of being Bethlehem born, he had Davidic connections.

Jesus' "first" or "Christian" name was itself, weighted vocationally. Recall that Mary and Joseph had no choice in the naming of their son, except the freedom to accept or reject Gabriel's command: "You are to name him Jesus, for he will save his people from their sins." (Matthew 1:21b.) "Jesus" translates a similar sounding Greek word with Hebrew connections, "YUSHR" or "Savior." "Christ" ("anointed" or "called") comes from a Hebrew word translated into English as "Messiah" or "Christ." Scripture used the term to identify his redemptive, saving work. Christ ("Messiah") combines both vocatio and persona, as goals and achievements related to the miraculous circumstances surrounding his birth, life, death, and vocational commission.

Jesus also bore the names, "son of man" and "son of God." The words do not necessarily signify two aspects of his being, nor even different vocational tasks. They tie him in with Old Testament descriptions of persons with a holy vocation. "Jesus" has different connotations from "Christos." Along with its connection with YUSHR Jesus signifies a family name, also a human being's name. "Christos" definitely refers to his anointment as King of Kings, and of David's line, and of prophetic announcement. Both Pilate and Herod had difficulty straightening out the implications of "Christ" when Jesus was under trial for "perverting the nation, destroying Judaism, and claiming a divine nature." He tossed the responsibility back into their laps: "You say so." (Luke 23:3.)

Both Jesus' names are extremely important: the one that he grew up and was baptized with, and traditionally associated with in his teaching career, the other dealing with his spiritual goals and vocational commission. Jesus as son of man adopted a slave's demeanor (often translated "servant;" the Greek is "doulos," and is most frequently used for a slave.) He was also the Christ, the Second Godhead person, essentially one with God, whom he frequently called "Father;" and one, of and with, the Holy Spirit God.

Jesus' sovereignty is embraced, among other places, in the title, "Kurios," or Lord. Thus The *Apostles' Creed* identifies him as "Jesus Christ, (God's) only son our Lord." He deserved and lived the title. His influence has proved more dominant than any person in history, in theology, in the Church, in the family, in society and in culture. His deeds are incomparable, particularly his raising dead persons, and his own resurrection, three days after his murder. He lived a vocatio dictated from heaven, and put on a persona that baffled and astonished his contemporaries, and irritated his opponents. He lived out God as essence, source, and deliverer, but with puzzling rejection.

From his beginning to his end Jesus Christ taught and ministered to certify himself as sent from God: the most authentic, powerful yet humble, and perfect human being who ever spent time on earth. He did the part as a slave-savior. He became the one person whose persona proved totally consistent with his person. In other words, when he was doing ministry for which he was called, "Jesus or Jesus Christ or Christ," or the Son of Man and of God for others, he was being the same being as he was and is now, and forever shall be, one with God, the world's Savior and Redeemer. His name was, is now, and ever shall be: "The same yesterday, today and forever." He came from God as God to bring the kingdom of God on earth. Jesus' S*on of God and son of man* formed a single title. Jesus lived it out, though while on earth he had left behind the totality of his "Godness" in exchange for "God-humanness." He died because of his vocatio and in spite of his persona. What human being has the audacity to claim childhood of God through him? Only the one who becomes a child by faith in him, and does his vocation and lives his persona in abject humility!

His baptism propelled Jesus into new commitment to his vocatio. It also united him more closely to the one who would soon become his "go-before" agent, his cousin John.

His messianic awareness had the advantage of an epiphany (a personal visit by God): "Suddenly the heavens were opened to him and he saw the Spirit of God descending like a dove and alighting on him. And a voice from heaven said, 'This is my Son, the Beloved, with whom I am well pleased.'" (Matthew 3:16b-17.) The baptism encounter served as his ordination: his vocation was to proclaim that he had been sent as a King, with unique and universal authority to inaugurate the kingdom of heaven on earth. Soon even his enemies—ironically, his own family to some extent, and his own race to a large extent—would confront him with threats, obstruction, and finally obliteration.

As the Jewish religious establishment began to hear about—some of them having firsthand experience of—his claims, and his deeds and his truth, they increasingly determined not to tolerate a young itinerant evangelist claiming oneness with God, having been "sent"—one of Jesus' most repeated vocatio claims. He was even challenging the powers of the world—particularly the Roman regime, under whose tutelage the Jewish establishment enjoyed pomp and pleasure and tolerance. Tolerance came easy to those whose challenge to Roman hegemony was forceless. Wait till they heard the Temple Choir singing, with Jesus as the inspiration behind the lyrics, "The kingdoms of this world have become the kingdom of our Lord, and of his Christ, and he shall reign forever and ever." (Revelation 11:15.)

Opposition against him increased as Jesus entered into a ministry characterized by three dominant activities: proclamation, instruction and medication. Finally, his death and resurrection confirmed, rather than condemned, his claim of having been sent. His ascension back to heaven forty days after his crucifixion climaxed his claim as the ultimate universal resurrection of the dead. Ten days later, on the day of Pentecost, fifty days after the Passover, with the official arrival of the Church, Jesus' kingdom was advancing mightily against the opposition, in large part, of course because of the coming of the presence and power of the Holy Spirit; but also significantly because of courageous vocatio and persona expression by the Church. It was becoming increasingly convincing that no demonic, worldly or other-spiritual power could prevail against the Church. The testimony to the Holy Spirit's replacing Jesus' incarnate presence on earth was too convincing. The effects of his crucifixion and resurrection began to become convincing that history would not need a repeat of Jesus Christ until the end of time. (Cf. Hebrews 7:27.) The Church had begun under the dispensation of Christ; the Church would triumph under the dispensation of the Spirit.

No one, Samaritan or Judean or Galilean or Asian, gained more from a personal encounter with Jesus Christ—hearing, and seeing and blinded by the encounter—than the feisty and brilliant former resident of Tarsus, Roman Citizen, Saul. It took knocking the man down to persuade him that further persecution of the Church would result in his eternal damnation. The final submission to the reality of the presence of the Kingdom of heaven on earth, and of the firm planting of the Church with Christ as the cornerstone, were affirmed in the most dramatic roadside encounter in history; more important, it resulted in Saul's seemingly impossible conversion. The knowledge and skills he had accumulated as an exemplary Pharisee were also converted and brought under the control of the Cross. Christ claimed Saul, whom he renamed Paul, and his reputation as a superior gifted Jew, for the Church. Paul had experienced total conversion: of soul, mind, talent, background, and future; his commission from his conversion on would be the vocatio of traveling, letter-writing, surviving, miracle-working missionary. His technique, as he himself expressed, was unique: "Though I am free, I have made myself a slave to all…. To the Jews I became as a Jew…. To those under the law I became as one under the law.... To those outside the law, I became as one outside the law. To the weak I became weak….I have become all things to all people, that I may by all means save some. I do it for the sake of the Gospel, so that I may share its blessings." (1 Corinthians 9:9-23.) The mission and expansion of the Church were guaranteed, primarily because of Jesus' promise, " I am with you always, to the end of the age." (Matthew 28:20.)

Paul was not the first person radically recycled vocationally for Church growth. Ever since the beginning of the world, God has ordained models of conversion and conviction and consecration to the vocatio and persona that would do his will. They have proved the truth of Paul's insight: "God chose what is foolish in the world to shame the wise; God chose what is weak in the world to shame the strong; God chose what is low and despised in the world, things that are not, to reduce to nothing things that are, so that no one may boast in the presence of God." (1 Corinthians 1:27-29.)

- Eve and Adam share the reputation for receiving the first vocatio assignment in the Bible. They bungled it, as they apparently did also their parenting: their elder son murdered their younger one. They also share the dubious reputation for inventing sin. Adam rated a Biblical obituary. (Eve's did not receive recording, or it has been lost.) "The days of Adam after he became the father of Seth (a third son) were eight hundred years; and he had other sons and daughters (not named). Thus all the days that Adam lived were nine hundred thirty years; and he died." (Genesis 5:4-5.) Another genealogical statement about Adam credits him—ironically in many ways—with the grandfather-hood of the Hebrew religion: "To Seth (the son of Adam) also a son was born, and he named him Enosh. At that time people began to invoke the name of the Lord." (Genesis 4:26.)
- Noah, the "Flood Man," received the vocatio from God to build a boat and save the world. His persona was as exemplary as his vocatio: "a righteous man, and blameless in his generation.…After the flood Noah lived three hundred fifty years. All the days of Noah were nine hundred fifty years; and he died." (Ibid, vss. 28-9.)
- Abram/Abraham had the distinction of being called as the progenitor "Covenant Man." He obeyed God's call to head the chosen Hebrew Nation that would grow to become as vast as sea sands. His wife Sarai(ah) shared the calling. The Patriarch's obituary reads: "This is the

length of Abraham's life, one hundred seventy-five years. Abraham breathed his last and died in good old age, an old man and full of years, and was gathered to his people. His sons, Isaac and Ishmael buried him in the cave of Machpelah, in the field of Ephron son of Zohar the Hittite, east of Mamre, the field that Abraham had purchased from the Hittites. There Abraham was buried, with his wife Sarah." (Genesis 25:7-19.)

- Jacob, also known as "Israel," reluctantly spent his last years in Egypt, in part because of a drought in Israel. In spite of entering into a conspiracy with his mother to steal his brother, Esau's birthright; and later of swindling cattle from his father-in-law, Jacob was regarded as reputable, and he became a heroic figure.
- Joseph was one of Jacob's twelve sons. As a result of mistreatment by his brothers, he ended up in Egypt. He spent several years there, and became powerful in government. When his brothers came to Egypt looking for grain—again a consequence of the drought just alluded to—Joseph recognized them. He persuaded the whole family to move there. His calling to serve in Egypt saved Israel, both the man of that name, and the emerging nation. The brothers' evil had served God's purpose. What magnanimity of character and control Joseph had!
- Moses as an infant was saved miraculously—due in large part to the courage of his mother and sister—from Pharaoh's genocide of Hebrew babies, and he was raised an Egyptian. Like Joseph, he became high in Government leadership. He received a call from YHWH that would rock anybody's retirement plan or medical coverage: "Come, I will send you to Pharaoh, to bring my people, the Israelites, out of Egypt" (Exodus 3:1-10.) Moses obeyed, and after radical miracles that robbed Pharaoh of combatant resources, including the loss of the firstborn of livestock and families, Pharaoh capitulated to Moses' request for Israel's departure from Egypt for Israel. Along the way, God again called Moses, to hike up Mt. Sinai, to receive the "Ten Words," (Ten

Commandments.) Because of a temper tantrum along the way, Moses was denied permission to cross the borders into Canaan. His obituary records that on the day he died in his 120th year, "His sight was unimpaired and his vigor had not abated." (Deuteronomy 34:7.)

- Joshua was called to a leadership vocatio, to replace Moses in the invasion and conquest of Canaan. Joshua succeeded in organizing Israel's tribes into a confederacy, offering them charismatic leadership.
- Samuel was born in answer to his aging "barren" Mother, Hannah's, petition of the Priest at Shiloh for a baby. Hannah gave the baby to the Priest for life at the Temple. One of his most memorable activities was to find Saul and anoint him as Israel's first King. The Prophet's Scriptural obituary reported: "Now Samuel died, and all Israel assembled and mourned for him." He made two remarkable re-appearances following his death (by a temporary time away from Sheol): the first, in connection with Saul's military dilemma (see "Saul" below); and the second, when he showed up at Jesus' "Transfiguratiaon," testifying to Jesus' vocatio, as one sent from God.
- Saul, Israel's first King by populist request rather than by divine wish was a tall, handsome man; he lived out a complex vocatio and he frequently bore an inconsistent persona. His life ended ignobly. A shepherd. (David), would replace him as King and a military defeat of Israel would humiliate him to the point that he ended up impaling himself on his own sword because his armor bearer would not do the deed. His three sons followed his pattern.
- David, for whom vocatio became a service, duty a privilege, and thanksgiving a piety, was born multi-gifted: shepherd boy as a child, musician and artist by natural endowment (and probably lots of rehearsal time), lover with a good supply of libido, adulterer by default, murderer by sinister abuse of his authority as the national Commander, ruler—again by default (he followed Saul); conqueror, composer, husband,

parent, saint—in short, the Renaissance man centuries before the Renaissance. David's son, Solomon, built the Temple that David had neither the time nor resources to complete. The King died at age 70, after forty years on the throne. By that time he had established Jerusalem as Israel's Capital. Music was his avocatio: he composed at least seventy-five of the Psalms. His son, Solomon, succeeded him to the throne.

Time fails for writing about Miriam, Rahab of Jericho, Solomon, Esther, Abigail, Isaiah, Job, Amos, Daniel, and a host of heroes, of whom, as has been and will probably be quoted again, the Hebrews Letter records, "The world was not worthy." (Hebrews 11:38.) Neither is the Church any more worthy.

A Reformer who lived centuries after the personalities who have just been introduced, John Calvin encouraged Church leadership and membership to model its vocatio obedience and persona development after great heroes of the faith; and as obediently and perfectly as possible, for the advancement of Christ's reign. He wrote: "The Lord commands every one of us, in all the actions of life, to regard his vocation as a "sent" commission. For he (God) knows with what great inquietude the human mind is inflamed, with what desultory levity it is hurried hither and thither, and how insatiable is its ambition to grasp different things at once. Therefore, to prevent universal confusion being produced by our folly and temerity, he has appointed to all their particular duties in different spheres of life. And so that no one may rashly transgress the limits prescribed, he has arranged for *vocations,* or *callings*. Every individual, therefore, lives out a role assigned to him by the Lord, so that one does not wander through one's years aimlessly, or stumble too frequently, especially not fatally. Thus all human action shares the accountability of being measured according to God's will. And so necessary is this distinction, that in his sight all our actions are estimated according to it, and often very differently from the sentence of human reason and philosophy."[1]

Several New Testament characters—of whom the world was no more worthy than of the likes of Abel, Rachel, Miriam, Jonah, Esther, or Ezekiel—emulated their Old Testament ancestors remarkably in vocatio. Their success is all the more remarkable in light of the obstacles that enviers, suspects, and opponents put in their way.

- Brothers Peter and Andrew, and James and John, and their colleagues, Thomas and Philip—among the first Twelve Jesus called as Apostles; and, of course, one of the most sensitive of all, the late-in-time genius, already cited for his conviction about his vocatio and his flexibility of persona, the Apostle Paul, (Saul), persecutor turned "Mission Marathoner;"
- a host of female saints—Mary, the Mother of Jesus, and Mary the Commemorator-Anointer, and Mary, the other Embalmer, and Elizabeth, Mother of John the Baptist, and Priscilla and Dorcas and Phoebe and Eunice and Lois and several of the ladies of "The Revelation;" others, women like the Samaritan woman at Jacob's well, whose testimony to Jesus as the "water of life, converted a number of men—and women—in her hometown of Samaria, enough to begin a church. And there were the other women who gained a reputation for supporting Jesus' mission "out of their own means." (Cf. Luke 8:1-3.
- Joseph of Arimathea, Nicodemus, Apollos, Timothy, Titus, first Martyr Stephen, Lazarus—both the rich one and his two sisters, and the poor Lazarus denied the left-overs from the meals of the rich man sometimes known as "Dives," and who in Hades begged Father Abraham in Paradise, to send Lazarus to cool the rich-turned-poor man's hot tongue. In the early history of the Church there were Irenaeus, Tertullian, St. Augustine, St. Francis, and Jerome. All these saints belonged to the corps of the righteous, of whom, again, the world was not worthy.

Other persons, comparably skilled, honorably motivated, highly intelligent, broadly educated, unequivocally committed and consistently perceiving that they had been called to serve Christ, have ironically faced opposition by Church leadership because of their gender: they are women. The Reformation did not considerably alter their eligibility for Church Office. Modern females bent on vocatio fulfillment justifiably blame obstinate and shortsighted gender policies for frustrating their ambitions. The *Second Helvetic Confession* exemplifies the obstruction. The text in Chapter XX, "Of Holy Baptism, The Minister of Baptism," reads: "We teach that baptism should not be administered by women or midwives. For Paul depriving women of ecclesiastical duties, and baptism, have to do with these."[2] Paul and other shortsighted endorsers of policies like *Second Helvetic's* are mistaken! The restrictions for which they claim to find Biblical guidance need rethinking. Ineffective, outmoded, and scholastically limited interpretations of the Bible have perpetuated Stone Age mentality on issues like women speaking up in Church. (Cf. 1 Timothy 2:11.)

The Presbyterian Church (U.S.A.) *Book of Order* bases its gender-nonbiased policies on its perception of the wisdom of God, as recorded in Scripture and advocated, and as discerned by the Church as the will of God, after years of shortsightedness. Like Jesus following his late arrival home from Jerusalem after forgetting to leave the city with his parents and the other traveling pilgrims—"Jesus increased in wisdom and in years (The Greek also translates the word, "stature"), and in divine and human favor" (Luke 2:52), so the Church is wiser and of a more tolerant stature in the 2000's than it was in the 1600's. Paul's statement about the Church's having no church—leadership basis based on nationality or gender has finally influenced employment policies. Many bodies of Christ order, but do not always practice, the election of Church officers without gender discrimination. The Presbyterian *Book of Order* is unequivocal: "Both men and women shall be eligible to hold church offices. When women and men, by God's providence and gracious gifts, are called (vocatio) by the Church to undertake particular forms of ministry, the church shall help them to interpret their call (vocation). The church shall pray for the presence and guidance of the Holy Spirit upon them and upon the mission of the Church."[3] (Chapter VI. G-6.0105.)

The PC (U.S.A.) currently suffers potential fracture over a different issue: homosexuality and church office. Several gay and lesbian persons have become convinced that their gifts for ministry and discipleship of Jesus count for more than the sexual behavior which they regard as a Biblically ambiguous issue. Many of them prepare for and seek ordination to Church Office. However, the *Form of Government* denies Church Office to persons who do not comply with the provision of G-6.0106: "…the requirement to live either in fidelity within the covenant of marriage between a man and a woman (W-4.9001), or chastity in singleness."[4] The final determination of who will be ordained into church office—minister of Word and Sacrament, elder and deacon—resides in a vote by the Presbytery, following the guidelines in the *Book of Order.* Presbyteries ordinarily abide by denominational standards. A 2008-2009 vote by the Presbyteries on setting aside the current standard has resulted in the defeat of the measure. The 2010 meeting of the General Assembly will vote either to ratify or not ratify the action of the Presbyteries. Many denominations face similar struggles over vocatio and gender or sexual practice.

Meanwhile, persons are living and dying, reminding survivors that we are surrounded by "so great a cloud of witnesses," (Hebrews 12:21), whose example of vocation serves as a pointer for us. The following excerpts rank among the forerunners:

CALLED TO MEXICO FAMILY MINISTRY; OCCASIONAL COCA COLA COMPENSATION: He was answering a call to mission in Mexico when he died, leaving a wife and ten children, plus seven foster children. The Couple's ministry focused on strengthening families and marriages, as well as promoting educational values in the surrounding villages. A family friend testified to the fact that on occasion, the Mexico Missionary's remuneration might have amounted to a bottle of Coca Cola. His vocatio deeply touched many lives "South of the Border." He died deeply satisfied with both his ministry, and the response to it.

DOUBLE FUNERAL FOR CHURCH ORGANIST AND PARTNER: With spiritual fervor the young man pursued his vocatio as organist and church musician. He was renown for his knowledge and love of the organ, sacred music, liturgy and congregational and choral singing. He and his "beloved partner," who had died earlier, shared a double Funeral Service. (cited earlier.)

MIGRANT'S SON'S SINGING INSPIRED HIS CAREER: The migrant's son's "twangy" voice matured while he worked in the Texas oil fields with other Mexican immigrants. He heard "blues" sung by Blacks, and foreign ballads by Mexicans. He marshaled his gifts and geared his persona into a career as a singer and composer. One of his hits catapulted him to the top of pop and country music charts. Shortly before his death at age 60, he remarked that he felt OK about himself, but, if he could have had his way, he would have extended his life a while longer.

FILIPINO PHYSICIAN OCCASIONALLY CALLED TO MINISTER BACK HOME: Born in the Philippines, he had a call—and found the resources to pursue it—to study medicine in the USA. He became an "Ob-Gyn." He returned occasionally to the Philippines to volunteer in medical practice. He organized church mission groups that took medical assistance to remote Philippine towns and barrios. At the time of his death he was raising funds to help the Nation's Children's Cancer Institute.

SCOTTISH LASSIE MADE A FRIAR: Born in Glasgow, Scotland, she studied Medicine and became an M.D. at age nineteen. After immigrating to the USA, she spent years working in Health and Welfare in the State of Washington. Later she and her spouse moved to San Francisco, where she conducted research on "Tay-sachs" syndrome, a genetic disorder that deteriorates brain and other cells, particularly in young children. She also felt called to ecclesiastical ministry, and became a full-time volunteer at the Friars' Infirmary in San Francisco. Her calling reached a pinnacle when she was eventually welcomed into the Franciscan Order as a "full" Franciscan friar.

TENOR, WALLPAPER HANGER, JOHN ADAMS IMPERSONATOR, SALES REPRESENTATIVE: A Sales Representative for major Corporations, he had avocations in music and friendship. Upon moving to Seattle, he joined a Church Choir and forged enriching friendships. His repertoire varied from spirituals to patriotic singing. His persona assumed patriotism. He traditionally led "The Sand Spit July 4th Parade." He beat his brass drum, wearing a costume reminiscent of John Adams. Memorial Services were held at his Church.

HONORED BY DALI LAMA: He died young from melanoma. Athletic enough to receive a full sports scholarship to the University of Michigan, he worked at hospitals and taught nursing students. On a Mission Trip to Dharamsala, India in 2004 with "Operation Smile," he became a recovery room nurse for hundreds of children operated on for birth deformities. The Dalai Lama once invited him to be his guest.

PULMONARY PHYSICIAN UNABLE TO CURE HERSELF: At 59 she ironically died during her own heart surgery. Her skills with pulmonary medicine pre-empted many untimely "last breaths." She changed many minds of those who felt hopeless about asthma.

Persona vies as voraciously as vocatio for obituary space. Persona arises from emotions and temperament, endowment and environment, and the general business of living and surviving. Parental and social environment make an impact. Health and preference play their role.

As with vocatio, Scripture abounds in both commendable and reprehensible persona. Conscientious Reformed believers searching for patterns on which to base "imitatio spirituality" cannot begin the search with any more assuring words than the following: "The word of God is living and active, sharper than any two-edged sword, piercing until it divides soul from spirit, joints from marrow; it is able to judge the thoughts and intentions of the heart." (Hebrews 4:12.) The Bible may not always tell the truth—especially when Satan talks—but neither do Bible characters live by the truth. Some deliberately disregard it. But do not despair or capitulate to lower common denominators. You will find some of the best models of goodness in history and literature by reading your Bible. You may even admire and desire to emulate some of the ones chosen for inclusion at this point; some you may want to ignore.

- Eve, tricked by a serpent, disobeyed God, and tempted her husband to be as naughty as she. Her persuasive plea was, "Eat from the tree in the center of the Garden." Adam bit, literally; he ate of the forbidden Garden fruit. The couple suffered the consequential humiliation of eviction: "The Lord God sent (the man) forth from the Garden of Eden, to till the ground from which he was taken. He drove out the man, and at the east of the garden of Eden he placed the cherubim, and a sword flaming and turning to guard the way to the tree of life."(Genesis 3:23-4.)
- Sarah eavesdropped behind the tent flap to hear the secret the visitors from far away had for her husband: she would become pregnant.

  She laughed. Later she lied about it—to her husband. She was centrally located in another incident: Sarah and Abraham shared complicity in a lie to King Abimelech of Gerar about their marital and relationship status, denying that they were husband and wife, and declaring that they were siblings—which had a distant truth connected with it. When a plague hit the palace, and Abimelech discerned that the curse was related to the couple's deceit, he ordered them off the premises. Abraham and Sarah decided to go back to where they belonged, unless Plan B comes along. They headed back to Israel, and eventually Sarah gave birth to a promised child. Isaac's arrival began to fulfill God's plan for the people of Israel to expand into a great nation. Hebrew Religion produced the Virgin Mary, Jesus Christ, the Apostle Paul and a host of other brilliant and martyred saints. Hebrew people have been abused and burned in Holocaust's ever since. Contextual decisions are not exempt from the maxim of "the truth, the whole truth, and nothing but the truth." (Genesis 12:10-20.)

- Delilah, the second wife of Samson, played a persona of sweetness and devotion with her Giant of a husband, Goliath. On one occasion she was bribed by Philistines to probe his secret about his strength. She found out: it was his hair. The tipping cost both of them peace and friendships. He became a "clava" (club) killer (Cf. Previous Chapter.) He had other marital problems; he gave his "heifer," as he called her, to the person who had been the "best man" at their wedding, because his companion had "ploughed with her." A short time later as he was killing innocent men in order to obtain their foreskins to pay a debt, he attempted to implode a temple, and he died in his misjudged ploy. "He had judged Israel twenty years." (Judges 16:31.) Samson showed more sense about revenge than about how properly to treat women, choose a good wife, and keep secrets.
- Jezebel, the wicked (surely not called by God to it) daughter of King Ahab, who was killed by a push from a windowsill, while disguised as a prostitute. Recall from Chapter VI how her remains—that is, those not eaten by the town curs—had to be scraped off the sidewalk for a decent burial. (Thanks to the mercy of King Jehu.) Her qualification for the dignity stemmed from Jehu's recognition of her as a "King's Daughter."
- Adorable, handsome, music instrumentalist, Psalm composer, intelligent, devout, adulterer, and a man of considerable administrative skill and spiritual charisma, and second King of Israel, David, moved by lust, became complicit in the murder of the husband of the woman he had raped (consensual?) His son Solomon succeeded him as King. Solomon completed his Father's Temple Construction project. His piety suffered judgment for his inconsistency. King David was "humanitia persona ironica."
- Queen Esther saved the Jews from a holocaust conceived by King Ahasuerus' court official, Haman. She had to assume the persona of a queen when Ahasueras' wife proved so obstinate that he divorced her. Her cousin-uncle (the Hebrew word allows either translation)

Mordecai, having learned of Haman's plot, along with Esther put on the persona of savior. The Jews were saved. A gala followed, and ever since on Month Adar, Day 14, the "The Festival of Purim (lots)" is observed with feasting, charity and gift giving.

- Judas Iscariot followed Jesus for probably three years, a devious wolf in sheep's clothing pretending to be a devoted Apostle. He was the embezzler-treasurer of the Twelve. He betrayed Jesus for thirty pieces of silver. His hypocrisy does not appear to have been detected by the other Eleven until the heinous act. Jesus had not, been fooled! For some reason Judas decided to return the money, but Jesus' enemies would not accept it. The traitor died on Crucifixion Day, either from hanging or as a result of a stroke that caused his intestines to burst.
- A Priest and a Levite (church attorney) ignored a seriously robbed and wounded countryman lying at the side of the road that they were traveling. (They crossed the road so as to avoid walking past the man.) A hybrid Jew, a Samaritan, came along, put the injured man on his own donkey, and led the animal to an Inn. The dying man received first-aid treatment, the bill for which the Samaritan paid. He went the second mile, committing his personal resources to the Inn Keeper for follow-up treatment. His Good Samaritan deed qualified him as a memorable model of Jesus' response to a Lawyer's question, "Who is my neighbor?" (He knew the Bible quotation to love your neighbor as yourself. He wanted Jesus to give him an answer that he could use to justify himself.) Suffering proves costly and inconvenient, but the lesson may teach you that you are justified by faith working itself out in love, and not by working it out yourself.
- Onesimus, a slave apparently "slaving" honestly and diligently, stole from his Master, Philemon. He absconded with the loot. Hearing Paul preach, he repented and promised to return to the Philemon household, confess his sin, and make amends for his crime. Did he? (Read the open-ended account in Paul's Epistle to Philemon.

Colossians 2:9 may offer a clue to a story with a happy ending.)

- Jesus himself, *El vocatio-persona non deceptio*, occasionally pardoned persons who had committed some of the worst ethical and moral sins, while at the same time he extolled some of the best examples of obedience and adaptation. He even on occasion conscripted questionable characters to make points in his parables. The "Parable of the Dishonest Manager" (Luke 16:1-9) typifies the practice. When the Vineyard Owner returned to his orchard after being gone for an extended period, he discovered that his manager was squandering money that did not belong to him. He called for an accounting. The Manager panicked, but he kept cool. He quickly contacted the debtors and drastically reduced their accounts. Jesus concluded the parable: "And his master commended the dishonest manager because he had acted shrewdly; for the children of this age are more shrewd in dealing with their own generation than are the children of light." And Jesus post-scripted the lesson: "Make friends for yourselves by means of dishonest wealth, so that when it is gone, they may welcome you into the eternal homes." (Luke 16:1-9.)

Later in the Gospel, Jesus told a "persona centered" story about a Nobleman whose persona turned out to be an imitatio issue. Before he left the country for a while, the rich and administratively skilled man left various grants of money with his slaves, commanding them to make the most they could with it while he was gone—for an unspecified time. After he had been away a while, he returned and called the slaves together for an accounting. Two had doubled their grant; one had kept his wrapped in a piece of cloth. Upon reporting the activity of the market, the Nobleman ordered the no-gainer to turn over the money he had hidden, and he gave the cautious man's "savings" to the man who had made the most. If that is not mystery enough, Jesus added that the citizens who had hated the Nobleman and had sent a delegation telling him that they wanted out from under him, were then summoned. The Nobleman said, "Bring them here and slaughter them in my presence." (As Peter said of Paul's writings, some of them were too difficult for him to understand.) Disciples of Jesus remark similarly about parables like the one just considered. Jesus was teaching, of course, about the Jewish persona of hypocrisy that would finally result in their rejection of him.

Reformed Catechisms and Confessions, while being realistic about human depravity, nevertheless applaud human effort toward perfection. The path to righteousness begins when you acknowledge your moral frailty. There is no one who has sinned, no not one. "If we say that we have no sin, we deceive ourselves, and the truth is not in us." (1 John 1:8.) Be honest. *The Heidelberg Catechism* calls us to this standard. It reminds us of the discrepancies in persona that characterize every disciple of Jesus Christ. The diagnosis has reform as its goal. Question One of the Catechism asks: What is your only comfort, in life and in death? A. *That I belong—body and soul, in life and in death—not to myself, but to my faithful Savior.... Therefore, by his Holy Spirit he makes me wholeheartedly willing and ready from now on to live for him.* Question 5. Can you keep all this (the Law of God) perfectly? (Sic. Law of God) A. *No, for by nature I am prone to hate God and my neighbor. (Sic. I have never been aware of that vileness in myself.)* Question 6. Did God create (me) evil and perverse like this? A. *No. ...God created me...to love him with my whole heart, and to live with him in eternal blessedness, praising and glorifying him.*

The answer to "Question 60" comments: *Christ imputes righteousness and holiness to persons of faith, "true faith," and by no other way than "faith alone."* "Question 61," and its "Answer," declare that good, acceptable-to-God persona are expressions of faith, as "fruits of gratitude." Question 70 asks: What does it mean to be washed with the blood and Spirit of Christ? A. *It means to have the forgiveness of sins from God, through grace for the sake of Christ's blood which he shed for us in his sacrifice on the cross, and also to be renewed by the Holy Spirit, and sanctified as members of Christ, so that we may more and more die unto sin and live in a consecrated and blameless way.* (Sic. persona.)[5]

The *Shorter Catechism* makes a connection between faith and persona: *Such as truly believe in Christ, and endeavor to walk in all good conscience (persona) before him may, without extraordinary revelation, by faith grounded upon the truth of God's promises, and by the Spirit enabling them....witness with their spirits* (**persona**) *that they are the children of God....*[6]

Obituaries sometimes give the impression that persona righteousness results more from human effort than from grace; and that vocatio results more from your searching for it, than its searching for you. Still others reflect the mystery and tension of sin that grip every human, and the need to adopt as your motto, "Christ died for us." We have to admit, with Paul, "I can will what is right, but I cannot do it." (Romans 7:18b.)

PERCEIVED AS POSSESSING AN ETERNAL SOUL: A thoughtful listener, he was regarded by many as their most pleasurable company. Friends said that one could talk to him, literally, about anything. He died in his early forties. He exuded the persona of maturity that "rubs off" on others, and helps make them better persons. He was described as a man who in his short life exhibited an eternal soul.

PERFECT ALL-ROUND "GUY" BREATHED HIS LAST IN A PLANE CRASH: When he died, he was engaged in what he liked to do best: fly. His character: passionate, compassionate, loving and giving, and, as frequently mentioned in obituaries, he reflected truly Renaissance persona. He "did" his religion, studied constantly, and developed his skills as an athlete, and he respected all persons. What a person to meet, play cards together, ski with and otherwise be inspired by?

ZEALOUS MARATHONER SUFFERERD THE WAY SHE RAN: Friends commented that she had fought her disease, cancer, as effectively as she had run marathons, spiritually kin enough to the Apostle Paul to boast: "I have finished the course, I have kept the faith." (2 Timothy 4:7.) Physically attractive, she held passionate beliefs and lived by high principles. She was enviably religious and tolerant, a devout Jew and a fervent Zionist. She promoted religious unity.

FATHER A WARRIOR IN MIDST OF FAMILY STRUGGLE WITH AIDS AND ALZHEIMER'S: By the time he died in his mid-eighties, he had had plenty of opportunity to show himself a warrior and a hero, versatile with persona. A family member insisted that his Father's emotional strength had proved a rock to the family during two major crises: first, a family member died from AIDS; second, the wife and Mother in the family had struggled with Alzheimer's.

TOURED WITH WOLF, READ EXTENSIVELY, EXPANDED HIS SOUL: The visionary, master builder, entrepreneur, mentor, poet, writer and friend died in his early forties. At one point in his life he had befriended a wolf, and he hiked across country with it. The companionship fulfilled an adventure in his love of exploration and of nature. He was perceived as having a revolving spirit, promoting every human being's good.

SYNAGOGUE EMPLOYEE AND MEMBER WHOSE SLAYER IS CURRENTLY (06/08) INCARCERATED FOR THE CRIME: A man angry at Israel made his way into the Seattle Jewish Federation Office and began shooting. He injured five, and killed the Synagogue President. Her obituary spoke highly of her vocatio with the Office, and her persona as a devout Jewish woman. Her Jewish friends praised her. So did Muslims and Christians. They appreciated her ability as a persuasive thinker, and her energy as a friendly worker. A gay man stopped by her office with sympathy, and complimented her staff for her standing up firmly and strongly for him at a time when few would. (The first trial of the defendant was overturned. The second trial convicted him.)

AN APPEAL: "LIVE AS I DID" (Note: an "Autobituary" paraphrased): I taught Sunday school at my Church and was busy with various women's groups and guilds. My home was filled with classical music, and the smell of cookies baking for many events. I loved piano so much that I took lessons all my life. I have had such confidence in the virtues of my best persona that I leave you this challenge: "Live as I have."

A ROBUST BARITONE, AND A TASTE FOR ANYTHING WITHOUT CHEESE: He served his Church in many ways, particularly with his baritone voice. He loved everybody and everything in life as long as it did not contain cheese. He was generous and positive, and he wanted people to be more aware more often, of whom we human beings need to thank for the good in all our lives. He aimed to live the persona he believed that Jesus wanted everybody to exhibit.

A FOUR-OUNCES' SOUL, WEIGHTED WITH LOVE: A son of the deceased shared a mystical experience with a friend. The event happened in the hospital room in which his mother had just died. Going into her room as soon as the nurses had left, he saw a peace about her and a light in her eyes; he perceived the countenance to be the presence of "The Lord." He claimed that the vision had given him an indication of where the Lord was taking his dying mother. She had been an amazingly devout woman, and she had expressed her desire that all people should live and love as unconditionally faithful as she had tried to. She had been weighed immediately before and after her death. The pre-death weighing registered four ounces more than the post-death one. The son concluded the four ounces difference between the two represented his Mother's "soul weight." (Ed. The Hebrew word, "nephesh" translates from the Old Testament as "breath and soul." "Ruach" is "spirit" and "wind." The Greek "pneuma" in English is "spirit." "Psuche" translates "soul." The Author of OBITUARY THEOLOGY is pleased with the son's comfort, but puzzled over where to find scales that weigh air. The son illustrated spiritual imagination, but more important, he expressed an offspring's loss and devotion.)

Paul C. Clayton, a United Church of Christ Pastor, has written a new book about the two principal issues of this chapter, vocatio et persona. The Book bears the title: *Called for Life: Finding Meaning in Retirement.* (A scholarly review of Clayton's book by a Mennonite scholar, John A. Esau, appears in the December 16, 2008 issue of *Christian Century.)* Mr. Clayton has just retired after many years of active ministry. He has continued to believe about his vocatio as he did when he had first begun his ministry: God had called him. He has concluded that living out your vocation fills three basic human needs: the need for affiliation, the need for power, and the need for achievement. (And the need for flexible persona!)

Other insights in Clayton's book about vocatio include this perception: "*Calling* has to do with identity (Who am I?); with gifts (those talents, abilities and aptitudes with which we are born, or that we develop); and with occupation, or the roles in which we exercise our profession or career. These concerns apply not only to our active work years for which we are paid, but they still figure prominently in our retirement. One reason is because the principles apply equally to every Christian, regardless of vocation, or all those other human differences which have perpetuated segregation in American society.

Clayton's conclusions make perceptive insights into vocatio and persona. He makes it clear that it is not only clergy who are called by God—as in the inadequate definition so often used in the past, "full-time Christian service." Every Christian has a calling, and it attends us whether we work or play, whether we slumber or have insomnia, whether we stay on the job or occasionally take a vacation, whether we are still employed or are retired. The theology about vocation that Clayton advocates conforms to insights gained from the examination of the subjects in this chapter; and with allowances for individualism and context, from obituary excerpts. He concludes: "Everyone's *call* (vocatio) is not just for how long one is healthy and happy, but for life, that is, a lifetime: to fulfill our calling to the end."[7]

This Chapter concludes with a reference to persona wisdom that comes from the prophet, Micah. His insight encourages pursuing vocatio critically, diligently and intelligently; and as consistently as drive and control make possible, expressing persona faithfully and sincerely. The

Prophet raised a question that has sounded down through the centuries with the same poignancy it possessed in his day—and still holds: "With what shall I come before the Lord…?" A social service answer that could have come from the lips of Jesus came off the Prophet's pen: "To do justice, and to love kindness, and to walk humbly with your God." (Micah 6:6-8.) Micah wrote as if he were previewing the Renaissance!

Paul assures us that we could all do more things than we ever thought possible if we more consistently relied on the strengthening power of God.

Let the Psalmist (Psalm 51:16-7) now frost Micah's persona dessert:

> "For you have no delight in sacrifice;
> If I were to give a burnt offering, you would
> not be pleased.
> The sacrifice acceptable to God is a broken spirit;
> a broken and contrite heart, O God, you will
> not despise."

VIII.

Gone Before And Left Behind

> *"I believe....in Jesus Christ (God's) only Son... born of the Virgin Mary ....was crucified, dead and buried.... He will come again to judge the quick (the living) and the dead....I believe in... the holy catholic Church, the communion of saints.... Amen."*
>
> The Apostles' Creed

....

ANCESTRY (Gone Before) PREPARED HIM FOR HEAVEN: He reverently appreciated the Roman Catholicism of his ancestors (the "gone before's.") He had constantly aimed at imitating his father's philosophy: "Live in the present as if it were preparation for living in heaven."

AEROSPACE INDUSTRY (Left Behind) WILL BENEFIT: A pioneer in the growth of the US Aviation and aerospace industry, from the beginning of the jet age to the space program, the deceased died in his early 80's. He had grown up within a few miles of Kitty Hawk, the birthplace of aviation. During the 1930's he frequently flew with his father, whose vocation necessitated flying. His engineering education led to a career with Boeing. He originated many mechanical aviation designs that are still in use. He left behind a wife of fifty-eight years, two sons and other family members, many of whom shared his interests.

FUTURE JEWISH THEOLOGIANS (Left Behind) WILL STUDY IN HIS (Gone Before) BUILDINGS: Born in London, he left behind several architectural European icons: in England, France, Germany, Spain, and the Netherlands. He eventually moved to the U.S.A. Some of his "left behind" projects in France rank among Europe's finest buildings, a tribute to his professionalism and drive for excellence. With a vision of contributing to a pool of well-educated Jewish religious leaders, he conceived and designed the Genesis Center, a campus in Tel Aviv, serving 150 Jewish students. He recently initiated construction of a new synagogue (Yakar) in Tel Aviv. (Sadly, a criminal assault at the Center a year ago resulted in the deaths of several students. Their tragedy was regarded as a "mini-holocaust." The victims left behind many grieving families.) (*Pittsburgh Post Gazette.*)

"I will remember in their ***(Left Behind)*** *favor the covenant (made) with their ancestors* ***(Gone Before)*** *whom I brought out of the land of Egypt in the sight of the nations, to be their* ***(Gone Before)*** *God." (Leviticus 26:45;) "Posterity* ***(Left Behind)*** *will serve the Lord, future generations* ***(Left Behind)*** *will be told about the Lord." (Psalm 22: 22 & 30.)*

....

Literature seldom reports positively on dying and death. Jesus Christ broke through the concrete negativism. He had something better to offer to replace belief in Sheol as the Old Testament place for the dead. Sheol painted such a dismal prospect that its depressive ambiance earned the title, "The Pit." The Hebrew people flinched at the prospect of ending up there. Their goal aimed at avoiding death as long as possible. The disconnect of ending up in "the Pit" meant a worse cut-off contact with family—and worst of all, with YHWH God—than simply breathing your last. The sentence was almost unbearable.

How fortunate for the New Testament believers that the view and the theology changed; to say "for the better" brutally slams Christian theology. Resurrection provided the fulcrum for the change. No viewpoints and convictions about the hereafter consequences of death come across more hopefully than in the Gospel, and in Jesus Christ's rising from the dead. For persons before Christ, aging and living with discomfort and pain, death held a stronger prospect than continuing to live; it was embraced with anticipation. More than any other writer, the Apostle Paul developed a consequent theology of hope. He wrote words which, if he had written them in the time of Moses or Samuel or Isaiah or Ezekiel, he would have been treated with disrespect similar to the "guff" Jesus had to put up with, and die for. Paul wrote: "To die is gain." (Philippians 1:21.) Jesus taught several parables about the gain, but he never spoke more dramatically or timely about it than when one of the criminals being crucified beside him, a repentant human being, turned toward Jesus and asked for mercy. Jesus had an answer that would soon take effect: "Today you will be with me in paradise." (Luke 23:43.) The news was almost beyond belief, but apparently the dying companion accepted it. Today the Church accepts it even more convincingly. In the Creed, the Church confesses about Jesus, "The third day he arose again from the dead." These victorious words, however, cannot be confessed apart from also admitting the death that made them possible and truthful. Paul's "sting," and Dr. Elisabeth Kubler Ross's "distaste" have to fit into the vocabulary as well.

This Chapter introduces a track for thinking about death—and resurrection—more in terms of its consequences than of its cause. The paradigm introduces a before and after reclassification of humanity into two classes: those who have died and those who still face death. They are designated the gone before and the left behind, the ancestry and the posterity. The gone before, the dead, have become the ancestry of the left behind; the left behind, the survivors, have become the posterity of the gone before.

Scripture has performed a helpful service for both the living and the dead. The dead, the gone before, benefit from being remembered; the living, the left behind, benefit from having the records. Summaries of the dead appear frequently, with careful attention to family lines. Folk of Bible times did not quite enjoy the genealogical privileges that the libraries of the Salt Lake City Church of Jesus Christ of Latter Day Saints Library of family connections and origins provide. But considering the primitive technology available, the records turn out to be helpful to the Church.

Reference has already been made to several identity passages about outstanding personages. Mention of a few follows:

- Adam and Eve, according to the scriptures, hold the unique role of having no ancestry, and almost losing one-half of their posterity when their elder son, Cain killed his younger brother Abel. Although the record does not tell how, it records that more family came on the scene, and probably through sibling siring, families were begun. Abel eventually lost his distinction of being the only gone before. Cain's ancestry is listed through seven or eight generations, but no mention is made of his dying. It is doubtful that he could claim the reputation that his nephew to the fifth generation could. Enoch, Great Grandson to the 4th Generation of Cain's second brother, Seth, is the only one in the line whose death is not reported. Did Enoch never die? Did he turn out to be the first miracle "gone before?" Here is the record: "Enoch walked with God; then he was no more, because God took him." (Genesis 5:24.) (The previous chapter noted Adam's death, at age nine hundred thirty; no record exists of Eve's. {Genesis 5:4-5.})
- Noah was born in the eighth generation after Adam, through Seth, Adam and Eve's third son, and brother of Cain. His father was Lamech, and his grandfather, the honorable, longest-lived person recorded in Scripture, Methuselah. After the Flood Noah—and his wife, and three sons and their families and all the saved animals—went out of the ark. The sons, Shem, Ham and Japheth, and their offspring played a crucial historical role, both in the re-peopling of the earth, and in a diversity of ancestry. "After the flood Noah lived three hundred fifty years. All the days of Noah were nine hundred fifty years; and he died." (Genesis 9: 18 and 28.) Shem became the "Ancestor" of the Semites, the Jewish people; Ham of the Hamites, or Canaanites; and Japheth, the progenitor of several tribes and lands bordering his brothers'

territories. By the time of their productivity, Adam and Eve had been joined by a number of gone before's; and of course, a larger number of left behind's.

- Abraham—son of Nahor, and of the ninth generation after Adam, again through Seth; and his wife, Sarah, have been publicized a few times before. They "jump started" the development of millions of people eventually known as the "Covenant Community." Their remarkable posterity provided leadership for God's "chosen people:" Grandson, Jacob, proved to be one of the most courageous and adventurous of his offspring.
- The Old Testament Prophets, Elijah, and his successor, Elisha, were closely connected spiritually and vocationally, and historically. Elisha became a professional colleague of the prophet, Elijah. They both served God as remarkable prophets in the category known as "the non-writing, non-publishing Prophets." Elisha pleaded for a "double-portion" of Elijah's spirit, and his plea was honored. At the time of his death a flaming chariot appeared and whisked Elijah away. A piece of his clergy robe was left behind, and it proved to be the answer to Elisha's plea. A group of prophets later witnessed a miracle in which the cloth was prominent, and they confirmed its source: "The spirit of Elijah rests on Elisha." Subsequently, Elisha found frequent and efficient use for his cherished "Elijah's double portion." On one occasion a dead man's body was hurriedly thrust into the grave where Elisha's body was being placed for burial, and the man revived! Ironically, the resurrected man belonged to a local band of marauding Moabites. (2 Kings: 5 and 12.)

The covenant inheritors who became left behinds by the above ancestors vindicated God's plan for a chosen people. They inherited both good blood and good spirit from Abraham. He gained a reputation for the unique quality of his faith—acting on trust and hope. Paul wrote that faith like Abraham's justifies a human being, and reconciles humans with God. Faith salvation stands in opposition to works' righteousness. God's word, accepted by Abraham, was coming true: "Go from your country and your kindred and your father's house to the land that I will show you. I will make of you a great nation, and I will bless you, and make your name great, so that you will be a blessing. I will bless those who bless you, and the one who curses you I will curse; and in you all the families of the earth shall be blessed.'" (Genesis 12:1 ff.) And so the religious tradition of the Hebrew people began. And the families of the earth have been blessed. Eventually, however, the covenant suffered damage, not because of any inherent flaw with the Old Covenant, but because of the human condition. "The Letter to the Hebrews" describes the transition: "But Jesus has now obtained a more excellent ministry, and to that degree he is the mediator of a better covenant, which has been enacted through better promises. For if the first covenant had been faultless, there would have been no need to look for a second one.... In speaking of a new covenant, he (God) has made the first one obsolete. And what is obsolete and growing old will soon disappear." (Hebrews 8:8-13, selected.)

Jesus, his Apostles, and the Early Church, and Paul and his missionaries and trainees held their gone before's in high regard. Jesus frequently alluded to them. He illustrated the Gospel by Old Covenant paradigms, personalities and incidents, in part, to nullify the accusation of his enemies that he felt otherwise about Jewish history and the Law. His discussion with the Sadducees on marriage, with his attention to Moses as a support, was one of his most brilliant performances. His ultimate argument, of course, was that his life and death and resurrection were the fulfillment of the Law and the Prophets. Years after his ascension back to heaven, he would receive support from Paul. The Apostle's position was in line with the Hebrews' truth: "The law is holy, and the commandment is holy and just and good. Did what is good then, bring death to me? By no means! It was sin, working death in me through what is good, in order that sin may be shown to be sin, and through the commandment may become sinful beyond measure." (Romans 7:12-3.) In Galatians he offered a tribute to the law, which could be regarded as its funeral commemoration: "Now before faith came, we were imprisoned and guarded under the law until faith would be revealed. Therefore the law was our disciplinarian until Christ came, so that we may be justified by faith. But now that faith has come, we are no longer subject to a disciplinarian." (Galatians 3: see 21-29.) The law, the Old Covenant, is the Church's doctrinal "gone-before;" faith is the Church's "left-behind." Thanks be to God through Jesus Christ our Lord!

Obituary excerpts show some of the same appreciation for gone before's and left behind's that the Biblical literature does. Compare the two:

DADDY'S LAST CALL FROM IRAQ: The little girl shared sadly with her mother about her phone call from her "Daddy" two days previously. He had died a few hours after their conversation. The child repeated his last words to her: "He said he loves me, and then he said 'Goodbye.'" His obituary described him as a deeply concerned family man. It could be a long wait before those whom he had left behind would join him. The gala family reunion would be worth waiting for.

THREE GREATS' IN GRANDDAUGHTERS' WOMBS: The Union Pacific Railroad Conductor was survived by his wife of 63 years, several children, grandchildren, and one great-grandson; plus three more "greats" in family wombs. He was gone before he would ever see them. Slightly in contrast with what was written earlier about ancestral descent: the retired Conductor had filled the roll of pre-natal ancestor; the yet-to-be-born were his post-natal posterity!

JEWISH BELIEFS PROMPTED CHRISTMAS GIFTS, AND JUSTICE: Born in Berlin, his Jewish faith was important to him; he had survived the Holocaust. On Christmas Day the devout Jew took Christmas gifts to families that could not afford them. He left a legacy of education, diversity, social justice, and remarkable strides against anti-Semitism. His obituary enjoined people not to labor in vain: do not allow religious bias to prevent you from setting an ancestral example before you go.

LEFT AN OUTDOORS LEGACY TO IMITATE: He developed skills both as a skier and as an instructor; he taught in Sun Valley and New Zealand. (Ed. I had the privilege of several seasons of skiing in Sun Valley, and two seasons in New Zealand. I wondered if he had taught me?) He participated in sports and outdoor recreation with the family: skiing, hunting and fly-fishing. His wife and four children have determined to perpetuate his legacy. He went before them, before he, himself, had had too many years behind him.

FORESAW ANTI-SEMITISM'S ULTMATE DEMISE: Anti-Semitism, beware! The noted psychiatrist and neuro-scientist, who died in New York at age 88, had written *The Myth and Madness: the Psychodynamics of Anti-Semitism.* In a 1986 *New York Times* article on terrorism, he had addressed terrorists' characteristic obsession with a final and self-justifying revenge. He was convinced that though the scourge may seem to prevail, looks and superficial bias are deceiving; the forces for good will triumph. Before he went, he had encouraged those left behind to wrestle with anti-Semitism. Many have met with significant success.

ALASKA HERITAGE WILL SURVIVE: He was born and died in Alaska (of gunshot wounds, at age 42). He had been educated at a U.S. Military Academy and had traveled globally. He was a member of the Cup'ok Tribe of Chevak, Alaska. He loved music, played the piano, and danced; and he was practicing on the piano when murdered. His loving extended family is determined to keep alive his delight in his Alaska Native heritage. He left, but not before he had left a heritage worth preserving.

In spite of the superlative examples already cited from the Old Testament, no person can claim a more remarkable, more richly blended, more socially diverse, and more perfectly spiritually beneficial gone-before and left-behind record, than Jesus Christ. Of all the New Testament literature, the Gospels of Matthew and Luke offer the most detailed list. Matthew ordered his three sections of biographical data under the title, "Generations." Matthew wanted the Church to remember first and foremost about Jesus, that he fulfilled Messianic prophecy, as the Son of God and son of "Man." Both Matthew's and Luke's Gospel identify royalty, commoners, and even non-Jews as contributors to the legacy. Luke's two volumes—the Gospel that bears his name, and the Early Church History, "The Acts of the Apostles"—document a considerable amount of ancestral and survivors' data about Jesus. Luke's goal was to highlight the salvation that Jesus Christ has accomplished, crediting Israel's role as a light to the nations, and the Church's chartering as a means to facilitate and fulfill the ancestral promises of God—through a Messiah. With the establishment of the New Covenant, and with literature like Matthew's and Luke's the demographics of both the gone before's and left behind's took on more spiritual homogeneity—both in heaven and on earth. The Messiah had perfected the possibility. Messiah's coming, in fulfillment of God's plan, challenged the Church as much with a vocational commitment as a spiritual mandate.

No more interesting a New Testament list of gone-before Old Testament celebrities can be found than the compilation in Chapter Eleven of The Epistle to the Hebrews, (11:39.) The iconic Biblical heroes "commended for their faith," invoke "imitatio" by the Church. The Epistle offers the reason why duplicating these saints serves the kingdom of God: "God had provided something better, so that they would not, apart from us, be made perfect." (Ibid. 11:40.)

The "something better" is both the example of Jesus and the obedience of the Church in its earliest founding days. Believers are challenged: "Therefore, seeing we are surrounded by so great a cloud of witnesses, let us also lay aside every weight and the sin which clings so closely, and let us run with perseverance the race that is set before us, looking to Jesus the pioneer and "perfecter" (Greek, "teliotein," also translated in English as "finisher") of our faith, who for the sake of the joy that was set before him, endured the cross, disregarding its shame, and has taken his seat at the right hand of the throne of God." (Hebrews 12:1-2.) The "cloud" honored him with more perfect faith; the Church can also—and must.

One more insight about the faith course that Church saints have chartered with Jesus as the model "finisher" comes from the Epistle to the Ephesians: it challenges Christians to finish the battle with evil, as a fierce combatant. Deceived by the expectation of prevailing against the Church, the serpentine enemy of the Church engaged in warfare. His opponents soon discovered that his formidability demanded that Christians dress for battle. Special armor is required. Keep it at hand, and in good condition, the Epistle to the Ephesians instructs, and in the end you will be the winner, the "perfecter" or the "finisher." See "Ephesians" Chapter Six, for a description.

The obituaries excerpted at the opening of the Chapter introduce persons who have lived intelligently and productively. After an exemplary life of faith and work the Boeing engineer went ahead. He bequeathed, "left behind," aerospace information and skills that proved helpful to both colleagues and the larger society. His success has energized and synergized other persons' talents and goals. His contribution to the development and improvement of air travel testifies to a well-used brain, imagination, education, experimentation, innovation and motivation— some of it developed by the man himself, and some of it picked up from colleagues. He did more than his share to guarantee a prosperous and productive future in the industry, and for human adventure, pleasure and accomplishment. His example inspired others to advance aerospace developments in the future, therefore guaranteeing career opportunities with a Company that would be productive and serve society for a long time. Besides, it would attract many residents to Washington State for employment. (This obituary required twelve inches of print.)

Look now at some other remarkable legacies ancestry has left to its posterity:

The "Lower Animal" Kingdom;

COW BREEDING MAY SUFFER: The young man was a bright and rising star in the dairy industry. He had enjoyed hands-on work with cattle: had vaccinated them, performed routine veterinary work on them, and had assisted with calving. He and his father had spent considerable time together in agricultural industry activities. The "wannabee" farmer had become an expert in the selection of bulls for breeding. He had shown cattle at County Fairs. People who knew of his love for cattle are convinced that a left behind herd will miss him. The lad had possessed and perfected a gift his father had bequeathed him: a special charisma with cattle. (*Florence Alabama News.)*

LAKE ERIE WILL HAVE FISH AGAIN: An environmentalist, protector of nature, and a fresh water advocate, she took on responsibility for aggressive pollution legislation that cleaned up and rescued Lake Erie. She left behind a Lake where Fish have returned, and if her work continues, the number of fish will increase. She also labored for fish preservation in North Carolina. She believed that an informed society makes the world universally cleaner and safer for Posterity, for "all creatures, great and small." *(Pittsburgh Post Gazette.)*

The Human Kingdom:

TIGER CREDITED DAD FOR GOLF TROPHIES: A friend of Tiger Woods' Father credited the elder Woods with raising, "Perhaps the most recognizable athlete on the planet." Tiger himself praised his Father as the most influential inspiration for his success: "I wouldn't be where I am today without him, and I'm honored to continue his legacy of sharing and caring." (An account carried in several newspapers.)

BETTER WATER, WASTE DISPOSITION: His knowledge and efforts will ensure better water and waste management for his survivors. The Pacific Northwest Clean Water Association had given him the Arthur Sidney Bedell Award for his lifetime contributions to the cause.

<u>AIDS</u> SUFFERERS WILL BENEFIT BECAUSE OF PARTNERS' CONTRIBUTIONS: At the time he died, both he and his partner of several years—he had died previously—were passionately devoted to the Northwest

Aids Foundation. They also supported medical institutions dealing with problems connected to the Disease. Their generosity and compassionate concern moved others. The partners were honored together in an inspirational funeral.

PIONEERED IN HYPOTHERMIC SURVIVAL SKILLS: The Pittsburgh Nurse's simple protocol established universal treatment for hypothermic victims. To prevent their death by shivering, she wrapped patients in warm towels, followed by the application of heat receptors to their hands and feet. As a tactic for preventing infection, she also promoted locating electrodes on the abdomen of paraplegic patients to determine when their bladders had filled. She served on the U.S. Deptartment of Food and Drug Administration and National Health Institutes. She died at age 82. *(The Pittsburgh Post Gazette.)*

TRAINED EAST GERMAN SPIES: A Spymaster of Cold War Espionage, he was so elusive that he was known as "The Man Without a Face." He was born in Berlin and died in Russia. He was once convicted of treason and kidnapping, but the convictions were overturned. He trained 4,000 spies for Stasi, the E. German Secret Police, for infiltration of the W. German Government. Though the wall between the two Germany's has gone, the Spymaster's strategies still apply. The deceased wrote in his Memoirs that he was not proud of what he had done, but he had become convinced that he had "not lived for nothing."

ENDOWMENT GUARANTEES ECONOMICS SCHOLARS: The Washington (State) Professor has guaranteed that future economists will serve society skilled in international business. She worked in Germany for the United Nations Relief and Rehabilitation Administration, lived in Hawaii, and saved her money to help students. Some of her estate went to establish scholarships at the University of Washington in her parents' names. Before she died, she had endowed Economics Department scholarships in her own name.

RENAISSANCE ATHLETE, SCHOLAR, TEACHER: HIS HERITAGE LIVES ON: He deserved his "Renaissance Man" persona. He excelled not only academically, but also in the gym. He became a Champion Arm Wrestler and Physical Trainer—in Turkey, Greece, Assam and elsewhere. In the Army he so despaired over illiterate soldiers that he developed a program that eventually taught 18,000 military service persons efficiency in literacy. Some of his students even attained the status of scholars. One of his male progeny became a Canadian National Weightlifting Competitor and World Masters' Champion, and he still competes at age 37. Of Greek heritage, the deceased became a "socialite" friend of shipping magnate, Aristotle Onassis (one-time husband of Jacqueline Kennedy). His family has established a Fund to enable disadvantaged youth to participate in sports. His philanthropy will keep many kids out of trouble. His brilliance was renowned. A liberal portion of it was passed on to his posterity.

HOPPY HAPPY, KODAK SNAPPY: Hoppy was a happy "Kiwi," homespun poet, and a friend of *Obituary Theology* author and his wife when they lived in New Zealand, 1994-5. Hoppy was happiest when snapping photos on the streets of the South Island village of Akaroa, near Christchurch. (The Christchurch, New Zealand daily paper, along with other newspapers, carried her obituary.) A devout Anglican, she frequently snapped photos of the Presbyterian Elgin's. She was known by almost every permanent resident of the vacation village, as well as by many "weekend batchers," as "Kodak Snappy Ellen Hoppy." Few people knew her real Christian surname. You could find her shooting pictures in sunshine and in rain. Among other consequences, her death recently (2008) at age 105, created a marathon of negative sorting. Her summons to posterity was read at her service at the local Anglican Church: "When the golden sun is setting, And your thoughts from care are free; When of others you are thinking, Will you sometime think of me?" RESPONSE: "Dear Hoppy, happy; smiling and snappy; dead, but smiling yet, how could we forget?"

The remainder of the Chapter will concentrate on the accountability which "left behind" posterity has because of the remarkably industrious and intelligent endeavors of their ancestors. The legacies are imperatives:

- Be humble. Paul laid out this directive to the Corinthian Church: "Not many of you were wise by human standards, not many of you were powerful, not many were of noble birth. But God chose what is foolish in the world to shame the wise; God chose what is weak in the world to shame the strong; God chose what is low and despised in the world, things that are not, to reduce to nothing things that are, so that no one may boast in the presence of God." (I Corinthians 1:26-29.)
- Be joyful. Sing a happy song, or whistle a happy tune. Tune yourself with a continuous Doxology, as in the "Revelation." You could as well be chanting the twenty-third Psalm. To God be all glory and power and dominion.
- Be studious. Have the persistence and diligence of the ancestors who took on the task of recording, sorting, and preserving sacred script. And remember the holy passion that prompted creatively writing it and continued effort carefully to preserve it. Be humbly studious reminding yourself of Paul's words to the Corinthians, "We have this treasure in clay jars, so that it may be made clear that this extraordinary power belongs to God." (2 Corinthians 4:7.) The task will be even more incumbent upon those of us who are "… carrying in the body the death of Jesus, so that the life of Jesus may also be made visible in our bodies." (Ibid. Vss. 8-11.) A 1947-56 fulfillment of Paul's realistic appraisal surprised the world, especially the world of Biblical scholars, when a wandering shepherd boy came upon the clay jars containing the amazingly preserved Dead Sea Scrolls. The translation of certain passages of Scripture has undergone perfecting. Exploration of other caves may result in even more unearthing of sacred text. The discovery of the scrolls leaves posterity with an even more accurate text of several pieces of Biblical literature.
- Be inclusive. Inclusiveness did not challenge the patriarchal culture of the Old Testament, or even the Apostolic culture of the New Testament, with the force

it has exerted on the Modern Church. Even misogynist extremist Paul, missionary especially to Gentiles, received Divine inspiration to record, "There is no longer Jew or Greek, there is no longer slave or free, there is no longer male and female. For all of you are one in Christ Jesus." (Galatians 3:28.) Fortunately, Jesus had burdened the Church's first Apostles with the Commission: "Go therefore and make disciples of all nations, baptizing them in the name of the Father and of the Son and of the Holy Spirit.... And remember, I am with you always, to the end of the age." (Cf. Matthew 28:19-20.) Remember also Jesus' eclectic friendship coterie: Zacchaeus, Jairus, Nicodemus, Mary Magdalene, the Samaritan woman at Jacob's Well, Mary, Sister of Lazarus, the "Ten Lepers," and a host of others; and his sermon on inclusiveness at the Synagogue in Nazareth that resulted in his dangerously being run out of town. (Luke 4:16-30.)

- Be genuine, natural, real. Avoid one of the worst pharisaical sins Jesus had to deal with: hypocrisy. Check the list of "woes" in Matthew 23.
- Be in awe of modern technology. Ancestors did not have computers, electricity, calculators, telephones, printers, and other means of recording, comparing, dating and preserving precious literature. Papyrus and animal skins had to serve as paper, and charcoal and berry juice had to write like pens with ink.
- Be both teachers and students.
- Be tolerant, without compromising doctrine. An example from the Early Church was a developing controversy over two of the most sacred Jewish pieties: Sabbath observance and circumcision. (See Acts 15.) The issue became so problematical that a Council had to be called, the first such in the neophyte Church. The Scriptural account of the setting and the record of the proceedings follow:

"The apostles and the elders met together to consider the matter." Peter reasoned with the group—based on gone before practice—"Why are you putting God to the test by placing on the neck of the disciples a yoke that neither our ancestors nor we have been able to bear?" Silence came over the assembly. It was time to listen to the "foreign missionaries." They began: "Barnabas and Paul told of all the signs and wonders that God had done through them among the Gentiles." (Acts 15: 12.) Moderator James took over. He based his argument on the fact that God had chosen the Gentiles, as had been the case with the Jews, "to take from among them a people for his name." James then offered his decision: "We should write to them (Gentiles) to abstain only from things polluted by idols and from fornication, and from whatever has been strangled, and from blood." (Vs. 20.) The wisdom satisfied the Assembly, and they "With the consent of the whole church, decided to choose men from among their members and to send them to Antioch with Paul and Barnabas." In the letter conveying their decision, a statement of authority was made: "For it has seemed good to the Holy Spirit and to us to impose on you no further burden than these essentials." (Vs. 28.) The letter was received enthusiastically. When the Antioch Church Congregation gathered to hear the decision, "They rejoiced at the exhortation." (Vs. 31.) A major schism in the Church had been intercepted by orderly Reformed procedure, fifteen hundred years before the Reformation.

- Be pious, without being judgmentally proud. "Do not let your left hand know what your right hand is doing." (Matthew 6:3.) Early in their spiritual formation, the first covenant people were commanded to do sacrifices, and keep such Torah traditions as Sabbath, circumcision and Festival days. One of the best pieties, besides prayer, is the Old Testament "Shema habit." A daily "Shema" routine gathered families together to memorize and repeat Deuteronomy 6: 6 ff.: "Keep these words that I am commanding you today in your heart. Recite them to your children and talk about them when you are at home and when you are away, when you lie down and when you rise. Bind them as a sign on your hand… and write them on the doorposts of your house and on your gates." John Calvin was insistent: "It is the duty of every Church often to stimulate themselves to a greater frequency of prayer, and also to be inflamed with more ardent devotion…." And at the beginning of his long Chapter on prayer, Calvin reminded the Church, "We must pray for no more than God permits."[1]

- Be evangelists, with follow-up Christian Education. The two hold priority in Jesus' Great Commission: "Go therefore and make disciples of all nations, **baptizing** them…and **teaching** them…." (Matthew 28:20.) Before they headed out on mission, however, the Apostles could well, if the Epistle had been written, have reviewed the Ephesians Chapter Six strategy for spiritual warfare; and even though their leaning was toward pacifism, they were to be sure to gird themselves with the "sword of the Spirit," that is, the "word of God." The left-behinds' meeting the challenge would guarantee that the posterity of the Church would be made up of faithful and devout believers. Reformed believers, parents, cousins, grandparents, elders, deacons, and church members—all participate in the covenant of baptism that requires such promises. Paul charged the young minister Timothy constantly to remember his journey to, and in, faith, and the strong example of, and influence by, his ancestry—that is, ancestry when they died, presumably before Timothy. The two women, his Grandmother, Lois, and his Mother, Eunice, had raised him in the faith. (2 Timothy 1:5 ff.)
- Be watchful. Jesus has commanded the Church to be watching and ready for the Grand Event. "The Parable of the Ten Bridesmaids," (in the King James Version of the Bible, "Virgins") teaches alertness poignantly and graphically. Five of the women had brought oil enough to keep their lamps burning for a welcome-home to the bridegroom in case he was delayed; five had not anticipated an emergency delay, maybe too much wine enjoyment at the reception, and they were out scouting around for oil when the bridegroom came. Jesus said, alluding to his second coming, "Keep awake therefore,

for you know neither the day nor the hour." (Matthew 25:1-13.) The wait for Christ's return has implications for both the present and the future.

- Be a persuasive evangelist. If you desire faithfully to keep the vows you take when you become members of the Church, you will want your family and other neighbors to be jolted out of their complacency, and to become enthusiastic participants in the faith-covenant family. Exhibit persuasive enthusiasm for the faith. Witness to and pray for drifters and floaters to come into a spiritual commitment to Christ. As much as possible, avoid the predicament Noah's neighbors found themselves trapped in when the rain started. Jesus cited their lackadaisical attitude: "For as the days of Noah were, so will be the coming of the Son of Man… they were eating and drinking, marrying and giving in marriage, until the day Noah entered the ark, and they knew nothing until the flood came and swept them all away; so too will be the coming of the Son of Man." (Matthew 24:36-44.) Most Churches know the Gospel truth, and diligently preach it. So many of our neighbors are "in the dark," or in a spiritual rut, in spite of the vows they might have taken following graduation from a Confirmation/Commissioning Class. Sponsors of new church members in the Presbyterian Church, that is, the whole Congregation, promise: "To guide persons into an active role in the mission of the Church…. Evangelism proclaims the Gospel of Jesus Christ in attitudes and works that appeal for commitment to God in Christ, and service to Him before the world."[2] (*The Constitution, Book of Order,* Directory for Worship, W-2.3013.)
- Above all, know Jesus, and walk with him continually yourself. Someone you know may die before you, and be in desperate spiritual need. Jesus is the one sent from God to the left behind with the Gospel of salvation, the balm of Gilead, the hope of the resurrection, and, with God the Father, the co-sender of the Holy Spirit. Listen again to Jesus' promise: "Those who love me will keep my word, and my Father will love them, and we will

come to them and make our home with them." (John 14:23.) A little space will do, but a wide-opened heart suits God better.

When he dies, Author Kurt Vonnegut may possibly give less priority to orthodoxy of belief—including believers like his pastor who had come and observed the Sacrament of the Eucharist with him—than to being a resident in a heavenly mansion where classical music is ubiquitous, the sound system is super digital, and access to DVD's is unlimited. Mr. Vonnegut revealed his perception about life in the hereafter in an Article in the *Christian Century* (11/13/07) by Jeremy Begbie, "Meaning in Music: Sound Theology."[3] The epitome of his appreciation of music could wait for his dying and death. The author said, "If I should ever die, God forbid, let this be my epitaph: 'The only proof he needed for the existence of God was music.'"

Most gone-before's left-behind's need a lot, lot more. Maybe Mr. Vonnegut, when his "time" comes, will realize that he does also. The living, and especially the dying, need their loved ones, but more importantly, they need God. If God participates in our listening, singing, or other musical offerings, and through the symphony also hears our crying and the gurgle of our last-breath dying, what a symphony will result! As Kurt Vonnegut observed, life is good with good music. Christians believe it is even better and more satisfying if Christ composes and directs it; even better yet, if he sings it with us. The apogee would materialize most appreciatively if the extravaganza were playing at our last breath.

Every human being dies in debt: indebted to ancestors, indebted to society, indebted to the Church, and indebted to God. I hope that like me, you pray the Lord's Prayer every day—aloud—"Forgive us our (use either "debts" or "trespasses") as we forgive...." Jesus told us: "From everyone to whom much has been given, much will be required; and from the one to whom much has been entrusted, even more will be demanded." (Luke 12:48.) The Old Testament "indebted" acknowledged their debtor status by offering sacrifices. The New Testament faithful respond with a different kind of offering: a clean heart, and a new and right spirit (Psalm 51:10); and money when the plate is passed. No response, however, can satisfy the debt, especially one given with that intent in mind. At this moment, or the next available one, refresh your memory about debt repayment with a refrain from the hymn, "When I Survey the Wondrous Cross," Stanza 4 (Traditional):

> Were the whole realm of nature mine,
> That were a present far too small.
> Love so amazing, so divine,
> Demands my life, my soul, my all.

Another Author, William Styron, once admitted a debt—again, similarly to fellow-author, Kurt Vonnegut—to classical music composer Johannes Brahms.[4] The Writer was convinced that the music genius' "Alto Rhapsody" had saved him from a fatal personal and family disaster.

Styron had slid into an emotional state where he was in dire need of being saved. (The 05/01/07 edition of the *Christian Century* relates his dilemma. The title of the article is "Brainstorm." The Reverend Norman B. Bendroth is the author.) Styron was no stranger to the episodes. Chronic depression frequently locked him in a paralyzing emotional state. The episode related in the *Century* article caused him to think about and plan for suicide. Early in the morning of the day that he was contemplating ending his life, the writer was convinced that he had arrived at the terminus. Like a boxer in the ring, he imagined himself prostrate on the floor, hearing his inner referee hurrying toward the count of "Five." (Sic. The author said "five." Did he mean "ten?") As each skirmish with sadness left him weaker, he became more convinced that suicide offered the only way out.

He had gone to bed that night feeling like that. His wife lay next to him. As far as he knew, she was unaware of his frenzy. He was watching a video, and listening to a soloist singing the "Rhapsody." The music began to penetrate to the deepest level of his psyche, the same region of his feelings where in his deep depression he perceived only darkness.

Styron's mind suddenly located a different track. He began to imagine how his suicide would ruin his creative work, his writing career, his family, his wife, and children, and friends. Reflecting on his love for the woman sleeping next to him, and for his children elsewhere in the house, he was catapulted into a nightmare: he saw himself, with others, in the pit into which his death had cast them all. Suddenly, at the darkest moment (like Moses coming down Mt. Horeb in the storm that heralded his having received the ten commandments—see Exodus 20), Styron experienced an epiphany; he arrived at a sobering insight: "All this I realized was more than I could ever abandon, even as what I had set out to do so deliberately was more than I could inflict upon those memories, and upon those closest to me, and with whom the memories were bound. And just as powerfully, I realized I could not commit this desecration on myself." The brilliant, weakening Author re-evaluated his good fortune, his personal responsibilities and his social accountabilities. Suddenly he saw light; he was being offered a final escape. He reached out and laid hold of the psychic power to change his mind. A hand seemed there for him to grasp. Peace began to possess him. He immediately fell asleep. How different his obituary would have read—as major newspaper headlines, no doubt—if the power of music and ancestry and posterity had not proved a lifesaver to him, had not brought him to a new level of self-control. Thanks are due God and Johannes Brahms that William Styron's obituary has not yet appeared in print! He may come out with another bestseller, if he has not already.

If death attacks you with a shrill cacophony, or if your last breath suddenly starts its gurgling rattle, try with as much openness and imagination as you can muster, to come into communion with your righteous ancestry and your promising posterity. You may not be conscious of their spirit, and you may not be awake enough to identify their image before it suddenly vanishes, but something about the theophany will afford you confidence. Maybe your glimpse of them will have the double blessing of an encounter with Jesus (alluded to earlier). He promised that he and the Father would come and make their home with "whoever will keep my word." (John 14:23.) Like Peter at the Transfiguration, you will have a compulsion to open the spaces of your heart (mind, soul, spirit) for a mystical conversation with them. You will realize that the only energy you need to exert at the moment is enough will to keep the door open, and to be grateful.

And, oh yes, be hopeful. Hope and trust that your name is registered in the heavenly Book of life. (Revelation 20:11-15.) And, oh yes, also, like at his transfiguration, you may hear Jesus telling you that shrines are not as urgent at the moment, as that suburban enclave of poor shacks in your inner city; they probably also need some of the tin cans and cardboard boxes on your pantry shelves. Be compassionate. Be generous. Those mendicants do more for depression than oxycodone or lipitor.

As Jesus was about to lift up his cross and carry it to Calvary, he had reason to lapse into depression. Perhaps he had already entered it; he had cried, "Let this cup pass from me. But..." As he walked on, a pre-Brahm's rhapsody might have been playing. He might have heard it before. He might probably have sung it frequently, maybe as recently as the closing hymn at the Last Supper. If so, the words familiar to him would have been: "For he will command his angels concerning you to guard you in all your ways. On their hands they will bear you up, so that you will not dash your foot against a stone." (Psalm 91:10-11.) Satan himself had teased him with those words, tempting him to turn stone into bread. (Luke 4:10-ll.) He had resisted in the wilderness; he would not abuse power for his own pleasure.

If he needed music at the moment as desperately as Styron had, Jesus could have recalled his Mother's frequent humming. One of her arias had been the Magnificat (Luke 1:46-53.): "My soul magnifies the Lord, and my spirit rejoices in God my Savior, for he who is mighty has done great things for me....God has filled the mighty with good things, and the rich he has sent empty away."

Before he disappears, glance behind Jesus. Peter and the beloved disciple may be there; they had accompanied him on the trek to his original transfiguration. You are important enough to Jesus for them to join the company again. Yes, they are there in spirit. Now start singing your favorite mantra. You could do no better than imagining words Jesus might have been mouthing as he carried his cross on his way to becoming a gone before. "Duty drowns out desire."

IX.

Knowhow

"I believe in God the Father Almighty...maker of heaven and earth, and in Jesus Christ his only Son our Lord....I believe in the Holy Ghost, the Holy Catholic Church, the communion of saints, the forgiveness of sins, the resurrection of the body, and the life everlasting."

The Apostles' Creed

PEACEFUL EXIT, AND OLD ENOUGH TO KNOW HOW: Age 90 and appreciated as a loving, devoted husband, father and grandfather, he died peacefully and was received by God. He had worked in the movie industry, Fast Food Franchising, and at other enterprises. His family and friends respected him as a Christian man who loved God. His virtues included honesty, tolerance, forgiveness, fairness, and generosity. His obituary quoted Scripture: 2 Timothy 4:7-8: "I have fought the good fight, I have finished the race, I have kept the faith...."

TAKEN YOUNG TO THE LORD, HE HAD ALWAYS STRIVED IN LIFE TO DO BETTER: Young enough to know how, but seemingly too young to go or to have appreciated why, he was called to live with the Lord. He had a reputation for always striving to have done, or to do, better. His family and friends are convinced that he had done well in death: he now walks with the Lord, in peace. Services were conducted at the "Christian Restaurant Center."

Few human experiences benefit more from knowhow than dying. By the time mortals' ends seem close, they have entered that era where age begins to exact its toll. One advantage accrues: they (we) have already gained considerable knowhow about living: how to make a marriage last, how to keep peace in our family, how to remain friends with neighbors, how to succeed in personal relations, and maybe even, how to know and please God. Common sense has honed our defenses against self-destruction, and in most cases, against plotting an unnecessary death-with-dignity—or last breath by self-destruction—way out.

No matter how experienced you perceive you are, however, either by your successes, or your suffering, or the fortune or misfortune of close loved ones near you, dying and death can still surprise and confuse you. Emergencies and exigencies you hadn't anticipated show up. You come to the conclusion that you could have gone the route easier and quicker, if only you had been wiser.

The last Chapter of *Obituary Theology* aims at correcting that mistake in judgment. Pragmatic measures will be examined for dealing with the inevitable fate that every mortal faces. Suggestions will be offered that may lead you nearer, in spite of your grief, to the rescue the Psalmist sang about: "I waited patiently for the Lord; he inclined to me and heard my cry. He drew me up from the desolate pit (Sic. Sheol, or where the dead go), out of the miry bog, and set my feet upon a rock, making my steps secure." (Psalm 40:1-2.)

You may recall the obituary excerpt of the trainer of Stasis spies in East Germany. Regardless of how culture, nation, society or the world may judge him for the nasty work he felt called to perform, he had made up his mind that as he approached death he would feel good about himself. He would die a pragmatist. Of course, if your life ends swiftly and tragically, you may have little choice about how to arrange your end-time feelings. It may be too late to wish you had lived a life of religious faith. On the other hand, depending on whether your vocatio was in the searching-out-and-killing industry or in a life-saving career, you may die with vocational pride or professional embarrassment, or persona satisfaction or personal disappointments; or with peace and satisfaction and a self-congratulatory, "Well done, good and faithful servant, you have been faithful in a very small thing; the bigger ones are now ready for you to tackle." (Luke 19:17, paraphrased.)

Obituaries relate that death sometimes comes pragmatically; it shuts off a miserable ordeal of suffering; or a disappointing relationship which neither you nor the other party had the courage to terminate. Some more fortunate last-breath statements report: "She died peacefully, trusting in God and embraced by her family." Or, "He died quietly at home, surrounded by his loved ones." And, "Her courageous battle with cancer ended as if Jesus were holding her hand, and saying, 'Come home.'" The deliverers of these statements had come to terms with the dying exigencies introduced in the first three chapters of the Book. Some of them give evidence of having accepted the invitation of Jesus: "Come unto me, all you who are heavy burdened…and I will give you rest." (Matthew 11:28.) Or they had memorized Paul's, "Rejoice in the Lord…." (The Book has already alluded to the verse several times.) The condition that the verse introduces is, "Let all persons know your forbearance." (The statement is hardly an invitation to hypochondria.) The person who complies with the conditions of the invitation will receive this gratuity: "And the peace of God which passes all understanding will keep your heart and your mind in Christ Jesus." (Philippians 4:4 ff.) Those of us of the Christian Faith cling—some better than others—to a life that may not be ending pleasantly, having incorporated into our trust the teaching that hope that is seen is not hope. (Romans 8:24.) You wait for what you hope for with patience and trust.

Dying as a believer can turn out very different from the dying of persons without faith and hope and endurance. You have enhanced tenacity. You have a better idea of where to turn and what to do when someone else dies, and, therefore, how to prepare for your own. You had anticipated that when the roll would be called "up yonder," it would affect you as inconsequently as a notice from your primary care physician that your annual check-up day is two days away. You want your responses, to both the roll call and the physician, to come out, "I'll be there." Knowhow about death can assure your doctor, and your God that you will make it; you will do all you can to make sure you will. On arrival you will be thanking God for your faith, your support, your confidence, your refuge and your strength, a very present help in time of sorrow.

Psychologist Bob Deits addresses some of the effects of death, and the knowhow of getting through them, in his book quoted earlier, *Life After Loss:* "Loss is painful beyond words." He continues: "No one can anticipate the emotional and spiritual agony major loss brings. Life can seem to lose meaning. You may find your sense of self-worth diminished. The sadness and loneliness you feel may seem to consume all your energy." The Psychologist offers hope: "You won't always feel as you do during the first months after a major loss."[1] A lot depends, the psychologist maintains, on how well you do your grief work.

If your knowhow seems shaky or absent, and you occasionally think of or do something "crazy" following the death of a loved one for whom you held deep affection, do not spank yourself. Do not think, "I am losing my mind!" Do not contemplate suicide! Unless you have other psychological or physical problems, you will hopefully have not lost hope; you sense a special close presence with you. Like Author Styron mentioned (see the previous Chapter) you wake up to the realization that resources are available for you to deal with grief; and as in Styron's case, with depression. Just as other family members and friends have grieved and have come to peace, eventually, and so will you. Pay close attention to neighbors and families who seem to have found the secret of victory over sadness. Suck up some of the energy and joy available through people who have recovered. Start talking to persons around you, but be careful not to bore them with too frequent recitals of your dilemma. Remember the angels, and their God, who are watching over you. Look out the window, and contemplate the recoverability of Nature. Something deeply spiritual and hopeful, even playful, may come back to you from your childhood, like Psalm Twenty-Three, with its comforting "rod and staff" reference. Congratulate yourself on your accelerating knowhow for facing the exigencies, the emergencies and the extremities of life.

Every mourner needs to know how to grieve. You need knowhow about the resources of faith and the power of your mind and will, and the help from outside—and "upside." The stronger your faith, the stronger your spiritual knowhow will prove to be, and the more certainty you will be able to muster to survive until your mourning is complete enough for you to live in a semblance of sanity and recovery. But be patient: you have been caught in an earthquake, which frequently visits you with aftershocks. You may come up against the dilemma my potential critical reader found, after I had had her offer to help read. She tried, but in view of her husband's dying recently, she could not do it; she suffered a "backlash." I sympathized with her. Together, we have decided that when I write *On Writing a Book, Good Grief Ministry, or Hitchhiking Foreign Highways,* she will hopefully be more totally healed, and possibly more ready to do critical reading.

Qoheleth, the "Preacher-Orator" of Ecclesiastes, may not be the first and most comforting grief counselor or spiritual advisor you should turn to while you are recovering. Nevertheless, he can be helpful; he ranks high among frank and pragmatic Scripture wisdom writers. The Preacher had arrived at that enviable state in life when if you can just be more rational, you can also be less fearful, and you will enjoy a life more fruitful. You will learn to swim with the tide if you are a distance swimmer; or wear the proper life jacket, if you are not. Qoheleth repeatedly used the word, "vanity" as his philosophical mantra. (Vanity literally translates, "having little substance or shape or form, such as breath.") Qoheleth had to acknowledge that death hits not only with a sting, but also like a fist in an iron boxing glove. Nothing as light as breath or "vanity" matches that kind of wallop, does it? Life can turn out that way in a hurry. But you survive. Your dizzy reeling from a blow wakens you to the fact that you have never before felt more in need of being pragmatic. Recall how Kirk Douglas' mother, in her last breaths converted him to realism about dying: "… it happens to everyone!"

Successful "knowhowers" who have befriended Qoheleth may also relate to Job's pragmatism, without wallowing in his pessimism. The Prophet demanded, both from God and human counselors, a rational reason for the wrenching that he was going through, painful enough to cause him to lament, "Why did I not die at birth, come forth from the womb and expire? Or why was I not buried like a stillborn child, like an infant that never sees the light?" (Job 3:11-16.) He wanted relief from his physical, personal and psychological trap that he felt only God could give him. Like some of the characters in Jean Paul Sartre's dramas, he had become convinced that he had already arrived in Sheol, here and now, on earth: "O that I might have my request, and that God would grant me my desire," Job petitioned, "that it would please God to crush me, that he would let loose his hand and cut me off." Except for the victory chronicled at the close of his Book, the Prophet had lived for some time without satisfactory answers to his—in his thinking—unnecessary and, according to his outlook, undeserved dilemma. As reviewed in some of the previous Chapters, the mechanical and traditional answers of his counseling friends, true to human tradition and customary theological dogma, which he had anticipated would help him, disappointed him. The psychological-spiritual counselors were coming at him with the wrong premise: "Repent of your sin, and your trouble will disappear." The counselors had never been, spiritually or psychologically, where Job currently found himself. Repenting of sin as the cause of his suffering in the assurance that he would have sudden relief, did not apply in his case. He had committed neither venial nor mortal sin so damnably, that he should be living in such misery.

Persons in good health and of good habits suddenly diagnosed with cancer or paralyzed in an automobile accident may identify with Job. Nothing in their congenital, physical or moral lifestyle seems to merit their egregious suffering. The Organization, Hospice, has assisted persons in this kind of situation. The service proved extremely helpful, and was extremely appreciated, two years ago when my younger brother's lung cancer metastasized. His apprehension compounded his physical condition. Hospice came for their first visit, and Ray had an entirely different attitude for the next six weeks, or until he died.

As frequently happens with human medical advancements—and many personal achievements, as well—Hospice had an ironic genesis. It was started in the USA by a woman who had learned first-hand how to deal with suffering. At a time when she was seriously ill, the woman, Florence Wald, born in the Bronx, incorporated Hospice and opened its first chapter. Born April 19, 1917, she suffered from an ailment that had so hampered her efficiency that she decided that becoming a nurse would offer her insight on how to be productive in spite of her debilitation. She studied nursing, and graduated from Yale University. In 1948 at the age of 41, she was appointed Dean of Yale's School of Nursing. Her interest in Hospice piqued when she attended a lecture by Dame Cicely Saunders, the British Physician who had opened the world's first Hospice facility in Sydenham, south of London, England. Dr. Cicely had observed that, "Terminally ill persons were going through hell, and the family was never involved." Ms. Wald added: "No one accepted that life couldn't go on ad infinitum." She made the decision to travel to Great Britain and work with Dr. Saunders.

Following her return to the United States, Ms. Wald persuaded several Yale colleagues to join in organizing the Connecticut Hospice. They consented, and Hospice came to birth. Its services and demands mushroomed. In 1998 the American "founder" was inducted into the National Women's Hall of Fame in Seneca Falls, New York, along with Madeleine Albright, Maya Angelou and Beverly Sills. The article about the ceremony says, "There are now more than 3,000 hospice programs in the U.S., serving about 900,000 patients a year." In recent years Ms. Wald concentrated on extending the hospice-care model to dying prison inmates. (With permission from the News Desk, Dennis Hevesi, correspondent, and his article in the *Seattle Times, 11/16/08* in the Section, "Local B7.") A scholarly Ph. D. Thesis could develop from a study of how, in cooperation with Hospice, institutions may teach people with chronic health problems to live longer and more comfortably; and, when the time seems to have come, to accept "dying at the right time." It is encouraging that several medical schools today offer courses in "Medical Ethics," with counselors more sympathetic than Job's taking troubled people through their trauma. Many of these counselors could be Christians who have learned how to die peacefully and spiritually.

Resources on how psychology may help abound. Investigate them. Practice. Read Church liturgies aloud. Meditate silently, or read classical meditations aloud, softly, and from the book or journal. Read other sacred literature, particularly poems and prayers; and participate in prayer-healing services. Visits in your home by church deacons or similar church leaders, and a frequent Pastoral presence, are important. Request the Sacrament of the Eucharist. If able, participate in sacramental services with a church. If immobile, ask church leadership to come and have "Communion" in the privacy of your home.

Not every alternative therapy has equal credibility. (The point has already been covered in the discussion earlier of my MnMnM—Miracle, Medicine, Mind—modality of healing, in connection with the prophet Elisha's healing of the Syrian Commander, Naaman. {2 Kings 5}). The effectiveness of any therapy, like the magnets mentioned above—and like any medical treatment that a dying person receives—depends considerably on the mind and will of the patient. This truth became evident in a less pragmatic modality demonstrated in a healing service held at the Church we were serving in New Zealand (1992-4.) Our Church hosted an evangelistic gathering, with the guest preacher a female evangelist from the Cook Islands. She was gaining in popularity in the area. The service combined "word and deed." It included healing by anointing, for those who needed it and wanted it. The local Anglican Priest, and I, the "non-conformist" Presbyterian, were the host clergy. After the preaching, and at the beginning of the healing invitations, several people "came forward" and were personally prayed for. Anointing with oil followed. Several ill persons found holistic relief. They had been previously invited to relax into the arms of the person standing behind them. At the end of the service Father Martin, over six feet tall and healthily athletic, came and stood in front of me. He went into an ecstatic mood. He started toppling toward me. He leaned his whole weight on my frame. He weighed at least sixty to eighty pounds more. I managed to stay on my feet, and eventually help him slide to the floor. I later concluded that I had had the bigger miracle of the evening: catching Martin before he fell on the floor.

Toward the end of the service, two persons present turned the event into a "Laughing Service." The Cook Islands evangelist had not indicated that that modality fit in her healing kit; it had not become part of her practice. She neither encouraged the laughing, nor criticized or attempted to intervene in it. She reminded the group later that "Laughing Services" were gaining in popularity in the British Isles, and Australia; and, to a lesser extent, in the United States. And she was considering becoming more skilled in the practice. I decided that night that I was both too old, and too weak, to be a "catcher." I appreciate the psychology behind the mode, but I receive more benefit from a more melancholy approach, more rational knowhow, than holy hilarity. I regularly quote, aloud or to myself: "Rejoice in the Lord always, again I say rejoice....(Pray with thanksgiving....) and the peace of God which passes all understanding will keep your hearts and minds in Christ Jesus." (Philippians 4:4-7.) And I have long ago memorized, "Be still, and know that I am God." (Psalm 46:10.)

Parishioners have shared with me that singing softly or silently at night, or when lonely or sick, proves sedative: it brings quietness and softness to the soul, and relaxation to the body. My experience with insomnia confirms theirs. I have fallen asleep in the midst of a familiar hymn. Among the most effective, both for myself and when shared with the ill, even dying, patients, are, "Go to Dark Gethsemane" and "Dear Lord and Father of Mankind," (*Presbyterian Hymnal,* Numbers 97 and 345 respectively.) Another, the name of which I cannot recall, has this verse: "Give to my troubled mind, uncertain and afraid, the quiet of a steadfast faith, the calm of a call obeyed." Other spiritual songs in which I have engaged the bereaved or anxious include: "Amazing Grace," "It Is Well with my Soul," renditions of the Twenty-Third Psalm, and even the children's hymn, "Jesus Loves Me." (It usually strikes a memory chord.) My comfort repertoire includes Psalm One Hundred Thirty-Nine; Hymns, "Jerusalem the Golden," "Glorious Things of Thee Are Spoken," "For All the Saints," "Christ of the Upward Way," "The Strife Is O'er." and, "Go to Dark Gethsemane." "Jesus Loves Me," as previously noted, invariably draws smiles from patients, and usually turns into a "Sing Along." (Author Styron, introduced in the previous chapter, would undoubtedly agree.)

If you have occasionally sung at worship, "For all the Saints," a hymn often sung at funerals, you might have asked yourself, "Why is a person of the Reformed Tradition singing to or writing about saints? Do exemplary holy dead people play a role in healing and dying and death? They must, or my Church would not be praising them."

My response is: Why not sing "For all the Saints?" Christians confess, "I believe in …the communion of the saints…." Some Protestants have remarked to me emotionally, "I don't believe in saints, just as I don't believe in a lot of the doctrine that the Roman Catholic Church confesses." At this point, I ask, "Do you know or occasionally say the Creed?" Others, mostly Non-Protestant friends, but also some who are not Roman Catholic, have shared their confidence in the help that prayers to the Saints have proved in their struggles. (Ed. When "saints" is capitalized, it refers to persons whom the Church has "canonized.") Being Reformed, and therefore more reliant on the authority of Scripture than of the Church, leads most Protestant Christians in interpreting sainthood as it traditionally applies in the New Testament. As used by the Apostle Paul, the traditional Greek word "agios," (the "a" pronounced as "h") translated "saint," means anyone in Christ who is of unusual holiness and piety; and spiritual maturity, in Greek, "telion," and translating as "completeness." The individual is recognized as a deeply spiritual believer, or devout church member.

When Reformed believers confess their belief in the communion of the saints, they affirm their fellowship with persons whom they regard as more righteous and holy than they, and they are making a commitment to approach imitation of their piety. Saints on earth who have died, and are believed to have gone to Paradise to join other saints, according to Reformed teaching, are not considered as legions or hierarchies of spiritual castes who have a special imprimatur from the Church. They are not particularly set apart in heaven in special spiritual palaces, and constantly in concert with angels. The Saint, the Virgin Mary, while respectfully revered by Protestants, holds no perpetually eternal favored status of the quality with which Gabriel greeted her for the annunciation of her miraculous conception. Her sainthood has nothing to do with perpetual virginity. She had a special role to play in God's incarnation; she performed it and she pleased God by it. She and Joseph also had other children, including four sons, and "daughters." (Matthew 13:55.) God blessed her, and the Church blesses her memory.

Mary's humble submission to God for the task for which she had been chosen ranks her high in the conclave of saints, but she rises no higher than Francis of Assisi or Augustine of Hippo or Teresa of Calcutta or Billy Graham of Montreat, North Carolina. Communion with the saints results from singing the songs they sang, reading and meditating on the Scripture that some of them have helped clarify for us, communing with Jesus in the same spirit they commune mystically with Jesus Christ, and showing compassion in the neighborhoods where the poor exist.

Reading about saints, singing hymns with lyrics from their poetry or contemplative literature, devotional use of materials composed by them or dedicated to them, and prayers (to God) of thanksgiving for them, support the creed, and do no violence to Reformed piety toward them or liturgical veneration of them. Saints are hailed in Scripture for their piety, not their divinity. At their death, believers who evidence some awareness and humility of what is happening to them—they are about to meet Jesus Christ face to face and become like angels—experience a deep communion available to any of the faithful. "Imitatio" of them, rather than supplication to them, fits better with Reformed theology. I occasionally aim for that communion by singing a hymn that features two of the most famous of them—one heavenly, one earthly; one genderless, one female:

"The Angel Gabriel from heaven came,
His wings as drifted snow, his eyes as flame;
"All hail," said he, "O lowly maiden Mary,"
Most highly favored lady, Gloria!

I sing my "Gloria" to God for Mary, but I do not supplicate her as I do God. Reformed believers who address prayers to Mary risk slighting God the Father, the Son and the Holy Spirit.

Baptism confers potential and moral obligation on every believer truly incorporated into Christ's Church. Death confers no additional sainthood on anybody. Where would the Church be without Saint Peter, Saint Paul, Saint Eunice and Saint Lois, Saint Patrick, Saint Augustine, Saints Martin Luther and Martin Luther King, Junior, Saint Clair Boothe Luce or Saint James Baldwin--some of them "canonized" or, in the Reformed tradition, recognized and honored for the work they have already done on earth?

Knowhow has less to do with the more esoteric or mysterious doctrines and practices of the Church, and more with the practical, useful and available insight and energy for carrying out Christ's mission. He taught about it by stories about daily life and existence in Judea, Galilee, and the contiguous territories—in "parables." Remember that a central feature of his ministry was not only calling people to come to him, repent of their sin, and accept eternal life; it was also about witnessing to the Word, first by accepting it, and changing their lifestyle because of it; and then sharing it with the spiritually mute and the piously suspicious. He often made reference to dying and death, and he encouraged serving him in this life. His message was less, "Believe, and you won't go to hell;" and more, "Behave as if you were in heaven right now." He frequently made the point that the kingdom of heaven is in your midst. The following sentences introduce several of his most salient points that relate to dying and death:

- As soon as a death occurs telephone 911. Offer brief detail to whoever answers. Or, if instinct tells you that death may be imminent, call immediately. Give clear directions to your location. Discern how soon someone will arrive. When they come, trust their experience in knowing what to do for you, or for the situation. Take a mild relaxation medication if available or needed. Be as helpful as you can to those around you, without being intrusive, unless you are one of the principal survivors. Obtain detail about where the person will be taken, if you have not already requested a venue.
- If you have been anticipating the death of the needy individual, have needed documentation available, or know where to find it in a hurry. Call a house-sitter, and give them a script for phone callers or doorbell ringers.
- Once you have information about what the next day or two will bring, take out your personal calendar, or make one, and arrange—in consultation with any other household members—for the necessary events of the next few days. If death appears or is ruled imminent, begin to think about commemoration services; call your Pastor if not already contacted. Phone the Church about the death, and begin to contact the family, using the list of emergency numbers you have previously compiled. Do you have previous plans for the disposition of the Body, or has the Hospital Staff or Chaplain assisted you in that matter?
- Once you have returned home—for brief business or for an undetermined time, locate all the legal, bank,

personal documents, check book and other materials that you know exist and anticipate that you will need. Set up an emergency mini-file cabinet.

- If you perceive the need of it, seek the special personal, psychological and spiritual support you anticipate will be helpful to you the next two or three days—in addition to family or neighbors.
- Begin to think "Commemorative Service," and if it is not in your memory, know where to find any written material connected with it. Do not immediately and perfunctorily accept the fact that there will be no services, even though the deceased might have let that option be made known regarding their own death and acknowledgment of it. Think the matter through lovingly. If you haven't already done so, phone your pastor. If there is any ambiguity about how to proceed, or if your household does not attach to a Pastor, talk to a friend or neighbor about spiritual direction and counseling.
- Obtain sufficient help needed for the many details that commemorative events and disposition of the body necessitate, and accept offers of help.
- Give yourself a "faith checkup," jotting down your most important and long-held, or recently discovered comfort-offering convictions, and what doubts and fears you have recently experienced. Write down your three favorite Bible verses. The sympathy cards that will soon be arriving in your mail will offer suggestions. Do not be distracted from reading them—each one at least twice! Ponder, "How do I sense God in all this upset?" Do not worry if depression skews your reason occasionally, and temporarily; you will improve, and you will soon be back on familiar spiritual trajectories. God has neither retreated nor traveled far distant.
- After a day or two, depending in part on your finances, begin to think about your social future; your financial future; your future housing, but not necessarily in detail, as it is too soon for that kind of planning. Fill out a broad, general calendar for the next six months, even if

it seems "wild" or impractical. As the days pass, revise it as necessary, and filter it through a confidant.

- Talk about—not to—the person who has died, but not as if you expect to see her/him next week, or even next year. If you have any unresolved guilt or negative feelings about unfinished business with the deceased, talk to a confidant or a Pastor.
- Re-introduce yourself to yourself, and take time to re-impress upon your soul and memory the resurrection and other hopeful theology which you might have learned earlier in your life, and about which you have been hearing many comments. Ask for patience as you wait for comfort—for, and of yourself, your family and friends, and God.
- By this time you ought to have become "obituary conscious." If you have not already done it, think of preparing one. Remember that Obituaries come with a price tag; be ready to pay the price. (They are worth it.) Review the relevant material in Chapters Four and Five.
- Obtain a manual on "survival after loss" like the one referred to earlier, prepared by an acquaintance. The Internet also lists resources, and most Funeral Homes gladly make suggestions. Go on a Web "Search" using words that currently describe your needs, and if you keep searching, as Jesus promised, "You will find."
- Re-evaluate the security of your personal and real properties: your home, your possessions, your income, your family, your driveway, your mail. Your personal walking and phoning and shopping safety may depend on your being careful. (If you do not already have one, purchase a new paper shredder.) Do you possess or do you need a Safety Deposit Box in your home, or is access to your Bank convenient, and your Box there spacious enough?
- Do not spend too much time alone. At times you want to believe that you are in communion with the deceased—not in flesh, but in spirit. Get past too frequent daily

visits to the Starbucks for the highest priced, highest caffeine-content latte. Occasionally assess your alcohol consumption. How does your liquor intake at present compare with how much and how often you were drinking before your grief? Avoid binge eating.

- Carry on with your regular schedule, balancing work and play and social contacts, and engage in other activities as your time and interests suggest, and your budget allows. Go to bed and rise on a regular schedule. On the day of the commemoration or publicized funeral services or memorials—again, be sure to have them—give your house special security. Devious minds read obituaries for opportunities for trespassing. Remember: you are enduring and living through the toughest times a person may ever face. On occasion, you may suffer temporary amnesia. Prove to yourself that you can, and will, make wise decisions about serious issues you have to decide upon, like matters related to the settlement of the Estate. Keep assuring yourself, aloud, "I am doing OK. I am sure my spouse would be proud of me. However, I must keep humble and realistic about my progress. I will check out my behavior with my best friend, or if necessary, a psychologist." Keep assuring yourself that you are progressing in your return to a normal schedule and lifestyle.
- Once again, to repeat, YOU NEED TO COMMEMORATE. Death inflicts such a painful personal and social disconnect that it needs suturing. A service of remembering, celebrating, comforting and eulogizing proves healing. If you are a Christian, connect with God-Jesus-Spirit; if you are a Jew, with YHWH; and if you are of some other religion, find a familiar path to your Supreme Being or higher power. Work out details with your Pastor, spiritual counselor, or any other professionals or close friends whom you consider helpful. Think of your own health and emotional survival, but remember also other family members or friends who have felt something of your loss and theirs. Do not forget the needs of significant others. Engage family members

in planning services or memorials; and if emotionally strong enough, engage them, and yourself if comfortable doing it, in conducting the service. If you have a church affiliation, and unless close family members object, have the service there. (Review Chapter VI.) Otherwise have the family join you in making a decision, but insist on a religious or spiritual setting. Exercise Veto Power if necessary.

- Become aware of and alarmed about behavior that is unnatural to you, and that you would not have expected or tolerated in them, if you had preceded your loved one in death. Do not, as far as you can help it, let guilt over failures in your past relationships, or unfinished business with the deceased, continue to cause you unease. Do not wait too long to put your case before those most closely involved with it, especially if it has become a frequently repeated bad habit. Confess your "perceived" or "real" (venial)—but not mortal—sin to a spiritual counselor or pastor, and wait for forgiveness from God. Restrict your mortal confessions to your Pastor, or between God and yourself. You may also need to make an appointment with a psychiatrist. If you are a Christian, remember that forgiveness begets—and demands—forgiveness.
- Do not feel guilty thinking about your own needs of forgiving or being forgiven; of grieving and needing sympathy, or maybe even of being pampered, at least, not for the first month of your grief. You may be misperceiving your needs, and overlooking simple means for their satisfaction. You deserve your own "first-fruits" of mourning. Humility—especially about our shortcomings or personal needs—ranks with love as one of humanity's most powerful mendicants. "I am weak" is an OK admission; it means you are normal. Another helpful Bible verse may be found in 2 Corinthians 12:10, "When I am weak, then I am strong…." The Apostle continues with the advice that the strengthening power of Christ heals bodies, hearts and souls. And minds.
- Extremely rarely have persons confessed to their pastor about inconsiderate treatment by a funeral staff person.

If a complaint keeps bothering you, check out whether perception fits reality. Remind yourself that Funeral Homes are staffed with well-trained professionals, but their Staff is human. They deal constantly with different temperaments in grieving clientele, people in deep distress; sometimes they err.

- Deceased loved ones who have served in a United States military service branch ordinarily have death and body-disposition benefits. If not already contacted by an Armed Services Official, reach a local Veterans Administration service for advice and action. Assistance with commemoration expenses—and plans—are available. Other needs may be addressed.
- If your "means" are limited, or you need to conserve your Estate, and if earlier arrangements had not already been made for commemoration of a loved one, or disposition of the remains, consider "Discount Services." Check them out before you need them, and proceed with caution. Information is available on computer Web pages, under "Discount Nationwide Funeral Services." Some Yellow Pages also list them.
- Those who have assisted you in dealing with death are professional; remuneration is polite, so paying funeral or memorial officiants is ethical. Funeral Home staff can advise you. Some churches offer recommendations on fees, especially if the funeral or memorial service is at the church facility. At the beginning, remember that Pastors do not lose sleep over unrequited remunerations for their services, especially for funerals or memorials; remember also that fees can be negotiated, if necessary. Families invariably provide clergy a stipend, either handling the matter personally with the pastor, or more often, especially in recent years, through the Funeral Home. My honorarium policy has been: "Remuneration goes to my Continuing Education or Personal Library fund." My honorariums have varied from $10.00 to $500.00—once only! On a rare occasion when I did not receive a check or cash, I eventually spoke about it to the Director, and they apologized, usually discovering

it had been the Funeral Home's oversight. The longer I was in the Pastorate, the less shy I became about the oversight.

- Inquire of the Funeral Home, especially when you are making plans for your own funeral or body disposition at the time of your death—also for your enlightenment in case friends, or if you are a pastor, parishioners inquire of you—about the various items and costs of ancillary services. Ask for an itemization of the costs. If the funeral is delayed, and the body is not yet buried, is there a fee for interim care? How do you respond to clients who prefer not to be embalmed? Can you provide space and reception services for a small group from out of town who plans only a simple graveside gathering for a burial?
- How does the Establishment arrange for and cooperate with the military, police or safety officers' services? What is the protocol on "gun salutes and other military participation?" How does the Pastor's order of the service fit into the discussion? Can service participation by fraternal orders or social clubs or church groups be accommodated, as far as seating as a group or special ceremonies of remembrance? Do you have space where a family from out-of-town may receive guests, and may have coffee and punch? How are burial arrangements covered if an out-of-town journey is necessary? Does State Law require embalming? (Some of these questions may also be answered by correspondence with an Agency like: Premier Funeral Services and Cremation Inc., Lake Worth, Florida 33460.)
- Within a few hours or a few days following the death, certainly shortly following the funeral, you will be emotionally assaulted, and physically and mentally overwhelmed, by related business organizations and salespersons. Does the Funeral Home have preferences for qualified agencies? Or individuals, or businesses to help you with dying and death legalities? Do they have recommendations for florists? If the Funeral Home offers to print funeral service bulletins—complimentary

or for a charge—is the Pastor/Officiant contacted about the service order before the printing? (I prefer that the Church I serve duplicate copies of the service that I have worked out with the family or friends of the deceased. Or I duplicate the material myself.) What about viewing fees, and viewing preceding a cremation? Are there restrictions on burial dress?

- Obituary: *Obituary Theology*, by way of reminder, suggests that you write your own autobituary; and encourage your spouse, if you have one, to do the same. (You may want to employ a creative or critical writer to exercise editorial privilege.) Writing your own obituary usually results in a more creative and accurate document. If you are a Christian and include material about where you believe your loved one rests, conform your statements to your religious ethos. At the same time review Biblical teaching on hereafter whereabouts and resuming of former on-earth relationships. In Biblical terms, as frequently stated in *OT*, "former things" pass away with death, giving way to "new things." (Revelation 21:1ff.) The Tent paradigm of 2 Corinthians 5 may sound too obscure and obsolete for sophisticated twenty-first century Christians. Seek other metaphors. You may want to review your manuscript with your Pastor or someone you regard as more Biblically attuned than yourself.
- Order of Commemoration Service: If someone other than your Pastor, or a designated spiritual leader, is the officiant, and if the venue is other than a church, consult with the Funeral Director of the service or the Funeral Home Staff about the order you want, or should follow. Accept their assistance if you ask for it, or feel you need it, but do not subject yourself to dictation. Examine spiritual resources on funerals or memorials other than those you are more familiar with. Sort out the Scriptures you prefer. If the commemoration is limited to a committal event, you will find help available in your Church's liturgical library, or your Pastor's office. The Presbyterian Church (U.S.A.) offers resources in

Hymnals and Worship Books, particularly in *The Book of Common Worship: Pastoral Edition.*

Be pragmatic about the attitude you take toward the dying and death event, memorial commemorations, body disposition, grieving, paying the bills, and especially, recovery from your loss. Recognize that you need help from others, both the Deity in heaven and the saints on earth. Your handling of these matters will testify to how smart you are, in the wisdom of this world, but especially in the wisdom of God. (1 Corinthians 2:6.) One very practical word of wisdom comes from Jesus: "The children of this age are more shrewd in dealing with their own generation than are the children of light." (Luke 16:8.)

"Knowhow" moves the last of Chapter IX, and of the Book, into a "Question and Answer," "Q&A" mode. Some of the material repeats earlier comments, intentionally; repetition reminds the reader that certain issues connected with dying and death are more important than others. The order is semi-sequential with the chapters.

Q. 1. How long can I expect to extend hospitality to family and friends, some of whom have come from a distance, with suitcases, indicating that they will be with me for a while? A. *Some of your guests will stay as long as they feel you want them to stay, or perceive that you need them. You may have to take a kind-but-firm confrontational stance, expressing your need to be alone for a while, and giving your guests assurance that you are making good progress with your grieving, and you will continued to do so.*

Q. 2. What constitutes good policy for post-spousal-death social re-entry, or socialization, particularly with the opposite sex? And for remarriage? A. *Review comments previously made in this Chapter. Do not rush, and do not let family or well-intentioned "fixer-uppers" pester you. Thank "do-gooders," and at the same time, inform them that you are capable of managing your own life. Acknowledge that post-loss adjustments will take time, and you do not want loneliness or any other similar feeling to cause you to slip, and act erratically. Be patient, and ask for patience from others. The following successful re-marriage account is excerpted from an obituary in a recent "Seattle Times."*

FIFTY-SIX YEARS OF MARRIAGE, TWICE MARRIED: He died peacefully at age 81, having lost his "high school sweetheart" more than two decades ago. After ten years of loneliness and bachelorhood, he married again. The couple enjoyed a variety of activities for another decade: traveling, visiting family and friends. They regularly joined the annual Mariner Baseball Team in Spring Training at Sun City West, (Peoria) Arizona.

Q. 3. What about acknowledging special kindnesses shown my family and myself—both during pre-death stress and post-death bereavement? A. *Keep records, and do hand-written timely appreciations. (Email only if necessary.)*

Q. 4. What about paying bills and handling financial matters? A. *(Again, see details earlier in the chapter.) Lean heavily on the primary family accountant, Attorney, Financial Adviser, bank authority—or a family member if necessary. Purchase or obtain a guide to post-mortem business administration. Be diligent about canceling or returning Social Security or Pension Checks, beginning with the month of the death. If you are the Estate Executor, investigate the legal process, "Setting Aside the Estate Without Administration." Learn the lesson I have learned from the funeral bill-paying neglect of my Father when his Father died, as related in Chapter VI.*

Q. 5. How long do I wait before I dispose of clothes, personal items, hobby memorabilia, library, tools, machinery or autos, and other personal properties? A. *Ascertain whether the items no longer serve a use for you, or a member of your family, or some non-profit agency like Clothing Banks, Thrift Stores, Goodwill, World Vision, your Church's mission, or Church Distribution Centers. Watch for Church Rummage Sales. Advertise more valuable items, and negotiate prices. Ebay and you may both benefit from your offer. Donate books to an education institution, but do not be surprised if they have neither space nor use for your collection; the books may be outdated, or of a quality where demand for use of them exceeds their remaining lifetime. Eventually re-decorate your most cherished living spaces, probably dismantling the personal living areas. Do not re-stock the spaces with imaginary characters, or imaginary persona, or cherished personal property of the deceased. Sort out mementos, like old colored slides, photo albums, cassette tapes, and home movies; transfer them to Flash Discs or less space-gulping technology. Be as practical as possible with items of continual usefulness. If you have use of some of the items your spouse cherished, make good use of them.*

Q. 6. How soon should I relocate? A. *Not too soon, unless finances dictate; maybe not at all, if living where you presently reside feels comfortable, and your upkeep expenses are affordable; and if continuing residence in a familiar setting does not delay or exacerbate your grieving; in fact, it may facilitate it. Be diligent about regular property maintenance where you own the property. Do not rent Storage for "stuff" you would like to save. Make your sort-outs thorough and final. Let pets remain pets. Provide them a good bed, better located in a room other than your bedroom. If no other space exists, let your room become theirs, but let not your bed become theirs, not even a share of it. Restrict their diet to pet food; they will live longer and healthier—and enjoy healthier "elimination" habits. If your pet happens to be a chimpanzee, lock it in a bedroom when strangers come for afternoon tea!*

Q. 7. What about special social, athletic, and cultural events, or pleasures that "we" attended or participated in together? A. *Go wherever, and do conservatively and enjoyably whatever feels good. If acceptable, visit or join—after thorough investigation—a "Singles Club." Wear his or her UW jacket if it fits, and if it keeps you warm at the Stadium. Do not give away your sports season tickets too soon, if ever. If you are in a donating mood, offer your family first choice—if they are interested. Eventually seek out opposite-gender companionship, unless you are gay or lesbian; or even if you are. Be wary of Internet alliances. Develop skills in doing and being alone, as well as being in company. Try a cruise, especially if you and the deceased had cruised occasionally, or regularly, and enjoyed the pleasure of it; or even if you never did. Go someplace you have never been. If you and your spouse had gatherings at your home, keep gathering. Research meaningful institutions, charities, organizations, and groups that need and can use your skills and experiences. Volunteer your time. Investigate church "Mission Trips," such as to help "Katrina" victims; or do volunteer labor with "Habitat for Humanity," restoring or building new housing. Develop new recreational and social skills: line or ballroom dancing, painting, woodworking, crocheting, mountain climbing, gourmet cooking, mountain motor-biking, skiing, landscaping, furniture restoration, or antique dealing. Males, remember that the greatest chefs are/were not all Julia Child's or Martha Stewart's! And remember that it requires more athleticism and fitness to be a ballet dancer than a quarterback or a marathon runner. Try live-theater, opera, Nashville or Branson; occasionally visit Las Vegas, unless you are a gambling addict. The Motel 8 has adequate amenities, and at the right price. It is even less expensive out in Boulder City, twenty miles from the "Strip."*

Q. 8. What about publicizing memorial gift suggestions? A. *If the obituary lists them, make certain the requests are honored, and the donors thanked—even if the agency recipients have already extended that courtesy. Use discretion about publicly attaching donor's names to them, checking with the donor first. Let them know if bronze plaques or other public identification will be made, and ask if they have objection. Use undesignated memorial money for memorials that are appropriate, and that please you. You may choose to memorialize the deceased from your own resources. Keep donors informed of the progress of projects in which their memorial donations have been invested.*

Q. 9. What about connections with "former" in-laws, or stepchildren, or offspring from a previous marriage? A. *If the relationship had been meaningful in life, maintain and nurture it in death! Avoid becoming over-possessive or protective. Assure the involved and related survivors that death did not drain the family blood out of their veins—or yours! If your children or grandchildren inherit new "step-relatives," become acquainted. If the relationships appear nurturing, do your share in sharing the nurturing. If you perceive that overseers, child-carers, or stepparents are abusing surviving children or grandchildren, contact your state or local "Child Protective Services." If survivors or relatives choose not to visit you frequently, accept their decision, and find surrogates—human, in preference to animal. If the "cool" persists, try a conference meeting with those involved, maybe in the presence of a mutually agreed upon third-party counselor, or Pastor. Do not let family prey on your free time with excessive child-care requests. Do not let family relations become divisive. Do not be over solicitous in offering parental advice, in case death has put one of the surviving spouses in a "Sole Parent" relationship with the grandchildren. Compromise on sensitive issues, if necessary, "for the kids' sakes." Talk it out. Do not act deviously in prejudicing the children's perceptions and feelings, spoiling them with the offer of rewards.*

Q. 10. What "will" matters and other legal documents and transactions and business involvements require attention? A. *Clarify them as expeditiously and amicably as possible with your Lawyer and/or the executor of the deceased's estate, unless you are the executor, or the "co-executor." Be patient. Have your own will written, rewritten and updated—especially if the deceased had been your spouse or offspring. (If you had a "joint" passport, apply for a new one.) Upon the death of your spouse, work with the proper authorities on undoing joint bank accounts and similar portfolios. Review and update your power of attorney and living will documents. If you live on a "border state," or occasionally travel either North or South of the border, obtain the special card that substitutes for a drivers' license or a Passport and facilitates international border crossings. (If your passport is current, you may not want to bother.) If you are not currently informed on family business assets, and legal and financial records, or medical coverage, expeditiously seek an update of the information. Do not unduly interfere with, or put time-line pressure, on the individual responsible for settling the Estate, unless you have been designated as a Co-Executor. Intrude only when you suspect or perceive that affairs are not being dealt with efficiently, or in a timely process. Settling estates takes time.*

Q. 11. Is it healthy to make occasional trips to the cemetery; or the place where the loved one's remains are, or were placed or scattered; and perhaps periodically leave floral or symbolic tributes, like a flag, a statue or a carving? How about a periodic donation to the institution to which the body had been donated? Should I encourage family members to visit accidental death scenes or cemeteries? A. *Occasionally plan cemetery visits (if you feel the need to, and it proves comfortable under the circumstances); do not linger long, or attempt to communicate with the deceased, except by memory. "Memorial Day" decorating is culturally expected, but the decision is up to you. It may help you to be "season-responsive," and make relationships with other survivors more comfortable. If you have grieving young children, discern the protocol best for them—and you. If you discern that you hear the deceased's voice, or voices, and the perception persists, see a counselor, or a pastor. If your church or another "values" organization has a grief group, join it. Community Mental Health or Counseling Centers often provide special groups. Remember that there is both appropriate and inappropriate grieving. If you occasionally visit the scene of death or burial, ask family members if they would like to join you or take you, but assure them that the decision depends on how they feel. Be appropriate; be healthy; be faithful; be restored.*

Q. 12. How will I be able to classify my psycho-spiritual discomfort, whether it is grief or depression or guilt; or another destructive, negative emotion? A. *First, discern the issue, if possible by yourself, but if not, then make an appointment with a spiritual counselor, or your Primary Care Physician; of if you perceive it serious enough, a Psychologist. Research the symptoms, again with professional help. Several widows and widowers report talking to the dead-and-buried spouse, but eventually, with a little determination and substitution, they stopped it. Decide on the basis of professional advice, whether you may be able to speed recovery faster by attending group therapy or swallowing an anti-depressant medication. Trust that well-being and good feeling will eventually return. Be hesitant to participate in talk shows or surveys, or be interviewed by broadcasters or reporters while still deep in grief. Speak personally and occasionally with your pastor or counselor about your adjustments. Observe the sacrament of Communion, the Lord's Supper or Holy Eucharist, as occasionally as you have been accustomed to, hopefully regularly; or according to your Church's schedule, or in a special sacramental gathering with and for you and close family and/or friends. Swallow Paul's grief pill from 1 Thessalonians 4: "Grieve as one who has hope...."*

Q. 13. When will I know that grief has given way to wellness, and that wholeness has arrived? A. *The question assumes a completion. (Make sure you read the closing paragraphs of this Chapter; they concentrate on one family's dealing with that issue.) The reality is: there may never be the one you have envisioned, and have hoped and prayed for. Handle your feelings as you would in any other major illness: treat them regularly and intelligently as real provisional emotions, while at the same time reassure yourself that you are progressing normally through an emotional bruising. Ask for interim medication, with zero refills. Do some satisfying, uncomplicated, not-too-brainy activity, like a board game; or go on an outdoor hike. Keep repeating to yourself, "Service begets comfort, rather than comfort begets service." Keep repeating, "Blessed are those who mourn, for they will be comforted." (Matthew 5:4.) Occasionally obituaries prove therapeutic, testifying that Gilead's balm works through wholesome mourning, as in: "There is a balm in Gilead that heals the sin-sick soul." ("Negro" Spiritual.) Maybe even organize a simple, tasteful "End of Grief" recognition event, as a kind of coming out and as an affirmation to yourself that you have survived—as you know your spouse or parent or child would have expected. A local super-market, grocery store, has this slogan on its doors: "Get in, Get it, Get out." I suggested one "Get" adjustment that I believe would soften the message and make it applicable to grieving: "Get in, get it, get it paid for, get on." Thank Abraham Lincoln (his memory) for these words: "The best*

> *thing about the future is that it comes only one day at a time." Jesus said, "Let the day's own trouble be sufficient for the day." Or as in newer translations, "Today's trouble is enough for today." (Matthew 6:34.) Do not attempt to squeeze two or three months of grieving into three weeks. You have already had several reminders of what to do about anxiety.*

With regard to the last question about the duration of grieving, a family named Bush—no presidential connections are mentioned—has advice to offer. Professor Harold K. Bush, Jr., and his wife, Hiroko, arrived at a healing insight about grief while painfully dealing with the death of their ten-year old, only child, David. Professor Bush has written a book about their experience, entitled, *"Grief Work. After a Child Dies."* The Professor and his wife have received comfort, among other ways, by co-founding "The Daniel Foundation." (See further details through www.daniel foundation.org.)

The experience of walking through "the darkest valley" (another translation of the Hebrew of Psalm 23:4) convinced Professor and Mrs. Bush that speed is not of the essence in grieving; neither is the pain of loneliness, if it is dealt with intelligently and emotionally. Nor does adjustment or recovery require treading through the experience with icy objectivity: "Research has shown that lifelong grief is normal after the loss of a close family member, especially a child," Dr. Bush wrote. He disagrees with Sigmund Freud's thesis that the healthy grieving period has ended when the death of a loved one leaves the bereaved without a trace of "gross (lifestyle or thought) change."

Grief recovery for the Bushes did not arrive as expeditiously as they had hoped. Nor did it totally relieve them of their pain, even over a period of time. Spiritual insight offered them crucial relief. Professor Bush related an important advance in their struggle: "One of the greatest consolations in my own experience has been the realization that I actually do believe in God." That belief, he continued, increasingly proved to be a rock for the family. It testified to

Jesus' teaching in a parable about two builders who chose different terrains for laying the foundation for their new homes: one settled for sand, the other for rock. (The parable follows the "Sermon on the Mount," Matthew 7:24-7.) The wise man's rock-foundation construction withstood wind, rain and a flood; his house stayed put through the storm. The foolish man's house toppled.

"Over these eight years (since the child died)," Professor Bush continued, "I have been thankful so many times to realize that there was a little bit of rock underneath my life." (Pp. 36-39.) The Bushes are convinced that the grief-healing bonds they have established with their son have stationed them solidly. The still-grieving professor-father concluded his article with: "Finally, since we are also told in scripture that 'the spirit will return to God who gave it' (Ecclesiastes 12:7); and that God will most assuredly 'wipe away every tear,' (Revelation 21:4), we do hold out hope for a reunion with our son. Soon enough, I suppose, we will know the truth about these matters. Until then, and hopefully for a long time, our bond with Daniel will continue."[2] (It appears unequivocal that the Bush's will stay grounded on their rock-like faith! The one who "hears these words of mine and acts on them," Jesus concluded, occupies that location. (V. 27.) Bushes fit that category.

Does the Bush approach sound like "Knowhow" to you? It does to me. Does it sound like critical thinking for living rationally—and peacefully? It does to me. After all, the still-grieving Father is a Ph. D., and a Professional; and he has a smart wife.

The article was recently recommended to two families who have recently lost only sons. An older couple—he is ninety, and she is not too far behind—had lost their sixty-year-old Clergy "only" Son. The McIver's have expressed appreciation for the help the article has given them in the 2008 Advent Season. The Texan, currently Australian, residents are the parents of David, the child whose dying and death early in 2009 were recounted in Chapter I. Both families are devout Christians, and they indicated that they had found help from the Bushes' experience. (Bob Dietz in his *Life after Loss* also validates their grieving.) All of them testify to the power of the Gospel of hope.

Father Thomas Merton of the Abbey of our Lady of Gethsemani, lends support as well. The Father is regarded as "one of the most influential and provocative spiritual writers of the twentieth century," per the book jacket on his *No Man Is an Island.* He was also occasionally censured for his outspoken social commentary. Father Merton warned somberly: "If at the moment of our death, it comes to us as an unwelcome stranger, it will be because Christ has always been to us an unwelcome stranger. For when death comes, Christ comes also, bringing us the everlasting life that He has bought for us, by His own death. Those who live truly, therefore, frequently think about their death. Their life is full of a silence that is an anticipated victory over death. Silence, indeed, makes death our servant and even our friend. Thoughts and prayers that grow up out of the silent thought of death are like trees growing where there is water. They are strong thoughts that overcome the fear of misfortune because they have overcome passion and desire. They turn the face of our soul, in constant desire, toward the face of Christ."[3]

The "Preacher-Author" of the Book of Ecclesiastes, Qoheleth—with whom Kirk Douglas' Mother must have had some affinity—wrote starkly about death's universality:

> "For everything there is a season, and a time for every matter under heaven: a time to be born, and a time to die….The same fate comes to all, to the righteous and the wicked, to the good and the evil, to the clean and the unclean, to those who sacrifice and those who do not sacrifice. As are the good, so are the sinners; those who swear are like those who shun an oath. This is an evil in all that happens under the sun, that the same fate comes to everyone…. whoever is joined with all the living has hope, for a living dog is better than a dead lion. The living 'know' that they will die, but the dead

'know nothing;' they have no reward, and even the memory of them is lost. Their love and their hate and their envy have already perished; never again will they have any share in all that happens under the sun." (Ecclesiastes 3:1-2; 9:2-6.)

Imagine that the free-thinker preacher, Qoheleth; the genius, adulterer, murderer, victor, organizer, former shepherd, and survivor, and second anointed King of Israel, King David; the giant theologian and courageous critic of creedal and papal decrees, and designer of grace theology, Reformer Martin Luther; and the American Civil Rights Martyr, Martin Luther King, Junior; —imagine the four of them in heaven singing in quartette, "Thine Is the Glory," to Handel's "Judas Maccabeus!" If I were listening to them, or singing with them, or if Author Styron were (for whom a requirement for an idyllic heaven is classical music), I doubt that we could have finished listening to the number without sobbing uncontrollably. I am certain that I would have choked up, if not before, at least by the middle stanza:

Lo! Jesus meets us, Risen from the tomb,
Lovingly he greets us, scatters fear and gloom;
Let his Church with gladness Hymns of triumph sing,
For her Lord now liveth, Death hath lost its sting.
Thine is the glory, risen, conquering Son,
Endless is the victory Thou o'er death hast won."

The hymn quotation might have elicited an, "Ah ha, finally, the end of the Book!" Not quite! How could a volume with the title Obituary Theology end without an excerpt? It can't, especially this one:

GOD IN MOTION: Heaven was made richer when she arrived last week. She had not even reached "three score and ten years." She was multi-talented: she was known not only as a "Master" teacher with abundant compassion and love for her students, she was also known as a dedicated gourmet cook. More importantly, she was a godly woman; her greatest joy derived from serving others. Her obituary composer surmised that his Subject had no idea how many hearts and lives she had touched. She was described as the hands and feet of God to those who knew her. (*The Birmingham News.)*

Do you regret that you did not know that woman? If you reside in the South, perhaps you did! If so, you are richer in soul and in knowledge, not the kind of knowledge that Paul said "puffs up;" (1 Corinthians 8:1-3;), but the kind that builds up: love. The souls who die in that virtue are of all saints most fortunate.

Autobituary
Vernon Gibson Elgin

"All in the April evening," the Lenten Anthem reminds the Church, Christians remember that God's lamb had been slain and laid in a tomb. All on an April evening in 1927, the 24th to be exact, the thoughts of my Elderton, Pennsylvania parents, Marie and Glenn, overflowed with joy; they had a new little lamb in the house. He had just been born in an upstairs bedroom of their house, with a Midwife and the local Doctor present. For the present they named him, "Baby Boy Elgin." Three months later in their local United Presbyterian Church he was baptized, "Vernon Gibson Elgin."

I was not the first child in the Elgin Household; I had a one year-old sister, Janice Kathleen. Later we would be joined by Ray Leland and Mary Florence.

All four of us Elgin siblings would be educated in our little village, in a one-room, then two-room schoolhouse; we ended up in four-rooms for High School. Upon graduation, two weeks past my seventeenth birthday, I was sworn into the United States Army Air Corps Reserves as a cadet, and was sent to Virginia Tech for a year of university studies. Following a year and a half of active Air Corps (now "Air Force") duty—in Biloxi, MS and Scott Field, IL—I studied at Indiana University of Pennsylvania. Perceiving God was calling me to Church ministry, I enrolled in the Pittsburgh (Xenia) Presbyterian Theological Seminary. There I met my future Wife, Marjorie Curry, from Kansas. In my senior year of Seminary I traveled on weekends to Cadiz, Ohio, to serve the United Presbyterian Church. Upon Seminary graduation, I was ordained a United Presbyterian Clergy in Cadiz. Meantime I had been awarded a scholarship prize to study abroad. The Cadiz Church gave me a leave of absence, enabling me to attend the New College of the University of Edinburgh, Scotland. I enrolled in the Ph. D. Program. Upon arrival back in the USA, Marjorie and I were married, setting up residence in Cadiz. Two years later we had our first Son, Mark. One year after that event, we left Cadiz for a return to Scotland, and completion of the Ph. D. studies. I stayed in Scotland for six months after the family had gone home to Kansas. I returned to Kansas, and assumed the Pastorate of the family church.

Besides Cadiz and Eskridge, we also served as Parish Pastor and spouse in Washington, Iowa (where our second Son, Paul, was born); from there we were called to The Little Church on the Prairie in Lakewood, WA; from Parish ministry to Church Fund Raising, first in Buffalo, NY; then back in Washington State, also working part-time in Alaska. After that "service," we began "Interim Ministry:" in Washington; Akaroa, New Zealand; San Juan, Puerto Rico; Bali Indonesia; and teaching in Bogota, Colombia. Marjorie gave considerable time to Presbyterian Women and Church Women United. Her health precluded her joining me in Malawi, Africa for a Professorship at the new Presbyterian University of Livingstonia.

Our two little lambs—neither one born on an April evening—grew into hefty, healthy young men. Son Mark owns a Commercial Construction and Real Estate Company in Birmingham, AL. His wife Lynn owns a Business there, and the two parent four children: Alexandra (18), Alaina (16), Olivia (13) and Curry (10). Younger Son Paul is the Director of Music at the Providence Presbyterian Church in Hilton Head SC, and along with his Occupational Therapist wife, Elizabeth, they are the parents of Lucas (13) and Sarah (10).

At the time of my death, we were living in Kent, WA. I had published, *OBITUARY THEOLOGY.* I was writing another book, *Hitchhiking Foreign Highways.*

My commemorative service will be held Friday, ________ at 3:00 P.M. at The Little Church on the Prairie in Lakewood WA. Earlier in the day my family had held a private service of burial at the Tahoma National Cemetery in Kent. I died in the faith in which I had been baptized shortly after my birth. My summary verses are: from Jesus, "Come unto me…and I will give you rest…." (Matthew 11:28); and from Paul, "Whether we live, or whether we die, we are the Lord's." (Romans 14:8-9.)

Afterword 062109

More emotion than I had anticipated attends the termination of my long and sweaty relationship with Obituary Theology. More than two years ago I foresaw needing a case of sparkling cider, or champagne for the non-alcoholics, to add foam to a celebration. Now I am harboring a degree of sadness. I also have anxiety: how will I reassign my time, how will I handle the criticism and reviews, and how will I decide on which book to write next? I breathe deeply, and then I see the answers: check my weekly program calendar, look out at my lawn and garden, peek into my clothes closet, spend minutes in my work shed, review an agenda of family for my wife and me, glance at my desk tray, and fill out my calendar for catch-up on recent movie releases. Realistically, on the day I send my manuscript to the Publisher, I think I can kiss nostalgia good-bye, and quickly take on a new journey.

As I prepare to say, "Adios" to Obituary Theology, and, "Mi gusta muchos pesos" from its publication and distribution, I will also prepare to say, "Buenos dias" to *On Writing a Book, Hitchhiking Foreign Routes,* or to one or two of the other titles my mind thinks of during insomnia tossing. Though future writing adventures may differ drastically from *OT* scenarios. I will welcome the difference. My neurotic creativity stifles on sameness.

Some of the duties that I have neglected while writing my first book since my Ph. D. thesis (submitted to the New College, the University of Edinburgh, Scotland in 1959) include:

- Rescheduling an appointment with my Ophthalmologist;
- My spare hearing aid needs adjusting; my wife says my "good one" does, too;
- My front and back garden both are crying for fertilizer and trimming;
- Strawberries are on the tail-end of their bearing, and I have not yet put any in the freezer;

- Friends in Montana have invited us for a visit;
- The Bally's Fitness membership is being wasted;
- Increased volunteer services for my church, and for the Community Club at our Residential Park will hopefully relieve my guilt for not finding time for such rewarding involvements the past two years;
- Morning exercises and Daily Prayer will not require hurrying up, and I may arrive at my work desk before 10:30 a.m., and leave before 10:30 p.m.
- Sleep deprivation will be reduced.

The plethora of neglected blessings cannot overshadow or clip away at my appreciation for the skills my writing *Obituary Theology* has either created or revived. I am pleased with the sustained peace and persistence with which the task has endowed me. Seldom during the writing did I come to the computer without excited anticipation, even about locating the chapter that I had decided my fatigue the night before had contributed to my losing. Nor did those interruptions I could not avoid frustrate me. Happiest of all is the fact that Marjorie and I are still wife and husband. I am grateful to God for these accomplishments, and I am hopeful in God for the Book's publication, sales, and use.

Finally, finally, I want to sign off with recounting the deepest sadness encountered during writing the Book. Ironically, the experience deals with death. Ironically also, I had just lost my younger brother and sister a few months previously. Of course, Mary's death created a different grief reaction from the somewhat unexpected deaths of my siblings. However, I had come to need, appreciate, and love her deeply.

On one rare freezing morning in December my most skilled, professional, and final Critical Reader was found dead beside her car at the back of her house. Neighbors who found Mary believe that she—a leg-below-the-knee amputee—had gone in search of help after a tree had fallen on her roof, cutting off her utility and telephone service. Did Mary die and fall, or did she fall and die? God has not yet revealed the truth, nor am I waiting for such a courtesy.

Needless to say, Mary had proved most helpful, and she was happy giving me the benefit of her life-long professional expertise. (She had once been a sometime-professional reader.) We worshiped God in the same Church, and we shared many similar interests and ideas. Mary Savela was one of the most joyful and intelligent persons I have ever known. My life is richer because of the years of our friendship, and my writing has arrived at whatever degree of possibility it has, because of her didactical expertise. *Obituary Theology* will be more worth the purchase and use because of Mary Savela's hand in its preparation.

My wife has stepped in where Mary did not fear to tread. Besides, contacting Marjorie does not require a telephone or a car. We have been able to agree or compromise on most of the issues connected with our literary partnership. I believe the camaraderie will persist, and at the end we can hear—if not from above, at least from each other—"Well done, good and faithful servants. Now get busy on the next book!"

Vernon G. Elgin

Study Questions For *Obituary Theology*

(Note: for a Short Course, study Chapters III, IV and V.)

Chapter 1. Coming to Terms with Dying. (Genesis 3:1–19)

1. What are the most significant issues about dying and death that modern society appears to give most attention to? What the least attention to? Why?
2. What are some ways that you can approach your mortality without anxiety?
3. What practical advantages accrue to thinking theologically about dying and death, their causes and their consequences?
4. How much does the average person think about mortality, their own or others: at age 18; 30; 55; 75; 95?

Chapter 2. Coming to Terms with Theology (1 Corinthians 1:18–31)

1. What is your definition of theology; how do you evaluate the author's? What is missing in both?
2. When and in what circumstance did you last think in a way that could be described as theological? Was it hard or easy? Did it come naturally? How were you made aware of its theological nature?
3. Besides Scripture, where do you turn, if you do, for theological guidance, on: God, Jesus, the Holy Spirit, Scripture, a tragic death, a seemingly unjust death, funeral content, disposition of the body, the Church, and salvation?
4. Write three words that best describe Pop or Current theological thinking about: a. aging; b. dying; and c. God. What are your three favorite references in Scripture on these topics?

Chapter 3. Coming to terms with Authority (Mark 1:21–27; Matthew 21:23–27)

1. How do you see your Church, or your own thinking and behaving, as authoritarian? In what ways is it healthy and helpful? In what ways obstructive?
2. What are the advantages of having the Bible as an authority, "in matters of faith and piety (religious practice")? What are the advantages of having the Church as an authority? Disadvantages?
3. What are the most significant values of the Bible that merit it the tribute made in the introduction: it "excelleth all the riches of the earth?"
4. In what ways is the Church you are affiliated with an authority? In what areas of common life do you welcome its positions and pronouncements, in what ways do you disagree with it? What would change about the Church's use of authority?

Chapter 4. Last Breath (Romans 5)

1. Of the three topics the author connects with death (circumstance, cause, consequence), which do you regard as the most important? What distinguishes it in importance to you? If you in good conscience deemed it possible, how would you choose to die? Give reasons.
2. What does your theology teach about what happens when you die? (If not already discussed in Chapter 1 Study Questions.)
3. Chose an obituary from a supply in front of you, and discuss its theological and personal merits.
4. The State of Oregon passed the legislation first. Now it is legal in the State of Washington as well! The issue is "Death with Dignity." Under what circumstances would you, or would you not, consider it for yourself? For a member of your family? What are the moral implications of your choice? Do you think the Bible offers a choice?

Chapter 5. Commemorated (John 12:1–7; 2 Samuel 1:11–27.)

1. What personal and communal needs do commemorative rites serve, regardless of whether they would serve yours in the same way?
2. When and how can the policy, "No services" have Merit? Demerit?
3. What features describe the most personally satisfying commemoration service you have attended in the past ten years?
4. What issues would you give priority to in planning your own "service," or "no service?"
5. What will be its main content, and organization if and when you write your own obituary?

Chapter 6. Buried, Cremated, Donated, (Or Other Method of Body Disposition). (Genesis 23; John 19:38–42)

1. Choose one of the traditional, or non-traditional, modes of disposition of one's corpse, and discuss its theological, psychological, social and financial implications.
2. What are the advantages/disadvantages of one method over the other?
3. How does your religious faith affect your decision about the disposition of your body after you die? How does "Alkaline Hydrolysis" sound?
4. Do you attend commemoration, funeral, memorial services, et al., and why? What characterizes the most memorable one you have ever attended?

Chapter 7. Vocation et Persona (Luke 1:39–56; Deuteronomy 34.)

1. Does your religious ethos about your work, or previous career, or your retirement suggest a theology of vocation? What are its characteristics?
2. What virtues make your favorite and most admired Biblical character stand in such high regard with you? How would you react if God were to call you thus? Why?
3. How does vocatio affect persona; and vice versa? What do you imagine, or intend that your obituary will say about yours?

4. What Scriptures mean the most to you about living your Faith?

Chapter 8. Gone Before and Left Behind (Ancestry vs. Posterity) (Leviticus 26:40–46; Exodus 20:12; Revelation 14:1–5)

1. How do the obituary excerpts in this or other chapters suggest ancestry as a determinant of posterity?
2. What dynamics in your ancestry still dictate your holiday observances? your reverence for the dead? your views of heaven and hell? your relationship with your family? your relationship with Jesus?
3. What can an individual or a family do to guarantee that your offspring will never shame you, never desert you or never be embarrassed by someone in the "dead" line of your family?
4. What standards of covenant loyalty do the best Biblical Ancestors offer for living in our society? What about gender domination by males or fathers? Do you believe that the Bible unconditionally condemns homosexuality? What can the Church do to promote appreciation for ancestors and imitation of their values by your/our posterity?

Chapter 9. Knowhow (Matthew 10:5–25)

1. What issues raised in the Chapter are the ones you need most help with as you face the inevitable consequence of your mortality? Or the deaths of your aging parents? Or a child? What suggestions are most helpful, adequate?
2. How do you evaluate the pragmatism for dealing with dying and death in the Apostle's Creed; and do the particular words, phrases, clauses or sentences appear to have the connection the Author implies by citing them? Has the Author overlooked a relative phrase or clause?
3. If your Church has a Manual for Death, Commemoration, Services, et al, what topics in it prove most helpful in times of sorrow—yours, or in case you are helping someone else with theirs? And what about grieving? Does your Church have a grief group, or where would

you search to find one if you need one? How would you proceed in starting one?

4. What criteria or standards of success can you use from what you have studied or read that will enable you to live a full, wholesome, and abundant life and die a peaceful and hopeful death? Where does God-in-Christ fit in? What "know-how" has not been covered effectively? (Please inform the Author!)

End Notes

Introduction

[1]James Halterman, *Christian Century,* 12/16/08, Review of Gustave Speth's Book, *The Bridge at the End of the World: Capitalism, the Environment and Crossing from Crisis to Sustainability,* (Yale University Press), p. 38.

Chapter I. Coming to Terms with Dying

[1]Jerry Brewer, *Seattle Times,* News Story in Twelve Installments, Ending 10/05/07.

[2]Don Colburn, *The Oregonian,* (Portland, Oregon Newspaper), Newshouse News Service, 11/07/07.

[3]Elisabeth Kubler-Ross, *On Death and Dying,* Macmillan Publishing Co., Inc., now Schuster&Simon, New York, NY, Elisabeth Kubler-Ross, Copyright @1969, Paperback Edition 1970, Eleventh Printing 1973.

Chapter II. Coming to Terms with Theology

[1]*The Constitution of the Presbyterian Church (U.S.A.),* "Form of Government," Chapter I. Preliminary Principles, G-1.0200, "The Great Ends of the Church", No. 2.

[2]John D. Davis and Henry Snyder Gehman, Editors, *The Westminster Dictionary of the Bible,* Copyright 1944 by the Westminster Press, The Westminster Press, Philadelphia. (Permission granted, but not necessary for the amount copied.)

[3]John Calvin, *Institutes of the Christian Religion,* Translated from the Latin and Collated with the Author's last Edition in French by John Allen, Sixth American Edition in Two volumes, Presbyterian Board of Christian Education, First Published 1559, Philadelphia.

[4]*Constitution,* Part I, "The Book of Confessions", "The Westminster Confession of Faith," 2.2.

[5]Robin Lovin, *Christian Century,* October 21, 2008, Book Review: *Sovereignty: God, State and Self,* Book Title, *Sovereignty,* by Jean Bethke Elshtain, Cf. Pp. 54-6.

Chapter III. Coming to Terms with Authority

[1]Virginia Sue Mackenzie—*Autobituary,* and Managing Editor, *News and Advance,* Lynchburg VA Daily Newspaper, Obituary Section, 11/07/08.

[2]Kubler-Ross, P. 276.

[3]*The Holy Bible.* The World Publishing Company, Cleveland, Ohio and New York City, NY, 1924. Pp. 27-8. (Note: Not able to contact. Mail returned. Publishing Company may no longer be in existence.)

[4]*The Holy Bible, Revised Standard Version, Containing the Old and New Testaments,* Revised A.D. 1952. Published by Thomas Nelson and Sons, New York, Edinburgh. 1952, Introductory Pages, see "Acknowledgments."

[5]*The New Interpreter's Study Bible, New Revised Standard Version, With the Apocrypha,* Abingdon Press, Nashville, Copyright @2003. (The Bible Text is quoted, with permission from the National Council of Churches of Christ, copyright 1989, Division of Christian Education. Permission from Geneva Press to quote Articles, "Guides for Interpretation.") The Next five end notes are from the "Articles" by Authors as listed.

[6]*Ibid.* Walter J. Harrelson. P. 2243.

[7]*Ibid.* Phyllis J. Tribb; PP 2248–54.

[8]*Ibid.* Robert J. Gnuse, pp. 2255-60.

[91]*Ibid.* John R. Donahue, pp. 2263-67.

[10]*Ibid.* Metzger, "To the Reader;" p. xvii.

[11]*Peace, Unity Purity, The Final Report of the Theological Task Force on Peace, Unity and Purity of the Church to the 217th General Assembly (2006), with Study Guide,* (Permission from the Office of the General Assembly, Presbyterian Church (USA), pp. 4, *et.al.*

[12]*Constitution,* Book of Confessions," "The Westminster Confession of Faith," Chapter 1.

[13]Calvin, Material from Chapters vi-viii.

Chapter IV. Last Breath

[1]Kubler-Ross, *p.2.*

[2]*Constitution,* Westminster Confession, xxiv.

[3]*Ibid.* Heidelberg Catechism, Question 105, Setcion VI. 3.

[4]*Ibid.* Westminster Confession, Sections vi and xxiv.

[5]Bob Deits. *Life After Loss, a Personal Guide Dealing with Death.* (Published 1992, Fisher Books, 4249 W. Ina Road; Suite 101; Tucson AZ. 1992), p. 215.

[6]Calvin, *III,* xxv., pp. 252-3.

[7]*The New Interpreter's Study Bible,* Study Note on Psalm 139:7 & 8, p. 836.

[8]Alan Richardson, *A Theological Wordbook of the Bible,* The Macmillan Company, New York, Copyright 1950, p. 106.

[9]Calvin, *III,* xx.

Chapter V. Commemorated

[1]*Constitution,* "Order;" "Directory for Worship," W-4.10003.

[2]William H. Willimon, *Christian Century,* 04/21/09, "Accidental Lessons, " *30.*

[3]*Constitution,* "Worship," W-*4.10003*

[4]*Ibid.* W-*4.10000*

[5]*Seattle Times,* 03/16/09, "After Seven Hundred Years, Teen Gets Funeral." News Editor, compiled with The Associated Press.

Chapter VI. Buried, Cremated, Donated, Hydrolysized

[1]Norma Love, *Associated Press,* and *St. Joseph MO News Press, "New Idea in Mortuary Science: Dissolving Bodies,"* with AP, *05/09/09*

[2]A.A. Gill, "*Where the Dead Don't Sleep*" National Geographic. February 2009, p. 124 *et.al.*.

[3]David Twiddy, *"A Boon in Scattering."* News Story by Mr. Twiddy for the Associated Press "Close Up" Section of *Seattle Times,* 05/17/07.

[4]Jack Broom, *Alternative Lifestyles. Seattle Times, 02/09//07.*

[5]*Constitution,* "The Heidelberg Catechism,0" Question 41, and Answer.

[6]*Ibid.,* "The Second Helvetic Confession." Chapter xxvi.

[7]*Constitution.* "Book of Common Worship." Pastoral Edition, Westminster John Knox Press, 1993. Louisville KY, Pp. 224ff.

[8]Richardson, P. 35.

[9]Calvin, *III.* xxv.

Chapter VII. Vocatio et Persona

[1]Calvin, III, x.

[2]*Constitution* ,"The Second Helvetic Confession," XX.

[3]*Ibid.* "Form of Government," G-6.0105.

[4]*Ibid.* W-4.9001.

[5]*Ibid.* "Book of Confessions", "The Heidelberg Catechism", Questions 1, 5, and 6 and Answers.

[6]*Ibid.* "The Shorter Catechism." Questions 8, 60, 61 and 70, and Answers.

[7]John A. Esau. *Christian Century 12/16/08.* "Called for Life: Finding Meaning in Retirement." Review of Paul. C. Clayton's, *Called for Life*, 12/16/08, p. 62.

Chapter VIII. Gone Before and Left Behind

[1]Calvin, *XXX.xx.*

[2]*Constitution,* "Directory for Worship," W-2.3013.

[3]Jeremy Begbie. *Christian Century* 11/13/07. *"Meaning in Music….Sound Theology,"* Pp. 20 ff.

[4]The Reverend Norma B. Bendroth. *Christian Century,* 05/01/07, *"Brainstorm."* P. 10.

Chapter IX. Knowhow

[1]Bob Deitz, Pp. xii and xiii.

[2]Harold K. Bush, Jr., *"Christian Century,"* 12/11/07, *"Grief Works: After a Child Dies,"* Pp. 36-9.

[3]Fr. Thomas Merton, *No Man Is an Island,* Barnes and Noble, Inc. 2003 Edition. @ 1955 by The Abbey of Our Lady of Gethsemani, @ renewed 1983 by The Trustees of the Merton Legacy Trust, P. 263.

www.ingramcontent.com/pod-product-compliance
Lightning Source LLC
Chambersburg PA
CBHW060011100426
42740CB00010B/1454
9781603500067